You've Got *Unwanted* Mail

Alan Jones

DEDICATION

To scambaiters everywhere and the wider anti-scam community.

CONTENTS

ACKNOWLEDGMENTS

Thanks should go to the individuals who have created, administered and frequent the scambaiting and anti-scam websites and resources.

Finally, the biggest thanks should be reserved for the amazing Steward – he knows why ☺.

AUTHOR'S PREFACE

This book explores the different types of scams, how they work and how to avoid being caught out by them. Each chapter of the book will look at a different type of scam and in the final chapters we will look at some other related subjects.

Due to production costs, this book has had to be produced in black and white, so some of the images are not done full justice.

1. INTRODUCTION

In the current world of global connectivity, communication is faster and more impersonal than ever before. An email sent from Australia could be with its multiple recipients in Europe and North America, before the sender has time to walk to the other side of their office. Customers can buy products from stores without the need to leave their front room. Individuals can find partners on dating sites or offer items for sale on classifieds sites. Global communications provides so many benefits, but with it comes a dark side, as everywhere people "meet" to interact online, criminals lurk trying to steal from innocent victims. From the unsolicited emails in your inbox to the handsome soldier who messages you on the dating site, pathetic Internet scammers hide everywhere looking to profit from others.

Many people think that the victim is at fault for being caught by a scam and that it is down to their stupidity, gullibility or greed. Perhaps this is in part true of the pure Advance Fee Fraud scams, where a random person writes to you asking for assistance to move a large sum of money out of their country. However there are countless other types of scam that take advantage of the victims emotional state or lack of knowledge of how a particular transaction is meant to work. There are many documented cases of innocent young women from third world countries being caught out by au pair scammers offering them employment in a country where they don't know the immigration rules, or people buying a large item from a flashy looking website and thinking that because the seller asked them to pay by bank transfer and not Western Union or Moneygram that everything is above board.

In this book, we look at the different types of online scams, how they work and how to avoid being caught by them. Each chapter will look at a different type of scam and includes examples of actual emails received for that type of scam.

Any names, addresses and telephone numbers shown in the sample emails in the following chapters either belong to the scammer or are the made up details of a pretend victim. The spelling, grammar multiple fonts, images and varying sizes and colours of text in the emails has been left where possible as it was in the the original mails, to show the poor quality of the typing, formatting, spelling and grammar used. These can often give a good indication that you are not dealing with the claimed educated person working for a professional organisation, but a barely literate, uneducated, work shy scammer.

This book is not intended to cover every type of risk that exists on the Internet and we do not go into depth about subjects such as spam, phishing, or malware. However, the final short chapter of this book provides some general hints and tips for staying safe on the Internet.

Justifying scamming

Scammers and their apologists will often try to justify their crimes by using excuses of poverty, lack of opportunity and even getting back at the rich individuals from ex-Colonial nations for the poor treatment of their ancestors.

In reality, these are just pathetic excuses used by criminals who are too lazy to get a real job to support their families, or are unable to get the types of job that they think they deserve, due to their lack of intelligence or useful skills. There are many people in many countries living below the poverty line, who would never think of turning to crime and will take whatever job they can to support themselves and their families. As for the excuse of the lack of opportunity, many scammers are well educated and the only thing stopping them getting a job is their laziness. The excuse of getting back at past crimes is perhaps the most pathetic of all, the scammers most likely have no idea of the ethnicity or location of their victims when they send out their mails and if they do find that they are actually writing to someone in a third world country (or even their own country) who perhaps has less than they do, rather than some rich American or European, that isn't going to make them stop trying to scam them.

The reality is that scammers are pathetic little creatures who hide behind the anonymity of the Internet to commit their crimes and have no thoughts or care for the consequences of their actions on their victims. They will happily steal every last dollar of a pensioner's savings and then try to persuade them to sell their possessions and beg, steal or borrow from friends and family to carry on sending the money. And even when a victim has begged, stolen and borrowed from everyone and really has nothing more to send, their nightmare is often not over as the scammers may try to turn them into money mules to help them steal money from others. Not only does the victim end un broke, but they may also face criminal investigations and charges for laundering money for the scammer.

The depths that scammers will go to in an attempt to steal from their victims know no limits. They will happily pretend to offer loans to people who are about to lose their home or need a lifesaving operation and have absolutely no qualms about assuring a victim that they will get their loan with no problems, even though they know that they could actually be causing someone's death. They will not give a second thought to a victim who may choose to take their own life after finding out that they been scammed, except to lament the fact that they will now have to find a new victim.

2. ADVANCE FEE FRAUD

The premise of Advance Fee Fraud is that the victim is offered a large amount of money for the payment of a relatively small fee. The money being promised can take many forms, such as a lottery win, an inheritance, assisting someone move funds from an unsafe country, but the basis is always the same - in order to get their hands on the non-existent payment, the victim is required to pay fee after fee until they have been bled dry.

Advance Fee Fraud is not an invention of the Internet age or even the 20th century, its roots can be traced back to the Spanish Prisoner scam of the late 19th century and even as far back as the 1830s. In the Spanish Prisoner scam, wealthy businessmen were approached by individuals claiming to be trying to smuggle a prisoner from a wealthy family out of a prison in Spain. In exchange for the businessman's assistance, the scammer promised a handsome reward from the prisoners family and all the victim had to do is provide a small amount of money to bribe the prison guards. An example of the scam dating back to the late 1800s will no doubt look familiar to anyone who has an email account,

Mr. W. _____

Dear Sir - Notwithstanding having not the pleasure of being aquainted with you, I taken the liberty of writing you this letter in order to trust you with a secret that I never had thought to be obliged to entrust nobody with, but the sufferings that I am induring in this prison and my love for a young daughter of 16 years old who is in the actuality in a collge in Badajoz to make you my revelation, in the hope that you will be good enough as to help me recover a sum of 840,000 pesetas (33,600l) in gold money and french bank-notes that I was one day constrained to hide in the neighbourhood of your locality.

These are the motives of that affaire: I was a capatin of cavalry and cash-keeper of my regiment, when I took part in an inserection in which I was seriously exposed and obliged to take shelter in foreing in carrying away 460,000 pesetas that belonged to the cash of my regiment, having this sum been increased by the Central Revolutionary Comitee til 840,000, giving me the charge of purchasing in forein the necessary arnament for to help in the revolution.

I went to England, when I was informed by a friend of mine that the Spanish Government had asked my extradition, feering then for my freedom, I hastened to put my money in safety and as I dared not to deposit it in a Bank on account of my situation of emigrant, I tooke the resolution to bury it, what I did with all the care in order that neither the rain nor bad weather could never deteriorate the money. As soon as the occulation was made I met with an old peasant to whom I asked of an honest person of your country, and he gave me your name. Then, willing not to leave my young daughter into the hands of my enemies, I returned to Spain with design to take her off from the college and conduct her foreign with me. But alas! in arriving in Spain, I was recognised, arrested, and put into the hand of military authorities, which court-martial has condemned me at 15 years of confiment into a Castle-fort, of our Colonies, where very soon I shall be condicted and obliged to leave my dear daughter alone and without resources.

I will reward your troubles with the thrid potion of the money hided if you consent to help me in recovering it, but on the following conditions:

1. You ought to promise, under oath of secrecy, to be faithful and never make to nobody the least revelation concerning the secret I am trusting you.
2. You have to come to Spain to take my daughter and a respectable lady who ought to accompany her till your country where my daughter will give you a topographical plane of the spot where the money is hided, and all necessaries instructions that you may discover it without any difficulties.
3. For the moment, you must supply the means and pay expenses that may cost the travel of my daughter and the lady her companion as I cannot do so in my present situaion.

If you accept to lend me your aid, let me know so by return of post, but as I canot receive your letters directly because I am too watched, you must have the goodness to answer me at the adres of a friend of mine who I fully trust, and who will carry me your letters as soon as their arrival, with all the care that the case *require.*

In order to avoid all responsibiliy, do not sign your name, you may sign this of your locality, thus: .... Chelmsford.

I beg your pardon me if I cannot write engllish wel, I hope to be understood and be soon hounured with your answer, I have the honour to be Sir, your truely, Cesar De Cordoba.

Advance Fee scams became popular during the 1980s when they were again sent by mail and also by the increasingly popular fax machines that were appearing. The wide-spread use of email and the ability to harvest email addresses and bulk send emails has significantly lowered the cost of scammers sending their scam letters. In modern times, Advance Fee Fraud scams have become known by the name 419 scams, after the Article of the Nigerian Criminal Code that deals with fraud. Although Advance Fee Fraud emails come from many areas of the world, Nigeria is often singled out as a centre for these scams, and it is common for young Nigerian men to use Internet cafes to send out their emails.

Many people comment on the unbelievable content of these emails and the fact that they are unlikely to get a single response, but researchers such as Microsoft's Cormac Herley have suggested that by sending an email that repels all but the most gullible, the scammer is increasing his chances of getting replies that will produce a payment, as they can concentrate on those that are the most likely to believe the continuing excuses used for the promised funds not being transferred.

Many of the scams covered in the following chapters are also forms of Advance Fee Fraud. For example, Lottery, Loan and Pet scams all work on the premise of paying a small fee to receive something from the scammer (your winnings, loan or puppy/kitten in these cases). In this chapter, we will concentrate on the more traditional form of Advance Fee Fraud – those where the request is to receive money or other valuables on behalf of the writer.

We will now take a look at an example of how an Advance Fee Fraud plays out (insofar as we can get without sending the scammer any money) and after that, take a look at some of the other different types of opening mails that the scammers send out giving the different scenarios they use.

This particular scam is a refugee scam, a young female (usually) writes as a refugee in an African country, but has a large sum of money that she wants the victim to receive for her and help her to escape from the camp she is in.

Here is the original email received, which is very bland and gives no indication of what the writer actually wants.

> my dear, please contact me so that i can introduce my self to you very well,
> i have something special to share with you, Waiting to receive your mail soon
> have a nice day
> Yours Faithfully Franca

A simple reply gets the next scripted email in the scammer's format, with a bit more information, but still no hint as to what is really required and as is usual for this type of scam is accompanied by a couple of pictures of a well-dressed young woman.

> my dear
> Thanks once again, I am more than happy in your reply to my mail. How was your night ? mine was cool over here in Dakar Senegal. My name is Miss. FRANCA DICKSON, from Ivory Coast in west Africa and presently, I am residing in the refugee camp here in Dakar Senegal, as a result of the civil war in my country. I was a first year student of law at the University Of Abobo-Adjamé Ivory Coast, before the incident that lead me into this situation of living in the camp
>
> My late father Dr William Dickson, was the personal adviser to the former head of states, also a successful business man import and exporter during his life time, before the rebels attacked my house one early morning killing my mother and my father Equally my mother was a senior lecturer at the university where i read before her death, it was only me that is alive now because I was the first child to my parents as we are two and the other one died with them, now I managed to make my way to near by country Senegal, where I am leaving now
>
> I would like to know more about you. Your likes and dislikes, as I love cooking, hand ball, basket ball, music, reading and so on. I don't like dishonest people. your hobbies and what you are doing presently. I will tell more about myself in my next mail
> Thanks I am hoping to hear from you soonest
> hugs and smile
>
> Franca

Another response from the victim gets the next mail in the format, with another picture. Here, the real reason for writing is revealed and a Pastor is introduced as a point of phone contact (the scammer is most likely a young male, so needs to introduce a male character to field any phone calls from victims).

Hello

how was your night? also everything around you hope fine, I am more than happy in your reply to my mail. Mine is a little bit hot over here in Dakar Senegal. I am 24years of age living in this situation. In this refugee camp we are only allowed to go out some time in the weeks. Its just like one staying in the prison and i hope by Gods grace i will come out here soon.

I don't have any relatives now whom i can go to all my relatives ran away in the middle of the war, the only person i have now is Rev. Basil kwarma who is the pastor of Christ the king here in the refugee he has been very nice to me since i came in to this refugee here, but i am not living with him rather i am living in the woman's hostel because the camp have two hostels one for men the other for women.

The Pastors Tel number is +221776779180 when you call tell him that you want to speak with me he will send for me in the hostel. here is where am sending you email at church office. As a refugee here i don't have any right or privilege to any thing be it money or whatever because it is against the law of this country. I want to go back to my studies because i only attended my first year as law student before the tragic incident that lead to my being in this situation occurred.

Please listen to this now very carefully, i have my late father's account deposit certificate and death certificate here with me which i will show you latter, because when he was alive he deposited some amount of money in a leading bank in Europe which he used my name as the next of kin, the amount in question is $5.7M (Five Million seven Hundred Thousand Dollars).

Dear please i would like you to help and assist me transfer this money to your account and from it you can send some money for me to get my traveling documents and air ticket to come over to meet with you. I kept this secret to people in the camp here the only person that knows about it is the Reverend because he is like a father to me here.

So in the light of above i will like you to keep it to yourself and don't tell it to anyone for i am afraid of loosing my life and the money if people gets to know about it. Remember i am giving you all this information due to the trust and love i deposed on you now. I like honest and understanding people, truthful and a man of vision, truth and hardworking.

My favorite language is English which i did in the school. Mean while i will like you to call me by 14:00 (GMT) like i said i have a lot to tell you. Have a nice day and think about me. Awaiting to hear from you soonest.
Many kisses and hugs.
yours franca.

A positive response from the victim sees the next mail, which introduces a bank officer who will arrange the transfer of the funds to the victim.

My Darling

Hope you're doing good over there, thanks once again for your kind mail, and understanding, as i said about trust, not that i know you before or i understand your language but the believe i have and i really suffer here, so please help me, that is why I gave you this information hoping that you will never betrayed me after the transfer of my money to your account. before i contacted you i pray over it and ask God to give me the right man that will help me and i know that he will never disappoint me now i know is you.

And I want to inform you that I'm interested in the glamour model you proposed, so how can i start, hope you can hellp me for that

I promise you that you will never regret in helping me, I have all the prove of this fund all needed legal document is here with me, Listen I have not told anyone except you and rev Basil about the existence of this money and I will like you to please keep it secret to other people because since it is (MONEY) all eyes will be on it. Remember I trust you honey that is why I am giving you all this information. My love is for you and you alone, please I have informed the bank about my plans to claim this money and the only thing they told me is to look for a foreign partner who will stand on my behalf due to my refugee status and the laws of this country. the pics you were asking was the one i took before because here in the camp they can not allow as to take any pic

You will have 15% of the total money for helping me and the remaining money will be managed by you in any business of your choice since am too young to manage the amount. In this regards I will like you to contact the bank immediately with this information, tell them that you are my foreign partner and that you want to know the possibilities of assisting me transfer my 5.7 million dollars deposited by my late father Dr William Dickson, of which I am the next of kin to your account in your country.

Deposit Certificate Number: RBS810101785
Royal Bank Of Scotland (RBS)

EMAIL   =   royalbkscotland1@gmail.com
                  =   royalbanktransferofficescothland@aol.com

Telephone;   +447042068952
Fax number; +44-7005-807-719
Chief executive officer: Sir. Stephen Hester

Contact them now on how to transfer the 5.7million dollars deposited by my late of which I am the next of kin. I have mapped out 15% for your assistance and 5% for any expenses that might come up in this transfer. My dear I am glad that God has brought you to see me out from this situation and I promise to be kind and will equally need you in every area of my life plus investing this money since I'm still too young to manage it.

As I told you before, this camp is just like a prison and my prayers is to move out from here as soon as possible. Please make sure that you contact the bank so that after the transfer you will send some money from that money for me to prepare my traveling documents as i don't have passport now and other thing to meet with you in your country. let kiss, as I Awaiting to hear you soon after you contact and heard from the bank .

Yours forever in love,
Miss. FRANCA.

A mail from the victim to the fake bank official gets the following response. This email was meant to have a lot of embedded images of RBS logos etc., but due to the scammer's incompetence they didn't work. An analysis of this email showed that it was actually sent from Senegal and not someone working for the Royal Bank of Scotland in the UK.

Attn: **MR ZIEGE TATER.**

Please see the attached letter and comply with the answers to the questionnaire for the help of MISS.FRANCA DICKSON as she has informed us about you For the transfer of her late father's fund deposit with our Bank.
SINCERELY
SIR. Stephen Hester
CHIEF EXECUTIVE OFFICER
ROYAL BANK OF SCOTLAND PLC

(+447042068952 / +447031973494)

Attached to the email was a JPEG file containing instructions, which is reproduced on the next page. To enable the instructions to be added to a scam warning website, the scammer was told the document would not open and was asked to send the contents in the body of the email, which he did.

No.36 St Andrew Square,Edinburgh EH2 2YB

In line with our security measures and allied administrative matters, your application is going under securitization by the executive management board of this bank and this will be approved upon the fulfillment of our official obligation after certifying our bank the following questionnaire.

1) A power of attorney permitting you to claim and transfer the funds, to your bank account on her behalf; from Senegalese high court.
2) The deposit certificate of the fund.
3) The Death certificate of the late father.
4) An affidavit of oath from the Senegalese high court.
5) The full information of your bank account number and your bank name, address, name of the account number,
  including your bank telephone number, fax number of your bank, where you want our bank to transfer the fund.

As you provide all the requires the transaction of this fund will be made to your account within 48hrs.

SINCERELY
SIR. Stephen Hester
CHIEF EXECUTIVE OFFICER
ROYAL BANK OF SCOTLAND PLC
(+447042068952 / +447031973494)

 **Royal Bank Of Scotland**

36 St Andrew Square, Edinburgh EH2 2YB.

Atten: MR ZIEGE TATER

DATE: 03 / 07 / 2014

(RE ACKNOWLEDGEMENT OF APPLICATION FOR CLAIM, FORWARD THE FOLLOWING QUESTIONNAIRE TO THIS BANK)

I have been directed by the Chairman Executive Director of Financial Officer/Wire transfer to write you in respect to your partner mail which we received earlier. We are hereby acknowledging the receipt of your application as an appointed next of kin to our deceased customer Dr. William Dickson.

In line with our security measures and allied administrative matters, your application is going under securitization by the executive management board of this bank and this will be approved upon the fulfillment of our official obligation after certifying our bank the following questionnaire.

1) A power of attorney permitting you to claim and transfer the funds, to your bank account on her behalf; from Senegalese high court.
2) The deposit certificate of the fund.
3) The Death certificate of the late father.
4) An Affidavit of oath from the Senegalese high court
5) The full information of your bank account number and your bank name, address, name of the account number, including your bank telephone number, fax number of your bank, where you want our bank to transfer the fund.

As you provide all the requires the transaction of this fund will be made to your account within 48hrs,

This Power of attorney and affidavit oath of support must be endorsed by a Senegalese lawyer. (Since the money is originated from Africa and the young lady is currently residing in Senegal)

Note: The above four document are compulsory, and are needed to protect our interest, yours and the next of kin after the transfer has been made.

These shall also ensure that a smooth, quick, and successful transfer of the fund is made within 48hrs from when our bank receives the above mention documents.

Should you have any question(s) please contact our Chairman Executive Operational/Director of Finance Officer Mr. Stephen Hester through his telephone number for more clarifications and directives.

We promise to give our customers the best services.

Yours Faithfully

Jennifer Smith (Ms.)
Protocol officer to Royal Bank Scotland (RBS)

Email: royalbankscotland1@gmail.com, royalbanktransferofficerscotland@aol.com
Tel: +447042068952   Fax: +447031973494
http://www.rbs.co.uk/
Credit policies are administered and are underwritten by the Professional Underwriters
Insurance Group Registered in Scotland Nº 90312
Address 36 St Andrew Square,
Edinburgh EH2 2YB.

The victim, obviously, doesn't have the required documents, so he writes to the "refugee girl" to see if she has them. This is the response from her.

My Dear,

Thanks for your good effort and ability to help me, in other to transfer the money to your position pending my arrival to meet with you, it shows you are a dependable and trustworthy man. I am happy for your good effort and life you have given me

Listen, before I gave you this in formations I saw your profile that you matched mine, I have never told any body about this money. Listen the only people that knows about it is you and me and Rev Basil that give me the lawyer's contact now, no one again knows about it (since my parent's are dead). So, I will also advise you to please keep it to your self because I am afraid of loosing my life and the money again to people, who will disappoint me when the money gets to there care. That was why it took me time to tell you all about it and I promise you this from my heart (I AM NOT GOING TO DISAPPOINT YOU) and I equally expect the same from you.

Now regarding the requests the bank needs from us. I have with me here the Deposit Certificate OF The Fund and the Death certificate which i have attached to this letter, I thought it's the only thing the bank will need from us but since they need A Power Of Attorney, and Affidavit Of Oath, I informed Rev Basil about it after reading your mail and he gave me the contact of this lawyer bellow, he is a registered lawyer in the United Nations and he is also a registered member in (Senegalese Bar Association) who will help in preparing the documents for us.

Please I will like you to contact him through email and phone today, when your contacting him, tell him that you are my Foreign partner and you want him to prepare a power of attorney he will do it in your name to enable the bank to transfer my (Late) father's fund in ROYAL BANK SCOTLAND to your account in Your country.

His contact information's are as follows,
Bar (Dr) Ohie domingo
E mail address (ohiedomingochamber@yahoo.com)
Telephone Number is (+221705832492)

So, I will like you to contact him for the preparation of the power of attorney and the Affidavit of Oath, please try and contact me when you are in contact with him and let me know if he agrees to help us, also forward your information to the bank as required for the transfer. A big hug for you, From my deepest heart.

yours franca

Attached are two fake documents, which are shown on the following pages and a fake barrister is introduced. Another email is received soon after, with a suggested wording for writing to the "barrister".

---

pls send this letter to the lawyer

SIR

MY NAME IS MR ZIEGE TATER, I AM THE FOREIGN PARTNER OF MISS FRANCA DICKSON WHO IS CURRENTLY STAYING IN SENEGAL REFUGEE CAMP AND ALSO THE DAUGHTER OF LATE DOCTOR WILLIAM DICKSON

BEFORE THE DEATH OF MY PARTNERS FATHER HE DEPOSITED SOME AMOUNT OF MONEY IN ROYAL BANK OF SCOTLAND WHICH SHE IS THE NEXT OF KIN

SHE WANTS ME TO STAND FOR HER AS HER PARTNER IN CLAIM OF HER RIGHT AND I HAVE MADE CONTACT WITH THE ROYAL BANK OF SCOTLAND AND THEY ADVICE ME TO GET A POWER OF ATTORNEY AND AFFIDAVIT OF OATH FROM A SENEGALESE HIGH COURT SINCE MISS FRANCA DICKSON IS CURRENTLY STAYING IN SENEGAL, I ALREADY HAVE OTHER DOCUMENTS THEY REQUIRED.

I AM CONTACTING YOU TO PREPARE A POWER OF ATTORNEY AND AFFIDAVIT OF OATH WHICH WILL BE DONE IN MY NAME TO ENABLE THE ROYAL BANK OF SCOTLAND TRANSFER HER LATE FATHER'S FUND TO MY ACCOUNT

PLEASE GET BACK TO ME AS SOON AS YOU RECEIVE THIS MAIL
SINCERELY ZIEGE TATER.

His contact information's are as follows,
Bar (Dr) Ohie domingo
E mail address (ohiedomingochamber@yahoo.com)
Telephone Number is (+221705832492)

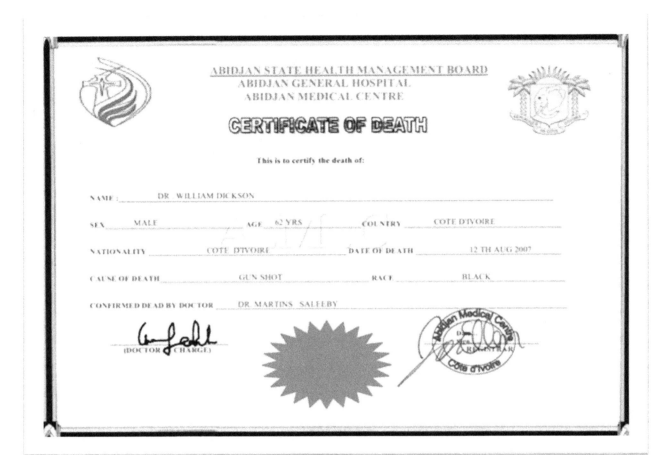

ABIDJAN STATE HEALTH MANAGEMENT BOARD
ABIDJAN GENERAL HOSPITAL
ABIDJAN MEDICAL CENTRE

CERTIFICATE OF DEATH

This is to certify the death of:

NAME : DR . WILLIAM DICKSON

SEX MALE   AGE 62 YRS   COUNTRY COTE D'IVOIRE

NATIONALITY COTE D'IVOIRE   DATE OF DEATH 12 TH AUG 2007

CAUSE OF DEATH GUN SHOT   RACE BLACK

CONFIRMED DEAD BY DOCTOR DR . MARTINS SALEEBY

(DOCTOR IN CHARGE)

ROYAL BANK OF SCOTLAND PLC

Banking & Finance
Address :36 St Andrew Square, Edinburgh EH2 2YB
Telephone Number: +447042068952
E-mail Address: (royalbscotland1@gmail.com) (royalbscotlandz@live.fr)

RBS The Royal Bank Of Scotland

RBS The Royal Bank of Scotland

CERTIFICATE OF DEPOSIT

DATE:27/06/2005

CLIENT NAME..: DR. WILLIAM DICKSON
NATIONALITY..: COTE D'IVOIRE
KIND OF ACCOUNT..: NON RESIDENTIAL
ACCOUNT No..: RBS810101785
SWIFT CODE..: RY0088XX5STD98
AMOUNT..: US$5.700.000.00 USD
NEXT OF KIN..: MISS FRANCA DICKSON

SECURITY CODE/ IDBS/117/#/SFC/ 2000   SERIES / IDBS / 733 /AC/F

DIRECTOR SIGNATURE

RBS The Royal Bank of Scotland

CUSTOMER'S SIGNATURE

12

12

The victim then writes to the barrister and gets the following response asking for personal details and attaching a fake ID.

Dear Mr ZIEGE TATER.

Sequel to the information which we received in our noble law firm on how to get an affidavit of oath and special power of attorney in your name to stand on behalf of your partner MISS FRANCA DICKSON as her trustee to transfer her late father's fund deposit to your nominated bank account in your country.

Note/ The following before we can proceed and render our legal service, we want you to forward your

1) full data name,
2) address and contact details
3) your telephone number, and date of birth.
4) Your ID or International passport number to our noble law firm, as you want it to appear in the (POWER OF ATTORNEY AND THE AFFIDAVIT OF OATH).
get back to me as soon as you receive this mail,
Thanks

Yours in service
Barrister Ohie domingo (senior advocate)
Barrister at Law, Ohie & Associates (General Solicitors and Legal Advocacy), Dakar Senegal.
Tel: <u>+221-705832492</u>
ADDRESS: UNIT 302 DAKAR SENEGAL
Email ohiedomingochamber@yahoo.com
Our priority is to render a good service to honest clients.

REPUBLIQUE DU SENEGAL
CARTE NATIONALE D'IDENTITE

Prenoms
OHIE
Nom
DOMINGO
Date de naissance   Sexe   Taille
27 MAY / MAI 1948   M   180
Lieu de naissance
DAKAR
Date de délivrance   Date d'expiration
09 SEP / SEP 10   08 SEP / SEP 16
Adresse
UNITE 302 DAKAR SENEGAL 3RD FLOOR

N° d'identification Nationale 290419484587

The victim sends the requested details and then gets a reply from the barrister, introducing the fees and asking for the money to be sent by Western Union or Moneygram.

Dear Mr ZIEGE TATER.

I wish to communicate you on the development of my inquiries from Federal High Court, Dakar Province today

However, it will cost the sum OF €580 euro for the registration and authentication of the power of attorney, €265 euro for Swearing of the affidavit of oath at the Federal High court here before it becomes validated, €215euro for the notary office registration stamping and my legal processing fee of €100 dollar euro.

Hence a total of €580 euro equivalent of Fcfa local currency here to get all your required documents prepared and validated as required by your partner's bank.

You will be required to provide this money immediately to enable me to proceed to make payments and securing all your requirements without further delay as your partner's bank has instructed.
Preferably, for easy accessibility, I request thatyou send the money through Money Gram or Western UnionMoney Transfer with the information of my secretary listed below

Sur Name .... NDOUR
Other Names .... MAME COUMBA
City...............................Dakar
Country............................Senegal.
Address.........No Unite 180 Grand yoffline -Dakar Senegal.)

Note: You have to inform me immediately you transfer the money to provide me with the information to enable me proceed with the preparation, registration and authentication of the legal documents as you do require which will take two working days to be completed.

Please be informed that i will receive all payments before rendering our legal service as i do not undertake the financial liability of my clients in the course of provision of legal service.
I am always ready to provide the best of my legal assistance at all times to my clients as an international advocate.
Thanks for your cooperation.

Yours in service
Barrister Ohie domingo (senior advocate)
Barrister at Law, Ohie & Associates (General Solicitors and Legal Advocacy), Dakar Senegal.
Tel: +221-705832492
ADDRESS: UNIT 302 DAKAR SENEGAL
Email; ohiedomingochamber@yahoo.com
Our priority is to render a good service to honest clients

If the victim had paid these fees, then the scam would have continued with more requests for different fees from either the barrister or the fake bank. If the victim realized they were being scammed and stopped replying to the scammer then some time later, they would have received an email from the "refugee girl" telling them she had succeeded in transferring the money with the help of someone else, but that she had left an amount of money for the victim (which would obviously require a fee for the victim to receive it).

Here are some other opening mails to Advance Fee Fraud scams.

This one gives no indication of what the business proposal is, just that it promises to make the victim a lot of money.

> Good day, friend.
> I have an interesting business proposal for you that will be of immense benefit to both of us. Although this may be hard for you to believe, we stand to gain $35 million between us in a matter of days. Please grant me the benefit of doubt and hear me out. I need you to signify your interest by replying to this email. md66bin@foxmail.com

Another unspecified business proposal.

> I am Andres Puyol the Director of Operations with a firm in Europe. Our firm is a Private Asset Management / Vaulting Company of high repute with years of outstanding service to various calibres of people. I have resolved to contact you through this medium based on business proposal that will be of mutual benefit to both of us. If your interested i will give you further details regarding the funds in question.
> Yours Faithfully,
> Andres Puyol.

Another vague email.

> We need to talk, please contact me with this email
> Address: info.tahapaul@accountant.com Thank you.

This one claims to have an investment proposal. Legitimate people who want to invest large sums of money get professionals to do it for them, not random people on the Internet.

> Greetings,
>
> I am representing an investment interest from Syria, interested in overseas investment involving large volume of funds, for which we seek your participation as an overseas representative to handle the investment in your country.
>
> These funds belong to my client who is a native of Syria but presently a political asylum seeker in United Kingdom due to the Uprising and Civil War in Syria. He wants to invest a large amount of funds in your country under qualified foreign partnership, these funds has no such illegalities like drug trafficking, money laundering or any financial crime attached to it. If you feel disposed towards the solicited role, please indicate by prompt response, so that I may provide you further details of the transaction, and also let you know what will be coming to you as remuneration for your solicited role. After that we shall then come to an understanding concerning the prospective areas of investment that will be conducive for investors of foreign descent. Bear in mind however, that this is a legitimate transaction, and the only reason why strict privacy is advised, is as the result of restrictions of the Syrian regulations.
>
> I look forward to your prompt response, send me an email in reply to standardtrust22@inbox.lv
>
> Your prompt attention to this matter would be greatly esteemed.
>
> Yours Truly,
>
> Dr Harvey L Spencer

This one is looking for someone to help him defraud his employer by buying a drug from a supplier and then selling it to his employer at a higher price. The drug doesn't exist, but the victim will have to pay to buy a sample.

Good day

I got your email from an e-marketing company, so i decided to let you know about the business opportunity of supplying us raw material from India. I am an employee of a multi-national animal vaccines production company in USA and UK working as the production manager.

There is a raw material which our company always send me to purchase from India. Right now I have been promoted to the post of production manager and the company cannot send me to India again, our director has asked me for the contact of the local dealer in India to enable them send the new purchasing manager to India to purchase the product directly from the dealer in India.

This material can only be found in India and Fiji only but cheaper in India. I want you to act as the dealer. I will present you to the company as the dealer in India where i was purchasing this product; You would now purchase the product from the manufacturer whom I used to buy from, and supply to our company with you as the direct dealer. After purchasing from original manufacturer, you would sell to our new purchasing manager at a higher price. The profit would be shared between you and I. This business is very lucrative and it is continuous.

Your role must be played perfectly and the least I expect from you is betrayal. I don't want my organization to know the real cost of the product because of my personal interest.

Kindly revert me if you are interested.
Get in touch with me through my mail id: gshimmar@gmail.com
Hope to hear from you soon!
Regards,
Shams Mohamed

Another one looking for someone to invest funds for them.

RE: SEEKING YOUR ASSISTANCE TO INVEST IN YOUR COUNTRY.

Sir,

I am Dr.Mathew Olunwa, writing to inform you of our desire to invest in your country on behalf of Hajiya Turai Umar Musa Yar'Adua the wife of former Late Nigerian President and former Katsina State Governor Umaru Yar'Adua.

Considering her very strategic and influential position, she hopes that the transaction is strictly confidential as possible. Also, want to disclose her identity at least for now, until the completion of the Transaction. Hence our desire to have you as our agent abroad to protect and invest their funds in a profitable business. The total amount she is willing to invest about $30.5M Only. Note, this transaction is 100% risk free and legitimate as these money originated from sales of crude oil and contracts executed. 25% of the total is for you, 5% for transfer expenses and 70% for her investment.

Further note: that every arrangement towards conclusion of this business has been perfected and $10,000.00, has been mapped out by the family just to take all legal process to obtain under the Security Diplomatic Immunity towards conniving of the fund through diplomatic means to your country for safety collection by you and once the agent arrive your country with the consignment will contact you for claim, as it will be deposited as (Valuable Family Treasury worth of $30.5M Only) once we secured all the backup documents under your name for the claim.

I have therefore been directed to investigate whether you would agree to act as a foreign agent in order to update this transaction. If you can handle this offer. Kindly send your Name, Contact Address, and Mobile Telephone Number to enhance our communications. Send your reply to: dr.mathewolanwa@outlook.com Or dr.mathewolanwa01@gmail.com.

I await your reply soonest OR Call No:234-7086-491-845 for more update thanks.

Regards.

Dr.Mathew Olunwa.
Email address:dr.mathewolanwa@outlook.com,

This one claims to be from the FBI, writing about unclaimed lottery winnings, with only a small fee required to have them delivered.

Anti-Terrorist And Monetary Crimes Division
FBI Headquarters, Washington, D.C.
Federal Bureau Of Investigation
J.Edgar Hoover Building
935 Pennsylvania Avenue, Nw Washington, D.C. 20535-0001
www.fbi.gov

ATTENTION: BENEFICIARY

This e-mail has been issued to you in order to Officially inform you
that we have completed an investigation on an International Payment in
which was issued to you by an International Lottery
Company. With the help of our newly developed technology
(International Monitoring Network System) we discovered that your
e-mail address was automatically selected by an Online Balloting
System, this has legally won you the sum of $2.4million USD from a
Lottery Company outside the United States of America.
During our investigation we discovered that your
e-mail won the money from an Online Balloting System and we have
authorized this winning to be paid to you via INTERNATIONAL CERTIFIED
BANK DRAFT.

Normally, it will take up to 5 business days for an INTERNATIONAL
CERTIFIED BANK DRAFT by your local bank. We have successfully notified
this company on your behalf that funds are to be drawn from a
registered bank within the world winded, so as to enable you cash the
check instantly without any delay, henceforth the stated amount of
$2.4million USD has been deposited with IMF.

We have completed this investigation and you are hereby approved to
receive the winning prize as we have verified the entire transaction
to be Safe and 100% risk free, due to the fact that the funds have
been deposited with IMF you will be required to settle the following
bills directly to the Lottery Agent in-charge of this transaction whom
is located in Cotonou,
Benin Republic. According to our discoveries, you were
required to pay for the following,

(1) Deposit Fee's (IMF INTERNATIONAL CLEARANCE CERTIFICATE)
(3) Shipping Fee's (This is the charge for shipping the Cashier's
Check to your home address)

The total amount for everything is $96.00 We have tried our possible
best to indicate that this $96.00 should be deducted from your winning
prize but we found out that the funds have already been deposited IMF
and cannot be accessed by anyone apart from you the winner, therefore
you will be required to pay the required fee's to the Agent in-charge
of this transaction

In order to proceed with this transaction, you will be required to
contact the agent in-charge (Mr.Ken Jackson) via e-mail. Kindly look
below to find appropriate contact information:

CONTACT AGENT NAME: Mr.Ken Jackson
E-MAIL;jackson_ken931@yahoo.es
PHONE NUMBER: +229-66043617
You will be required
to e-mail him with the following information:

FULL
NAME:

ADDRESS:
CITY:
STATE:
ZIP CODE:
DIRECT CONTACT NUMBER:
OCCUPATION:

You will also be required to request Western Union or Money Gram
details on how to send the required $96.00 in order to immediately
ship your prize of $2.4million USD via INTERNATIONAL CERTIFIED BANK
DRAFT from IMF, also include the following transaction code in order
for him to immediately identify this transaction : EA2948-910.

This letter will serve as proof that the Federal Bureau Of
Investigation is authorizing you to pay the required $96.00 ONLY to
Mr.Ken Jackson via information in which he shall send to you,

Mr. JAMES COMEY
Federal Bureau of Investigation F B I
Yours in Service,Photograph of Director
JAMES COMEY, 111 JAMAS COMEY
III Director Office of Public Affairs

This scammer is after a quick payout, by asking for a small fee in the opening mail, again so that some
unexpected funds belonging to the victim can be transferred to the victim.

Attn beneficiary ,

We are hereby inform you that your total funds $1,200,000.00 USD has
been released, however your daily tarnsfer of $5000usd have made, your
daily transfer payments is still (on hold)till your fund transfer
ownership certificate is obtained which will cost you $96usd only.Also
reconfirm your transfer details where your daily transfer of $5000usd
will be sending to you to avoid mistake till your $1,200,000usd
complete.

Meanwhile this is your first payment transfer informations you can
track it and confrim that your fund is available online waiting for
you to do the needed thing and start receiving your daily transfer of
$5000usd.
Here is your first payment information which is onhold till you send
the $96usd for your fund transfer ownership certificate .

1,Tracking infromations
https://wumt.westernunion.com/asp/order ... try=global
2,Money Transfer Control Number: 8845115202
3,Senders First Name: Darlena
4,Senders Last Name: Pike
5,Amount $5000usd
6,Text question Peace
7,Answer good
8,City address Cotonou
9,Country Benin Republic
10,Total amount $1.2musd

Send the $96usd through Western union,money express or money gram for
your fund of $1.2musd transfer ownership certificate with this
informations below,as soon as you send the $96usd then your first
$5000usd will be free onhold .Send it with this thress names complete.

Receivers name John Onyebuchi Chukwuemeka.
City Cotonou
Country Benin Republic

```
Text Very
Answer Nice
Mtcn,,,,,,,,,,,,,,,,
Amount $96usd
Senders name and address.
Email; fundfilesoffices@yeah.net


Regard,
Dr Sani .T.Israel.
Western Union
Department
headofficedepartment91@gmail.com
```

This one claims to have funds in a dormant bank account that he can pay to the victim and is using news reports relating to a real person to back up his scam.

```
Mr. Sunny Louie
Vice President/Branch Manager
Industrial and Commercial Bank of China (ICBC) USA
Oakland Branch, 401 9th Street
Oakland, CA 94607, USA

Greetings,

I have tried reaching you on the phone severally but no response until last night that a lady picked and informed me that I have been calling a wrong telephone number so I decided to reach you by email today. I will be brief in this message for safety reasons though I would not have used this medium (Internet) if I had reached you through the phone though email is also the fastest, surest and good secured medium of communication. However, this correspondence is un-official and private, and it should be treated as such. I also guarantee you that this transaction is hitch free from all what you may think of.

I am Mr. Sunny Louie, Vice President and Branch Manager, Industrial and Commercial Bank of China, (ICBC) Oakland Branch California USA. I am contacting you based on Trust and confidentiality that will be attached to this transaction. The Management and the Legal department of our Bank, (ICBC) in a recent meeting recommended that the account of LATE ROMAN BLUM, who was one of my branch depositors, should be declared Dormant, confiscated and the depositor's fund sent to the Bank Treasury according to American Banking and financial law. He died in January 2012 at the age of 97 years leaving no heir to this account. The bank has made series of efforts to contact any of the relatives to claim this money but without success, you can confirm through this site:

http://www.theepochtimes.com/n3/34142-roman-blum-no-heirs-to-receive-40-million-fortune-after-death/
OR
http://www.nytimes.com/2013/04/28/nyregion/holocaust-survivor-left-an-estate-worth-almost-40-million-but-no-heirs.html?pagewanted=3

LATE ROMAN BLUM own an account in my branch; he owns a dollar account with the sum of US$68.2M (Sixty Eight Million, Two Hundred Thousand United States Dollars Only) deposited in a Secret account with my branch. In fact, since his death, no next of kin to the account holder (the brother) nor any relative of his have shown up for the claim, this is because he has the account as a secret account thus he left all the documents for the deposit with me.This is where I am interested and where I want you to come in. I want you to come in as the relation of the deceased; I will give you the relevant documents and contacts to file the application and then effect the approvals for the transfer of the money, I will be the one to provide the vital documents for the claims of the money and then advise you exactly how we should handle it.

Please include your telephone/fax number/ Home address when replying this mail and I will give you more information as soon as you indicate your willingness to assist in this transaction. we will use our positions to get all internal documentations to back up the claims. Do not be bothered that you are not related in any way to him as I am in position to affix your name as the next of kin.

The whole Procedures will last only 9 working days to get the fund retrieved successfully without trace in future. After the transfer of the money we shall share the money 60-40.that is I will have 60% while you will have 40%. Kindly respond promptly so that I can advice you on the next step to follow.

I will be waiting to hear from you.
```

Yours truly,

Mr. Sunny Louie
Vice President/Branch Manager
Industrial and Commercial Bank of China (ICBC) USA

This one has found some trunk boxes with a fortune in them in a war zone and wants help getting them out of the country.

Dear XXX,

Thank you for your prompt response to my proposal. I will be glad to go a long with you towards actualizing this rare business opportunity.

I am Dr. Kerry Martins 60 years and comfortably married with three kids (two girls and a boy). Currently i am serving under the United Nations in helping the new Syrian authorities deliver immediate emergency aid and provide a democratic transition.I and my colleague discover USD$56.5 Million in Cash concealed in a Trunk Boxes which we deposited with a security company.

I would like to partner with you to claim these funds with a sharing Ratio of 50:50 should this offer interest you. However, there is no legal implication attached on these arrangements.I will like to inform you here that this is real and free without a risk attached and also bear it in mind that this business will cost both of us money before the truck boxes can get to your door step and if you are ready to work with me to achieve this golden opportunity then kindly furnish me your complete details

I am a man of my words and had a whole lots of integrity to protect.May i at this juncture request of the following information in other to build a solid mutual back ground before we proceed:

1. Your full name and address
2. Age and marital status
3. Occupation and international passport for proper identification.
4. Your direct telephone number for oral conversation.

I am leaving further details of this business till i receive the aforementioned requirements, after which we can discuss on phone on the best approach to the deal.

Be rest assured that all necessary arrangements had been concluded and since we are both foreigners, we are not exposed to any risk; hence this is 100% risk free.Though you may be engaged with myriad of commitment, may i crave your indulgence to give this business the urgent and confidential attention it deserves.

Regards,

Dr. Kerry Martins

This one claims to have compensation to be paid to victims of scams. There will of course be fees involved in getting the compensation.

Attention Beneficiary from the New Governor of Central Bank of Nigeria (DR GODWIN EMEFIELE),

We hereby inform you that the Scotland Yard Police, Interpol, Federal Bureau of Investigation, (FBI) United States of America, the Economic and Financial Crimes Commission (EFCC) of Nigeria and all the African Crime fighter leaders have come together to stop scam/internet fraud in Nigeria and all round Africa. We have recovered over US2.6 Billion Dollars from the people we have behind bars, also we have recovered you $15.5 million Dollars., Your 2.6 Billion Dollars is in a consignment vault box, the same application with your $15.5 Million Dollars.

Our duty is to make sure we stop internet scam and money laundering. As for today we have put a lot of fraudsters in jail. We go all over Africa to pick this thieves/internet rats. We have over 8,273 of them in our jails round Africa and we are still looking for more. We are aware that a lot of foreigners out there have been deceived and lost their hard earn money to these fraudsters after promising them percentages in their letters/e-mails for their impending help to move funds out Africa including fake lottery winning notification and at the end of the day, they will collect thousands of dollars from you without a successful end.

We have received the express mandate and instructions of the president, federal republic of Nigeria: Jonathan Goodluck GCFR together with the EFCC Nigeria, the Interpol and the FBI to commence the immediate release of your funds into your nominated account but we can not transfer this funds direct to your bank account,because we are having problem with the International Monetary Fund (IMF) so our method of payment is via Diplomatic Courier Service.So your diplomat has arrive with your consignment box worth One Million, Five Hundred Thousand United State dollars at John.F.Kennedy International Airport New York USA. Dr. Aaron Cohen Brcih now with your Full names,home Address,Phone Number also the name of the closet airport near to you via his email (servicediplomaticcourier@gmail.com)

CONGRATULATIONS.
DR GODWIN EMEFIELE
EXECUTIVE GOVERNOR
CENTRAL BANK OF NIGERIA.

It took this lowlife scumbag less than 2 weeks after the Malaysian Airlines flight MH17 was shot down to get his script together and spammed to potential victims.

Dear Friend,

I am KERRY FERGUSON a solicitor at law. I am the personal attorney to MR. JOHANNES VAN DEN HENDE a Dutch national, who owed series of businesses here in London. Herein after shall be referred to as my client.
On the 18th of July 2014, my client Mr. Johannes Van Den Hende, his wife Ms. Shaliza Zain Dewa and their three children(Piers, Marnix and Margaux) Aged 15, 12, 8, were involved in the Malaysian MH17 flight which was shot down in Ukraine Russian border.

All occupants of the MH17 flight unfortunately lost their lives. Since after the death of my client and his family then I have made several enquiries to Dutch embassy to locate any of my clients extended relatives but was unsuccessful. After these several unsuccessful attempts, I decided to track his last name over the Internet, to locate any member of his family hence I contacted you.

I have contacted you to assist in repatriating the money / properties left behind by my client before they get confiscated or declared unserviceable by the bank where this huge deposit were lodged.

Particularly, the bank where the deceased had an account valued at about £9.2 million pounds sterling. I have submitted a formal letter to the bank here in London informing them about the death of my client and I have been issued a notice to provide the next of kin or have the account confiscated within the next Sixty days of official working days.

Since I have been unsuccessful in locating the relatives for over days now, I humbly seek your consent to present you as the next of kin to the deceased so that the proceeds of this account valued at £9.2 million pounds sterling can be paid to you and then you and I can share the money. 60% to me and 35% to you then 5% will be mapped out for reimbursement of any expenses incurred during the processing of the funds release to your bank account.

I have all necessary legal documents that can be used to back up any claim we may make. All I require is your honest cooperation to enable us see this deal through.

I guarantee you that this will be executed under a legitimate arrangement that will protect you from any breach of the law. Please get in touch with me by my email and send to me your telephone and fax numbers to enable us discuss further about this transaction. EMAIL; (kerryferguson12@gmail.com)

Best regards,
Kerry Ferguson (Esq.)

How to avoid being scammed by Advance Fee Fraud

In many countries, unless you actively opt-in to receive marketing emails from a particular company or allow companies you do business with to pass your detail to "selected third-parties", then no legitimate business should be emailing you with sales or marketing requests. So any unsolicited emails that you receive should be viewed with suspicion, even if they appear to come from a trusted source. They are either spam or a scam. The points below, apply not just to Advance Fee Fraud, but in many cases to the other scams that I will be describing throughout the book.

- Legitimate individuals do not send emails to random people asking them to receive inheritances.
- Bank managers, Government officials and deployed servicemen do not "find" large sums of money that can be transferred elsewhere without being noticed.
- Governments, the United Nations, the military, banks, multi-national companies etc. do not use free email providers such as Yahoo, Gmail, Outlook.com or AOL – they have their own domains (see the chapter on Fake Websites for more information on domains) and any emails will be sent to and from those domains.
- Large companies, Government departments, and International organisations like the United Nations do not use mobile phone, VoIP or other non-landline telephone numbers as their main point of contact.
- Bank managers, barristers and Government officials do not offer to split the proceeds of a deal with you 60/40 (or whatever other random percentage they come up with).
- True orphans in refugee camps in Africa do not have large amounts of money from their Cocoa/Gold/etc. merchant father and do not send model quality pictures of themselves wearing designer clothes.
- Diplomats and "Diplomatic Couriers" do not deliver packages for people.
- There is no legitimate international database of email addresses that allow people from overseas to contact you individually. The only lists available are those used by scammers and spammers to contact their victims.
- Legitimate individuals do not write from one email address and ask you to reply to another (or set the email up so that the reply automatically goes to another).
- Legitimate individuals do not write from an email address that is in a different name (and often gender) to their own (i.e. "John Smith" would not be writing from the email address marybrown1953@gmail.com).
- Legitimate individuals do not send what appears to be a personal email where your details are actually in the Bcc: field rather than the To: field – that indicates the email has been mass-mailed to multiple people at the same time.
- Banks, barristers and courier firms do not ask you to send fees by Western Union, Moneygram or similar money transfer services – only scammers do that as it allows them to pick up the money anonymously. They will also not provide you with bank account details of a totally unconnected person or in a totally different country.

If you receive an unsolicited email and any of the above criteria are met then you are dealing with an Advance Fee Fraud scammer – hit the "delete" button and ignore it.

3. LOTTERY SCAMS

Lottery scams are a subset of the standard Advance Fee Fraud scam and work on the premise that the recipient is the winner of an online lottery. They will normally involve the receipt of a congratulatory email telling the "lucky winner" to contact a "claims agent" to claim their winnings (which will usually be cash, but often includes a luxury car as well).

A variant of the lottery scam is the use of the identity of a real lottery jackpot winner from the UK, USA etc. with a claim that they are donating a proportion of their winnings to people and you have been randomly chosen to receive a large $/£/€ payment. Those winners may well be donating part of their winnings, but it will be to a recognized charities or friends and family – not random strangers on the other side of the planet.

We will now take a look at an example of how the two variations of lottery scams play out (insofar as we can get without sending the scammer any money)

Here is the original email received for a standard lottery scam. In this case, the name and website of a legitimate lottery are mentioned in the mail, but they have no involvement with it and the scammer has even left the site's scam warning at the bottom of the email.

FROM: GOVERNMENT ACCREDITED
LICENSED LOTTERY PROMOTERS.
FREELOTTO AFFILIATED OFFICE U.K,
82 VICTORIA STREET VICTORIA LONDON
SW1 U.K
TEL:+44-7031-863-689

NOTIFICATION OF WINNING

We are pleased to inform you of the release of the recent results of the FREELOTTO INTERNATIONAL EMAIL PROMOTION PROGRAM held on the 1st of August 2014. You were entered as dependent clients with: Reference Serial Number:F2-003-036 and Batch number FR/45-300-07.
Your email address attached to the ticket number: 54-20-17-52-34-30 that draw the lucky winning number,which consequently won the Daily new year Jackpot in the first category,in four parts.You have been approved for a payment of $2,000,000.00 (Two Million United States Dollars) in cash credited to file reference number: TFR/9900034943/JPT.

All participants for the online version were selected randomly from World Wide Web sites through computer draw system and extracted from over 100,000 unions, associations and co-operate bodies that are listed online.This email promotion takes place every month. Please note that your lucky winning number falls within our European booklet representative office in Europe as indicated in your play coupon.

In view of this, your $2,000,000.00 (Two Million United States Dollars) would be released to you by our payment office in United Kingdom.Our Fiduciary agent will immediately commence the process to facilitate the release of your funds as soon as you contact him. For security reasons, you are advised to keep your winning information confidential till your claim is processed and your money remitted to you.

This is part of our precautionary measure to avoid double claiming and unwarranted abuse of this program,Please be warned.click on the website link below to view the photo page of some of our recent lucky winners. http://www.freelotto.com/winners.asp FreeLotto Winning Draw Results for 28th July, 2014.

$50,000.00: 4-5-34-41-3-37

$200,000.00: 22-43-6-9-28-26
$10,000.00: 12-32-17-14-24-10
$100,000.00 : 2-27-22-47-16-21
Monthly Jackpot $2,000,000.00: 54-20-17-52-34-30
Super Bucks $10,000,000.00 : 37-2-48-41-46- 25-43

To file for your claim, please contact your fiduciary agent immediately
via the email below:
Mr. Williams Ford
(Freelotto Fiduciary Department)
82 Victoria Street
Victoria London SW1 U.K

Email: uk.freelottooffice@yahoo.com
Email: uk.freelottooffice@yahoo.com

Provide him with these following details with which he will begin the processing of your winnings.

1.NAME IN FULL:
2.ADDRESS:
3.AGE:
4.PHONE:
5.FAX:
6.SEX:
7.MARITAL STATUS:
8.OCCUPATION:
9.COMPANY NAME/POSITION:
10.COUNTRY:
11.NATIONALITY:
12.EMAIL:

****
The freelotto Internet draw is held every month and is so organized to
encourage the use of the Internet and computer worldwide. We are proud to
say that over 400 millions U.S Dollars are won annually in more than 118
countries Worldwide. Warning!!!: Fraudulent emails are circulating that
appear to be using Free Lotto addresses, but are not from The Free Lotto.

PLEASE REPORT IMMEDIATELY
TO:abuse@freelotto.com

Once again congratulations.

Sincerely,
Kevin J. Aronin
Chairman & CEO Copyright © 1995-2014 The FREELOTTO National
Lottery Inc. All rights reserved. Terms of Service - Guideline
++

NB: You are advised to keep your winning strictly confidential until your
winning is processed and received by you.
This is to avoid double claiming which could lead to disqualification.

An email to the "agent" gets the following response introducing the "delivery agent" who will deliver the winnings.

FREE LOTTO EMAIL PROMO OFFICE
82 VICTORIA STREET,VICTORIA ,SW1
UNITED KINGDOM.
Tel: (+44)703-186-3689

===============================
Ref: TFR/9900034943/JPT
Batch: FR/45-300-07
===============================

ATTN: **Mike Hunt**,

We have received your claims email, based on this, your prize money shall be remitted to you accordingly.

On behalf of the Management and Staffs of FREELOTTO, we officially congratulate you as the beneficiary of the cash prize of $2,000,000.00 (Two Million United States Dollars) and your cheque have been issued in your name (Mike Hunt)

We advise you check the spelling and order your name is arranged so as to avoid problems at your local bank.

The order is.... Surname :- / Firstname:-/ Othernames.

This is real and not a hoax. You can click on the website link below to view the photo page of some of our recent lucky winners.
http://www.freelotto.com/ThisWeeksWinners.asp

As you already know, your email was randomly selected along with others from over 100,000 networks on the internet. Each email was attached to a ticket number.

A certificate of prize claims and some vital documents will be sent along side your winnings cheque. The documents to be sent are; Winning cheque,Winners Certificate and Certificate Of Lodgement.
Contact our Affiliate Delivery department with the contact information below for futher instructions on how to send the consignment to your location.
Find below the contact information of the delivery Agent for your immediate action.
================================
Handling Agent: Rickky Howard
Swift Express Courier Services.
241 Horton Road, West Drayton,
Middlesex, UB7 8HT, London
United Kingdom
Email: swiftcourier.deliveryservices@yahoo.com
Tel: +44-703-186-6991.

=====================================
Have it in mind that your won prize cannot be deducted from , this is because the total amount has been insured to the real value . This is in accordance with section 13(1)(n) of the national gambling act as adopted in 1993 and amended on 3RD July 1996 by the constitutional assembly. This is to protect winners and to avoid misappropriation of funds. Its is imperative that you add your IDENTIFICATION NUMBERS{CPEL/OWN/9876}as the subject of any correspondence with the delivery department to ensure they respond in a timely manner. I will require a concise update on proceedings with the firm as soon as you are in contact with them.If you need any assistance whatsoever, please do not hesitate to let me know and you are also advised to keep your winning strictly confidential until your winning is processed and received by you. This is to avoid double claiming which could lead to disqualification.
Accept our congratulations.

Sincerely,
Fiduciary Agent,
Mr. Williams Ford.

An email to the delivery agent gets the following response and the request for money to be sent by Western Union.

SWIFT COURIER SERVICES (OFFICE & ADMINISTRATION)

241 Horton Road, West Drayton,
Middlesex, UB7 8HT, London
United Kingdom
===
OUR REF:UK/CL24
DATE: 21st August, 2014.

ATTENTION : Mike Hunt,

This is Swift Courier Services (Passion to deliver) and welcome to our bespoke courier service. A certificate of winnings and other certificates including a winning cheque has been sent to us by the claims officer of overseas Winner, Freelotto Email promo. This is to inform you that after verification of your claims emails,we have therefore decided to deliver the package to you.

Please re-send to us your contact information and your winning package would be delivered at the address you would provide as parcel will not be delivered to P.O.Box address or street corners but to your residence.

With regards to this, you are required to select the most convenient of the two options below for a smooth delivery of your package to you:

Note: You will be given your PARCEL TRACKING NUMBER for you to track your parcel Online for delivery status as soon as you make the payment for delivery.

NOTE THAT YOU WILL PAY FOR THE COST OF DELIVERY TO ENABLE US PROCEED WITH YOUR DELIVERY.

SWIFT COURIER FIRST CLASS DELIVERY
Max Delivery Duration...............................48hrs
Mailing /freight cost...................................£300.00
Handling Fee...£140.00
Fuel surcharge..£85.00
Insurance..£100.00
Vat(5%)..£25.00
TOTAL £650.00

SWIFT COURIER SECOND CLASS DELIVERY
Max Delivery Duration....................................72hrs
Mailing /freight cost..£250.00
Handling Fee..£140.00
Fuel surcharge...£85.00
Insurance...£100.00
Vat(5%)...£25.00
TOTAL £600.00

Respond to this email by making a selection from the two options above. Also send to us a scanned copy of either your driver's license or any form of legal identification.

Be reminded that the deadline for the claiming of package is exactly one week after the receipt of this email. After this period, your package will be returned back to the office of the Freelotto office as unclaimed winning.

Please be rest assured that you will receive your winning package within 48/72hrs of we acknowledging receipt of funds from you. This is our business and when we promise to deliver at a specific time, we don't fail. Also we have no provision for cash-on-delivery(COD) for any customer.

For speed and convenience sake, do make all payments for your delivery via MONEY GRAM to the name of the office cashier,

Receivers Name: Mr. Ginery Kaufers.
Receivers Address: 241 Horton Road, West Drayton, Middlesex, UB7 8HT, London,United Kingdom.

After Payments must have been made by you, you will then proceed to send us the following information below as regards the very transfer as well as a scanned copy of the transfer slip from MONEY GRAM via an email attachment.

Sender's First Name.
Sender's Last Name.
Sender's Address.
Money Gram Reference Number.

We hope you are able to send the funds for your delivery as soon as possible because your winning package is here in my office ready for onward delivery to you.

IMPORTANT NOTICE FROM FREELOTTO PROMO
You are advised to keep your winning strictly confidential until your winning is processed and received by you. This is to avoid double claiming which could lead to disqualification. Also have it in mind that your won prize cannot be deducted from , this is because the total amount has been insured to the real value . This is in accordance with section 13(1)(n) of the national gambling act as adopted in 1993 and amended on 3RD July 1996 by the constitutional assembly. This is to protect winners and to avoid misappropriation of funds.

Thanks for your anticipated corporation.

Mr.Rickky Howard,
SWIFT COURIER SERVICES
+44-703-186-6991.
Email: swiftcourierdeliveryservices2014@yahoo.com

SWIFT COURIER DELIVERY SERVICES

If a victim pays this initial fee then there will be various other taxes and fees requested from them until they realize what is happening or are bled dry.

Here is the original email received for a lottery scam claiming to offer a proportion of the winnings of a real lottery winner. It was received in Russian and a translation is shown below.

Личное пожертвование USD 2,000,000.00 был дар для вас связаться со мной для более подробной информации

Private donation USD 2,000,000.00 was a gift for you to contact me for more details

A reply gets the following, more details explanation.

Thank you for writing to me, I want you to know that i did not make my donation public please take note, because of fraudulent people in the internet,am sorry for my spellings if you find any errors, i don't speak English very well,i used the internet translator to write you this message.
I am Pedro Quezada, A Native of Jarabacoa (Dominica Republic) like you already know i won the Powerball Jackpot of $338 million in the Month of March and the money have change my life and the life of my humble family, but it won't change my heart, my family is a very humble family and we're going to help each other out i and my family decided to do God's work after having a long talk with some ministers of God and prayer sessions by donating few good heart individual in the world. I don't have much to say about my self now but am over excited, So I want you and your family to be happy as we are happy today, So we decided to donate $2,000,000 us dollars to you and your entire family also to help people around you.

I am very grateful to you for the interest shown in my plight and I want to assure you that you will be greatly rewarded for what you have chosen to do. Although we know each other for the first time but I believe our father has directed me to you as I prayed and searched over the internet for assistance because I saw your profile on a list of registered email addresses provided to me by Microsoft list from which I picked you.

Be assured you stand no risk as this is my money,for source and verification please see the link below:

http://www.dailymail.co.uk/news/article-2302503/New-Jersey-338m-Powerball-winner-Pedro-Quezada-pays-30k-resolve-child-support-debt.html

We decided to donate Individuals and i told some Ministers about this which they said was a welcome idea and promised they will get me a list of some people who can help others with my donation and put smile in the face of the needy, i decided to select my self by going to Microsoft and Google to make a research. I decided to elope to United Kingdom with my family because, since i won this lottery different taxes have been fallen upon me and much are coming, my pastor and my able minister's of God advice me to move to United-Kingdom with my family rather than paying Tax each week.

MY PHOTO.
My donation OF $2,000,000 us dollars may not be much to you but i believe it will go a long way to improving your standard of living like my Powerball Jackpot did to me, I would like you to fill the below and return back to me and my entire household will be glad for you to visit us after my donation gets to you. Do this on time so you can contact the payout bank for further directives to receive donation,

Name:
Country:
Age:
Sex:
Occupation:

Thank you
Pedro Quezada

A reply supplying personal details gets a request to contact the fake bank.

Greetings Ziege Täter,

How are you doing? On behalf of my entire family i have now issued a letter of authority to my finance firm appointing you as our beneficiary and you are now the sole beneficiary to this fund totaling $2,000,000.00 USD for you and your family. also write to me as soon as the funds get to you please let me know.The contact details and email of our finance firm is below and you have to contact them immediately via email (lloyds-tsb-enquiries@hotmail.co.uk) OR Accountant Officer Mr.Tim Baker on Email (tim.baker.1@hotmail.com) or you can also reach the bank via phone as I have already issued the authority to them and they will be expecting to hear from you so that they can arrange on how the funds will be transferred to your personal account via an online bank to bank wire system, You have to provide them with every assistance the bank will need to effect the transfer to enable the funds released to you without delay. I want you to contact the finance firm stating only my deposit Reference: International Application ID no: (IPB/AVL2010/28392/UK) and your full name..... For easy trace of my file.

Note that you "MUST"first open a new online paying bank account with our paying finance group before your $2,000,000.00 USD will be paid to the new online bank account so you can have an open/secured access to your new bank account online and then information will also be provided on how you can personally transfer your $2,000,000.00 USD to your local account within 24 hours without providing your personal bank account information to anyone, if you follow the instructions from our finance firm directly within the next three (3) working days you will have this funds transferred to your account and available for use.

Bank Name: LLOYDS TSB BANK PLC AND FINANCE GROUP
Contact Person (Foreign Exchange Supervisor) : Mr.Tim Baker
Bank Tel Number: +44 7012908851
Fax: 442080432934
Bank Email Address:(lloyds-tsb-enquiries@hotmail.co.uk)
Bank Email Address:(lloyds-tsb-enquiries@outlook.com)
Mr.Tim Baker Email: tim.baker.1@hotmail.com

PLEASE NOTE THAT: The agreement/contract signed with the LLOYDS TSB BANK AND FINANCE GROUP London, United Kingdom for online transfers of the funds states that whoever is authorized to receive the funds will complete it through the use of an online account that must be opened by the new customer, therefore note that your contact with the LLOYDS TSB BANK AND FINANCE GROUP London will involve the opening of a new online bank account in your name which they will automatically credit $2,000,000.00 USD into the new account then you would have to transfer your funds online yourself from your house computer OR office accessing through their online database to any other account anywhere in the world. That is LLOYDS TSB BANKING GROUP Electronic Online - Banking policy so you should be ready to open an account with them upon your contact.
I wish you and your family the timeless treasures of Christ, the warmth of home, the love of family and the company of good friends because alot of friends will come around now. Good luck

Regards,
Mr Pedro Quezada

An email to the "bank" gets the following response, with the multitude of fonts and colours proving the fact that the email is not from a real bank.

LLOYDS TSB BANKING GROUP

24Hours On-line E-Banking Service
REGISTERED IN ENGLAND.
GREAT BRITAIN OF UNITED KINGDOM.
REGISTRATION NUMBER: 990LLOYDS/UK/ENG

ATTENTION :

GOOD DAY WELCOME TO LLOYDS TSB BANK,We have been waiting to hear from you please we will like you to send us the Reference Number which links to Mr Pedro Quezada's account that he gave to you so that we can confirm it very well before we can open an account for you.because he has told us that you are his beneficiary.

we are hope to read from you soon.
We thank you for banking with us.

Yours Sincerely,
Mr. Tim Baker.
BAcc CA (SA) H Dip BDP MBL
Tel: +44 7012908851
Fax: 442080432934
Group Risk and Finance Director

An email to the bank with the reference number, gets another reply and a form for the victim to complete (shown on the next page).

LLOYDS TSB BANKING GROUP
24Hours On-line E-Banking Service
REGISTERED IN ENGLAND.
GREAT BRITAIN OF UNITED KINGDOM.
REGISTRATION NUMBER: 990LLOYDS/UK/ENG
REFERENCE NUMBER :IPB/AVL2010/28392/UK

ATTENTION:Ziege Täter,

We receive your mail from the direct office of the LLOYDS TSB BANK.this is the proper information on what to do before this fund can be transfer to you as the beneficiary of our client Mr Pedro Quezada.Kindly choose from different account options and fill out the form attached along side with this email correctly.

Your email in regards to the reference number (IPB/AVL2010/28392/UK) which links to Mr Pedro Quezada's account, we also got confirmation from Mr Pedro Quezada that you are the beneficiary to be paid the sum of $2,000,000 and in line with our corporate policy, the beneficiary who will receive this donation is required to open an account with our Bank. This online account will be set up in your name by our Bank (Lloyds TSB Bank plc). As soon as you meet up to our corporate policy, you will have your account setup. Please be informed that setting up of an online account with us is a simple exercise that involves simple steps, which you will have to choose the type of account you want to open from the options below.

1. PERSONAL ACCOUNT: This type of account requires a minimum initial deposit of £470.00 GBP equivalent to $750.00 USD (Seven Hundred And Fifty USD), this amount is required to set-up your new account to a fully operational account. The maximum transfer possible within a month with this Account is £7,000,000.00 (Seven million pounds) within one month or the equivalent amount in another currency; and with this account you can apply for a gold membership credit card after a good business relationship with us for one year minimum.

2. CORPORATE ACCOUNT: This is a daily business account and the initial opening deposit is £664.00 GBP equivalent to $1000.00 USD (One Thousand USD) this amount is required to set-up your new account to a fully operational account. The maximum transfer possible within a month with this Account is £15,000,000.00 (Fifteen million pounds) or the equivalent amount in another currency; and with this account you can apply for a gold membership credit card after a good business relationship with us for five months minimum.

3. PLATINUM ACCOUNT: This is a daily personal and business account and the initial opening deposit is £940.00 GBP equivalent to $1500.00 USD (One Thousand Five Hundred USD) this amount is required is to set-up your new account to a fully operational account. The maximum transfer possible within a month is unlimited; and with this account you can apply for a gold membership credit card after a good business relationship for three months minimum.

Please note that the initial deposit is refundable upon request if you decide to close your account. As soon as your account is set up, you will have an account number and an access code with which you can access your account through our online facilities from your home which will also enable you check your account balance and also make transfer to any account in the world.

Please choose the type of account you wish to open with our bank so we can provide you with information/requirement on how to setup the account. We wait to receive response from you soon; if you have any questions do not hesitate to contact us via phone or email.

Note: The initial deposit cannot be deducted from Mr Pedro Quezada Account, this is as a result of the insurance policy bond he placed on his account which makes it impossible for us to deduct any amount from his account unless the funds is transferred in full to the beneficiary's account with our bank.

We thank you for banking with us.

Lloyds TSB Finance Account Team
Mr.Tim Baker(Foreign Exchange Supervisor)

LLOYDS
BANKING
GROUP

311 Barlow Moor Road Chorlton Manchester Greater Manchester M21 8AJ

PERSONAL INFORMATION

TITLE: MR/MRS/MISS/MS/Others		
FULL NAMES IN BLOCK LETTERS		
FIRST NAME	MIDDLE NAME	SURNAME

DATE OF BIRTH	YEAR	MONTH	YEAR

FULL RESIDENTIAL ADDRESS	

COUNTRY OF RESIDENCE	STATE

RESIDENTIAL STATUS	MARITAL STATUS	NATIONALITY

OCCUPATION/PROFESSION	ANNUAL INCOME

POST CODE	IDENTIFICATION TYPE	IDENTIFICATION NUMBER

HOME PHONE NUMBER	OFFICE PHONE NUMBER	MOBILE PHONE NUMBER	FAX NUMBER

EMAIL ADDRESS	PURPOSE OF ACCOUNT	TYPE OF ACCOUNT

NEXT OF KIN INFORMATION

FULL NAMES IN BLOCK LETTERS		
FIRST NAME	MIDDLE NAME	SURNAME
RELATIONSHIP OF NEXT KIN	GENDER	EMAIL ADDRESS

FULL RESIDENTIAL ADDRESS	PHONE NUMBER

COUNTRY OF RESIDENCE	NATIONALITY

- SIGNATURE (For mandate purposes)

PASSPORT
PHOTOGRAPH

NOTE: ATTACHED SCANNED COPY OF ANY VALID IDENTIFICATION CARD (IMPORTANT)

Lloyds TSB | for the journey..

Completing and returning the form gets the following response

LLOYDS TSB BANKING GROUP
                    24Hours On-line E-Banking Service
                    REGISTERED IN ENGLAND.
                    GREAT BRITAIN OF UNITED KINGDOM.
                    REGISTRATION NUMBER: 990LLOYDS/UK/ENG
                    REFERENCE NUMBER :IPB/AVL2010/28392/UK

                    ATTENTION:Ziege Täter,

WELCOME TO LLOYDS TSB BANK. Sequel to your previous email to this office We recieve the form and it was well filled please you will have to choose from different account options the account you want us to open for you then you will have to send to us any of your identification of your (International Passport)for us to know.

1. PERSONAL ACCOUNT: This type of account requires a minimum initial deposit of £470.00 GBP equivalent to $750.00 USD (Seven Hundred And Fifty USD), this amount is required to set-up your new account to a fully operational account. The maximum transfer possible within a month with this Account is £7,000,000.00 (Seven million pounds) within one month or the equivalent amount in another currency; and with this account you can apply for a gold membership credit card after a good business relationship with us for one year minimum.

2. CORPORATE ACCOUNT: This is a daily business account and the initial opening deposit is £664.00 GBP equivalent to $1000.00 USD (One Thousand USD) this amount is required to set-up your new account to a fully operational account. The maximum transfer possible within a month with this Account is £15,000,000.00 (Fifteen million pounds) or the equivalent amount in another currency; and with this account you can apply for a gold membership credit card after a good business relationship with us for five months minimum.

3. PLATINUM ACCOUNT: This is a daily personal and business account and the initial opening deposit is £940.00 GBP equivalent to $1500.00 USD (One Thousand Five Hundred USD) this amount is required is to set-up your new account to a fully operational account. The maximum transfer possible within a month is unlimited; and with this account you can apply for a gold membership credit card after a good business relationship for three months minimum.

We thank you for banking with us.

Lloyds TSB Finance Account Team

Tim Baker

Choosing an account type and returning a non-opening file and saying it is a copy of the passport, gets us to the request for the money to be paid, by Moneygram.

LLOYDS TSB BANKING GROUP

24Hours On-line E-Banking Service
REGISTERED IN ENGLAND.
GREAT BRITAIN OF UNITED KINGDOM.
REGISTRATION NUMBER: 990LLOYDS/UK/ENG
REFERENCE NUMBER IPB/AVL2010/28392/UK

ATTENTION:Ziege Täter

WELCOME TO LLOYDS TSB BANK. Sequel to your previous email to this office and you have selected the PERSONAL ACCOUNT:This type of account requires a minimum initial deposit of £470.00 GBP equivalent to $750.00 USD (Seven Hundred And Fifty USD), this amount is required to set-up your new account to a fully operational account. The maximum transfer possible within a month with this Account is £7,000,000.00 (Seven million pounds) within one month or the equivalent amount in another currency; and with this account you can apply for a gold membership credit and Debit card after a good business relationship of one year minimum.

We recieve the identification of your(International Passport)it was correct and ever thing was fill by you all you need now is for you to send to our transfer department the sum of $750 USD via MoneyGram Transfer to the below officer.

Receiver's Name: Fred Johnson
Receiver's Address:5 floor,25 Gresham street, EC2V 7HN, United Kingdom.

And you are to send to us the below information for us to confirm your payment:

Sender's Name:
Sender's Address:
MTCN:
Amount Sent:

As soon as the payment receipt is received, Your Account will be activated in the next 24-48 banking hours, and Mr Pedro Quezada funds will be credited to your PERSONAL Account with us, Then you will be given an online USERNAME AND PASSWORD which will enable you access your account from your Home, Make transfer to any account in the world.

You can also upgrade your account anytime you wish to.

Note: The initial deposit fee is refundable after closing your account with us and also you have to scan and send the receipt of payment to us via email attachment for official use only.

Thank you for your patronage.

Yours Sincerely,
Mr. Tim Baker.
BAcc CA (SA) H Dip BDP MBL
Tel: +44 7012908851
Fax: 442080432934

We thank you for banking with us.

Lloyds TSB Finance Account Team
Mr.Tim Baker(Foreign Exchange Supervisor)

How to avoid being scammed by Lottery Scams

In general, any email received telling you that you have won something should be viewed with suspicion unless it relates to a competition that you have specifically entered and comes from an official email address of the organization running the competition. In addition to the identifying signs in the Advance Fee Fraud section, here are some additional sure fire signs that you are dealing with a lottery scam:

- If you didn't buy a lottery ticket then you haven't entered the lottery, so you can't win.
- Lotteries are regulated in the vast majority of countries and cannot be run by random companies.
- Google, Yahoo, Microsoft, BMW, Coca-Cola, Pepsi, etc. do not run lotteries.
- Legitimate lotteries do not require you to write to a "claims agent" who uses a free email address.
- Legitimate lotteries do not require you to pay fees or taxes up-front and not allow them to be deducted from your winnings.
- Lottery winners do not donate a proportion of their winnings to random strangers on the Internet.

4. LOAN SCAMS

Loan scams are another subset of the standard Advance Fee Fraud scam and are targeted at people who may be looking for loans. In particular, people with poor credit records or other problems that stop them from getting loans from their own bank or another recognised lender in their own country are often hit by these types of scam. The initial email is often characterised by promises of guaranteed loans, low interest rates and inconceivable amounts being able to be borrowed.

A variation of loan scams is those scams where the leasing of a Bank Guarantees, Standby Letters of Credit and other complex financial instruments for 7 figure plus sums is offered – the premise is the same, but the potential rewards for the scammer are much larger, there is no guarantee, the scammer just wants to steal the fees he charges.

We will now take a look at an example of how a loan scam plays out (insofar as we can get without sending the scammer any money). Here is the original email from the scammer.

Good Day To You,
Are you looking for a very genuine loan? at an affordable interest rate ? processed within 2 to 3 working days. You were constantly rejected Your Banks and other financial institutions, ? The good news here!

We offer loans ranging from $ 1,000.00 to $ 30,000,000.00 Max . 3% interest rate per annum. Credits for the development of competitive business EDGE / business expansion. We are certified , trustworthy, reliable , efficient, fast and dynamic . and cooperate financier for real estate and any kinds of business financing , we give out long term loan for one month for a maximum of 50 years .

We offer the following types of loans and many more ;

Personal Loans (unsecured loans)
Business Loans (unsecured loans)
Consolidation Loan Combination Loan
Company loan.
Home Improvement.

Please , if you are interested in our financial offer , note Please contact us if you are in need of our services , as you will be required provide us with the following information to begin the process Your loan amount , respectively.

Name:
Surname:
Gender :
Age:
Marital status:
Contact Address :
City / Zip :
Country:
phone number:
amount of loan needed:
duraction of the loan:
purpose of the loan:
private email:
do you apply for a loan before:

---

once you finished filling the loan application form kindly send it back to us so that we can start the registration of your loan transaction, reply to this EMAIL contact : privateloantrust@gmail.com

THANKS

An email by the victim providing the requested details gets the following response.

Welcome TO WEND PLANET FINANCIAL HOME

Hello XXX,

I am in receipt of your mail, and also i will be able to offer you the Loan Amount as you required 750,000.00,for the purpose of borrowing 750,000.00 is to fulfill your Business expansion. for us to fully proceed with the loan processing ,stated below is the loan terms / repayment plan,if you are in agreement to these terms,we want you to get back to us so that we can continue with the loan processing for approval by the board of management of these company.

LOAN TERMS AND CONDITIONS/REPAYMENT PLAN

Loan Balance: 750,000.00
Loan Interest Rate: 2 %
Loan Term: 5 years
Monthly Loan Payment:13,145.82
Number of Payments: 60
Cumulative Payments:788,749.20
Total Interest Paid: 38,749.20

Note: The monthly loan payment was calculated at 59 payments of 13,145.82 plus a final payment of 13,145.82.

(1)The borrower will start to be paying the monthly payment at least four months time after the loan have been granted and transferred to the Borrower.

(2) Borrower must be willing to pay back at the appointed time.

(3) Theloan will be transferred to you exactly 4 hours after the transaction is completed.

Loan Approval/Processed

In regards to the approval of the loan,your loan will be Approved by the K.G.S Approval's Department {B.O.D} Board Of Directors of the loan.

Loan refund:

The loan must refunded back to the lender at the end of the tenure to the loan seeker which is seeking for the loan without any delay.for this reason, will agree to the duration of 30 Years as stated by the loan seeker, to the loan seeker so that you will be able to repay the loan with in that period.

Interest Rate:

The Interest rate applicable to all Loans amount is 2%

Transfer Of Funds

Considering the above condition: If the LOAN TERMS AND CONDITIONS/REPAYMENT PLAN are acceptable by you,you will have to give me a fast response so that we can proceed further getting the Loan Approved.

Best Regards

Loan Financial Service

Confirming acceptance of the terms, the victim gets the following response.

Attention XXX how are you doing with your family, I want to inform you that your mail was well noted: which stated that you have be in agreement with our terms and conditions.

Right now i want you to send down your id card and banking details with the sum of $190.89 as your loan approval charge which will be remit through western union money transfer but first your id card and banking details is needed to enable the facilities to provide the western union details which you are to remit the approval charge.

I await your positive response to proceed.

Mrs Wilson

Sending the bank details and ID card to the scammer gets the following response.

Hello,

we got your mail, but we want you to know that before this loan will be transfer into your account we have two option of given our loan

BELOW ARE THE FOLLOWING OPTIONS OKAY:

1)THIS FIRST OPTION IS THAT YOU ARE TO PROVIDE A COLLATERAL FOR THE LOAN, SOME THING MORE THAN THE LOAN AMOUNT THAT YOU ARE LOOKING FOR AND ONCE YOU ARE UNABLE TO PAY BACK THE LOAN THE PROPERTY WILL BE TAKING BY THE COMPANY OKAY,

2)IN THIS OPTION YOU ARE NOT TO PROVIDE ANY COLLATERAL BUT THE LOAN WILL BE INSURED BEFORE THE TRANSFER AND AN INSURANCE CERTIFICATE WILL BE OBTAIN AND WILL BE SEND TO YOU TO SIGN AND ALSO BE SHOWED TO THE BANK BEFORE THEM CAN TRANSFER YOUR LOAN INTO YOUR ACCOUNT, BUT THE POLICY OF THIS OPTION IS THAT YOU AS THE BORROWER IS GOING TO PAY FOR THE COST OF THE LOAN INSURANCE AND THIS IS THE FASTEST OPTION OKAY,

SO I WANT YOU TO KNOW THE OPTION YOU WANT,SO THAT WE CAN TRANSFER YOUR LOAN IN GOOD FAITH

BEST REGARD

I AM WAITHING FOR YOUR URGENT RESPONCE

Selecting the second option gets the following response.

Good day,
I receive your mail, i will advice you to send the fees directly to the person in charge Please note that you are expected to send the fees via western union or money gram.

You are to use the payment information below.
Receiver's Name: Best
last name;Uduebholo
Country: Nigeria
State; Edo state
Amount To Be Sent:1000$

As soon as you make the payment, you are to forward to us the information's as below

SENDERS NAME:

SENDERS ADDRESS:

MONEY TRANSFER CONTROL NUMBER(MTCN#):

Regards

The initial email sent out from the scammers can range from the detailed one shown earlier to a simple one-liner such as:

> We give out loan for just 2% interest rate, both local and international loan

Fake Certificates

Loan scammers will often send out certificates to prove the legitimacy of their business. Here are a few examples of some of their attempts at producing a certificate.

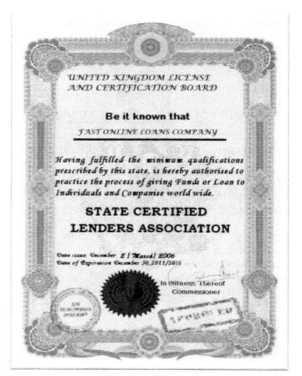

How to avoid being scammed by Loan Scams

As mentioned in the earlier chapters, any unsolicited email received should be viewed with scepticism, particularly when dealing with financial matters. Some other sure fire signs that you are dealing with a loan scam are:

- Claims to be a private lender – these do not exist in the real world. Loans are made by banks, building societies, credit unions etc. (or the equivalent in your country).
- Claims to be able to lend to any country - The Financial Services industry in every country is regulated in some way and to be able to offer Financial Services products (such as loans and mortgages) in a particular country you have to be authorised in that country. To offer loans worldwide, you would have to be authorized in **every** country, which would probably mean having a physical presence in each country.
- Use of titles such as Rev or Dr – people working for banks etc. do not tend to be titled. Scammers love to use titles as in their minds, it makes them seem trustworthy.
- Low interest rates and guaranteed loans - If your financial situation is such that you are having to resort to looking for loans on the Internet then you will not be getting 2% or 3% interest rates or a guaranteed loan.
- Arrangement fees – many countries do not allow the charging of upfront fees for loans and where they are allowed, they are added onto the loan and not charged as a separate payment.
- Ridiculous amounts – lenders do not lend multi-million dollar (or whatever currency) amounts by email or without any form of credit checking.
- Overly religious wording – businessmen, no matter how religious they may be do not tend to use religious references or quotes in their business dealings as it may offend those of other faiths or who are not religious. This is another scammer trait, due to their imagining that religious people will be seen as more trustworthy.
- Multi-million (or even billion) dollar bank guarantees cannot be leased on the basis of completion of a few forms. Anyone who was offering complex financial instruments like this, would not be approaching people by email, posting on forums or using free email addresses.

5. RECOVERY SCAMS

Recovery scams target those who have already been scammed, with the promise that money lost to a previous scammer can be recovered or compensation given. This is another variation of the Advance Fee Fraud and the scammer claiming to be able to retrieve the previously stolen funds will eventually ask for fees of some sort to enable them to get the funds.

Often, this scam will be run on the victim by the original scammer that stole from them as a means to get even more money from them when the original scam has been exhausted. However, sometimes scammers will just mass mail a recovery scam format in the same way that they would any other scam, hoping to get someone who will respond.

The email exchange below is an example of an opportunist scammer who just mass mailed his recovery scam script. The first mail is the original mail, which is made to look as if it came from another victim, who has been successful in getting her compensation

---

Attn: Beneficiary,

I am Mrs. Webber Katheren, I am a US citizen, 66 years Old. I reside here in Centreville Virginia U.S.A. My residential address is as follows.14852 Rock Landing Court Centreville Virginia 20121 United States and my email address id (webberkath@gmail.com) I am one of those that fall victims to scammers in Africa two years ago. I had lost over US$174,000 + for the past years while in the US. I was trying to get my payment all to no avail. And they always stopped my funds with one reason or the order. So I decided to travel with my Son to WASHINGTON D.C with all documents, there the (FBI) was amazed and contacted the Nigeria embassy in the US. After some hours in that office, I was asked by the FBI officer to come back the next week.

When I did the FBI officer gave me the contact of one Barrister Mohammed Peter who is a representative of the (FBI) and a member of the compensation award committee, currently in Nigeria. When I contacted him he explained everything to me. He said whoever is contacting us through emails are fake that we should fly down to Nigeria to see things for myself which I did and he took me to the paying bank for the claim of my compensation payment. This was paid to me successfully. Right now I am the happiest woman on earth because I have finally received my compensation funds of (US$4,300,000.00) Four Million three Hundred Thousand United State Dollars. Moreover, Barrister Mohammed Peter showed me the full Information of those that are yet to receive their compensation funds and this was how I came across only your email address and your full name.

The only Money I paid after I meet with Barrister Mohammed Peter was just $340 for processing of all paper works and legal modalities attached to the release of my payment. Considering the above explanation, I advising you to contact Barrister Mohamed Peter via email(cityexpress75@hotmail.com) for your own money including the money you lost or you can as well call him on his direct telephone number (+234 909-916-4327) please take it very serious. Thank you & God bless you.

Webber Katheren

14852 Rock Landing Court, Centreville
Virginia 20121 United States.

An email to the address given gets the following reply.

Dear Sir

How are you today? Mail well noted and I must tell you that Katherine just called me this morning about this your issue now
Yes I will help you facilitate the release of your funds into your nominated bank account within 7 working days from today
Send me your full contact and banking details so we can start from there
Full name and address
Banking co ordinates
Copy of identification
Copy of utility bill
Payment of $340 for documents
As soon as I hear from you, I will send you the payment details where you will pay the fee required

Yours faithful
Barrister Muhammed Peter

Providing the details requested, gets the following details for a Western Union payment

Dear Tater,

Mail well noted, the documentation process will commence as soon as i receive the fee, all documents will be send to you by dhl which you will present to your banker for immediate confirmation of the funds into your nominated bank account
Send the fee with details below

Receivers Name: JAMES OLAMIDE
Address: 10 Allen Avenue, Lagos Nigeria
Text Question: What for
Answer: Lawyer

Send me all details here on email and also call me

Your requirements are also needed for the paper works

Yours Faithfully

Barrister Muhammed Peter

The victim refuses to send money by Western Union, as he was scammed previously and asks for the "Barrister's" bank details.

Dear Tater
Mail received, the fee is small and can mis on account, that's why I advice you send it through express money transfer so that the receiver can pick and go to the court and pay the required fee to enable us proceed with documentations on your behalf.
I will advise you do so to faciliate the whole process as we have limited time to accomplish this task before the big holidays coming. If you wire the funds it may take up to 3 working days to arrive on th account and with bank charges and other taxes, the fee will not be complete again, so it will be better you go and send it by money gram or western union for faster and easy way to cash it for the purpose it was meant for.
Am a very busy person and will be going to london and switzerland to meet with delegates from bank of england and world banks with the beneciaries those that I have finalse their paper works and will like to go with yours too. So go ahead and send it. Yes there is fraud going on now, but am not among and will never let you down.
Kindly send me your details as requested previously , let it come with the fee so we can meet up
Regards
Barr. Muhammed Peter

NB: WANT TO CALL YOU TODAY, GIVE ME YOUR MOBILE PHONE NUMBER

A further refusal by the victim, gets the following response (a delaying tactic while the scammer finds a bank account he can use).

Dear Tater

I will provide you with the account details today, let me go to the office and send it to you in 5 hrs time
Regards

Bar. Muhammed Peter

Followed a few hours later by bank details.

Dear Tater

Per my last mail to you this morning, kindly find the account below
Make the payment and confirm the slip to me here, as soon as i confirm the payment i will get back to you.
Also send me the details of your bank and contact address so we have to open your file with the presidency and finance ministry before the arrival of the funds

find account

Account Name: Amobi Mercy Adaeze
Acct : 00008824xx
Bank name :UBA Bank
Bank address: Oba Akran Ikeja Lagos-Nigeria

Confirm to me when this is done

Your

Bar. Muhammed Peter

The victim responds to say he will go to the bank and the scammer sends the following email asking for the "payment slip" – he needs this to give to the account owner to show the money is his.

Dear Tater

Mail noted , waiting for the slip and other details needed
Regards

Bar. Muhammed Peter

The account details provided are insufficient to allow an international transfer from the victim's location, so the scammer is asked to provide the additional details required. Instead, the scammer provides details for a totally different bank outside of Nigeria.

Dear Tater

Happy Xmas in advance , sorry for the delay in given you the correct wire details for the fee
Find below the correct account details for the agent appointed by the government since your funds will be released through a prime bank in London
Send me the copy of the wire slip here
AIB BANK, TAILAGHT VILLAGE DUBLIN 24, BENEFICIARY: ETHELBERT THOMAS. A/C: 485790xx, SORT CODE: 933317, IBAN: IE89AIBK933317485790xx, SWIFT CODE: AIBKI2D

Waiting to have your full details for the documentations

Regards

Bar. Muhammed Peter

How to avoid being scammed by Recovery Scams

There really are only two things that you need to know to understand that you are dealing with a recovery scam.

1. If you have been previously scammed then it is highly likely that it will be impossible to retrieve any money you have lost and no Government body in any country offers compensation for money lost by being scammed. Also, the police, FBI, Interpol, EFCC etc. do not email you to tell you they can get your money back or pay you compensation.
2. If you haven't been previously scammed then no one would be offering you compensation or claiming that they can retrieve the money that you haven't actually lost.

6. ROMANCE SCAMS

Romance scammers prey on the emotional weaknesses of their victims and target those that are looking for romance on dating boards and social media sites. The scammer will take time to build the victim's trust in them and often profess to have fallen madly in love with the victim.

The actual form of the scam can take many guises, but will involve a request for money of some type. This might be because the scammer has a misfortune overseas and needs help getting back to his country or the scammer may claim to be a soldier stationed overseas that needs help moving funds, arranging leave to visit his victim or needs a special type of phone to speak to the victim.

Below is a step by step progress of a two romance scams, the first a Military scammer picked up from a profile on a free dating site and the other a Russian scammer posing as a young woman who emailed a victim directly.

Military scammer

Here is the profile that the scammer had on the free dating site.

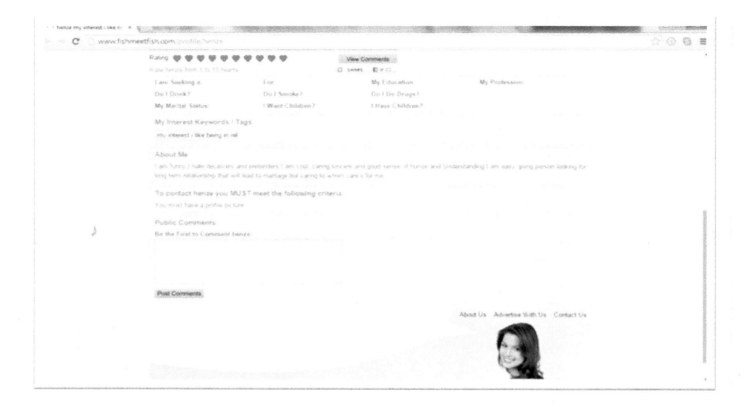

This particular scammer PM'd a female profile on the dating site and the first part of the scam takes place in the site's PM system, where the scammer is quick to get the victim onto email in case his dating site account is closed.

> I must confess that you look astonishing. Do you mind if we get to know more about each other? if yes, kindly send me an email on henzewilliams440@gmail.com

The victim mails the scammer and gets the following response.

> Am henze williams a captain of the USA army currently deployed in camp Dwyer Afghanistan, I just came across your ad on CL. Can we be friends and get to know more about each other?
> Thanks a lot, you got nice pic. Tell me more about you, like your occupation, hobbies and marital status.

There is then a period of exchanging small talk and pleasantries while the scammer gains the victim's confidence and tries to distance her from friends and family to make her dependent on him. This can go on for many months before the first money request is made. In this case, though it was a relatively quick process.

> am so sorry about your husband okay, can i ask your one question whats your idea of an ideal woman?

> For me, my ideal woman would be someone who is loving, caring and understanding and knows that family is an important part of any relationship and should be taking seriously. I am a type of guy who looks beyond the beauty of a woman, I look at her qualities, character and lifestyle.

> yeah, can we be friends? and get to know each other,,,
>
> I am looking for a committed relationship, someone I can call my own, my best friend, lover and confidant. I would like a relationship whereby there is love and affection, other factors are secondary as long as there is love and affection in a relationship it will stand the test of time. even if we have our differences some times, we make up with a make up sex. Someone who I can share my secrets with..

tell me a little about you like, hobbies, likes and dislikes, etc
And what is the first thing you look at when you meet someone?

we design and construct most military facilities for the army,.. most pics being taken here are mostly official there are rules here in the camp here.. We are not allowed to receive calls but can make only when its important, taking leisure pics is not allowed unless for official purpose.... a whole lot of rules especially when on deployment in a high profile location. or maybe am inthe duty okay.

What's the nature of your job like??

my honey thats job for you okay...

honey we've been communicating for sometime now and I think its really nice getting to know you. I think you are a very pretty woman who seeks for the simple things in life and so am I, guess we share the same ideologies when it comes to dating and that's a plus. I would like us to be very close and hopefully when I come to Canada we can kick it from there.

will come back very soon,

I want you to know that since the day we meet I've fallen deeply in
like with you. There are no words to express the gratitude I feel in
my heart that you came into my life. you make yesterday so special for me.You are my life, my heart, my soul. You are my best friend, my one true friend that i can talk to,my one and only. I like you more today than I did yesterday, and I'll
like you more tomorrow than I do today.I know this is coming to you so
fast Omg i don't think i can hold it again
I left a big part of me with you. It is yours now so, take care and
tread lightly. I wish that I could be with you now to kiss your lips
and tell you to your face how much i want you as my friend, but know
that I am there in spirit and am praying for everything to work out
for you. No matter where this life takes us, together or not, know
that you and your family will always be in my heart and "my favorite... promise to remain in love with you ...

I feel more happy the closer I am to you. For me love is life and love is you. I love to talk to you on phone and my talks never end. There is always a new topic to share with you. I can indeed share every minute and every silly incidence of my life with you. I have wowed you from the very day I met you...
take care of you self for me honey......

I feel more happy the closer I am to you. For me love is life and love is you. I love to talk to you on phone and my talks never end. There is always a new topic to share with you. I can indeed share every minute and every silly incidence of my life with you

I used to feel strange how people can sing love songs, and write love stories, but after meeting you I feel even I can do that. can i count on you honey?

So what are you up to today?

i am doing good, its been a busy week for me at the camp.
so far so good am been thinking about you.
hope you are fine. what did you think about me and our friendship?

yea that good, can i see you latest picture?

Wow I love that, its a beautiful picture. Now I want to remove my profile from Fishmeetfish, I want this to work between us, Are you talking to other guys? I am not talking to other women because they can be an obstacle. Would you like to come to the USA once my deployment ends in the camp or should I come to Zürich? You are very beautiful and you left me smiling when I saw more of your pic, I am convinced now that it is you I want and I am praying that when we meet you will be all that you are on here.

hello,i just got you message now,i am working sence I am into the engineering aspect that why i am so busy this time around okay....

how is my little daughter and son 'ope they are okay, mean while I left a big part of me with you. It is yours now,so take care and tread lightly. I wish that I could be with you now to kiss your lips and tell you to your face how much I want you as my friend, but know that I am there in spirit and am praying for everything to work out for you. No matter where this life takes us, together or not, know that you and your family will always be in my heart and "my favorite. i am busy working today.
how are you doing?

Finally we get to where the request for money comes in. In this case it is for a "care pack", which will be purchased from the scammer's other ID.

Babe boo can you send me a care pack? that is the most essential thing we need here, care packages. Most care packages we get are mostly voluntary contributions from family and friends, being in a war zone it is difficult to get them here so we depend on what the government sends and other contributions. We also don't have access to our credit cards and online banking here in case we want to get them online ourselves since the government will be taking care of us but we both know that what the government provides is just the little they can and cant be compared to the ones sent by loved ones. I am running short of my care stuffs and its really bad when that happens. The last care pack I got was from my ex wife because we decided to remain friends for the sake of my daughter, but we had a quarrel few weeks ago and I stopped talking to her. Since you came into my life I have decided to end the friendship with her (only on important issues) because I want to be serous with you and don't want anything to come between us, let me know what you can send so I can direct you on how to go about it. Kisses.

In this case, the victim agrees and then receives an email from the care pack supplier

STUFF FOR SOLDIER DELIVERY.

UNITED STATES OF AMERICA

Kindly choose your options below.

(1)Basic Care Package:

2 Condiments
5 Dental floss
8 Deodorant
10 Dry soup
6 Laundry detergent
1 Lip balm
5 Pringles
4 Crackers
4 Cookies
4 Pack of chocolate
2 Lotion
10 Toilet paper
1 Pack of Aspirin
5 Toiletries
10 Toothpaste/toothbrush
1 Food Supplement
8 pack of Inner wears

Total Amount plus Delivery fee is $250.90(25% Discount)

(2)Medium Care Package:

2 Hand Warmers
2 Foot Warmers
2 Sun Glasses
3 Tooth Brushes
2 Mouthwash
1 Frebreeze
4 Body Wash
7 Body Spray
7 Pringles
6 Crackers
6 Cookies
4 Cereals
5 Powdered Milk
8 Pack of chocolate
2 Condiments
5 Dental floss
8 Deodorant
10 Dry soup
6 Laundry detergent
1 Lip balm
2 Lotion
10 Toilet paper
5 Toiletries
10 Toothpaste/toothbrush
2 Pack of Aspirin
7 pack of boxers
1 mp3 player
2 Supplements

Total Amount plus Delivery fee is $400.10(15% Discount)

(3)Extra Large Care Package.

2 Hand Warmers
2 Foot Warmers
3 head Warmers
3 Sun Glasses
1 Mp3 Player
1 Sony Psp
3 PSP Games
3 Tooth Brushes
2 Mouthwash
2 Frebreeze
2 Shampoo
4 Body Wash
2 Eye drops/wash
10 Electrolyte replacement drink mix
1 Foot powder
7 Body Spray
6 Pringles
6 Crackers
7 Cookies
7 Canned Food
7 Ceraels
10 Chocolate packets
3 Powdered Drinks, especially Gatorade
8 Pack of suplement
5 Suntan Lotion
2 Condiments
5 Dental floss
8 Deodorant
10 Dry soup
6 Laundry detergent
1 Lip balm
2 Lotion

10 Toilet paper
5 Toiletries
10 Toothpaste/toothbrush
3 Pack of Aspirin
15 pack of Inner wears

Total Amount plus Delivery fee is $650.75(10% Discount)

Let us know if you have any additional item you want to add so we can include it to the option that you have choosed. we deliver under 3 days to Afghanistan, kindly indicate once you are ready to make payment so we can provide you with the payment options available.

Stuff for Soldiers Deliveries International

Once the victim confirms which package she wants, the payment instructions will come, with the money to be sent by Western Union. In this case, the money is to be sent to someone in the USA – they will be a mule, who is receiving money for the scammer and sending it to them. In some cases, the mule will be complicit and know what they are doing, but many times, they will be another scam victim who think they are doing a favour for an Internet friend or even have a job receiving payments.

Dear Customer,

Below is the payment details for medium pack $400.10 USD.

Receivers Name: Axxxxx Mxxxx
Address: #### Fennwood Sacramento, California USA 95831.

Payment Option: Wire Transfer

You can visit the western union store/outlet nearest to you or you can visit thier website at www.westernunion.com for online payment to the address above. Once payment is made, kindly forward us with the mtcn number and your address for confirmation. Payment can also be made via money gram, just visit the nearest money gram outlet to you and make payment to the payment details above. Once payment is made kindly provide us with the 8 digit reference number and senders address for confirmation, thank you.

Ms Portal

If the victim had paid, the scam would have continued with further requests for money, until the victim realized what was happening or had no more money left to send.

Russian romance scammer

Here is the first email from the scammer, received out of the blue

How is your mood?
Hope, you are ok! I am good, because I can send first message to you! Okey, you can call me Ekaterina, I am 28, but I don't have man of my dreams in real life. And what about you? My friends thinking about me, that I am energetic female. I have many friends in my life, but they are only friends.
I have many hobbys. We can chat about us and more, if you will write me back. I will send you my photo, hope you will like my imagine. Please write me back soon! I will be wait your message. Your new friend.
Yours friend Ekaterina.

A generic response gets a reply from the scammer and yet more photos.

Hello my new friend ! My name is Ekaterina. I am very glad to get acquainted with you. And I hope we can become good friends. I am not very good at using internet but anyway I decided it is a good way to get new friends. That is why I want to explain the reason why I am here right now. It is possible I will visit your country soon and I made my mind to get acquainted with a person from your country. And at this point I am writing to you. I have never been abroad and I don't have friends outside Russia. I really want to know more about you. Could you please tell me about you, about your lifestyle in the next letter. I hope it is not difficult for you. I will also write about myself. It is interesting to find out about your family, maybe about your job, friends and hobby. Ok, I am 28 years old. And I am sure it is a good age for a lady. Because I am still young but nevertheless have got a good life experience. My height - 170 sm and my weight 55 kg. You know I am fit because I like sports. One of the most important things is to look after myself .In a sound mind ,a sound body. I am sending my photos so you can see me. You know I am not very photogenic. The photos are usually not very beautiful. But they are important for correspondence so one can see another. I hope you will like me. By the way I am looking forward to see your photos in the next letter. It is very interesting for me to see a person you writing to. So I want to ask you a few questions so we will know each other better. What about sport? Alcohol? Smoking? Please tell me about your habits. As for me I am an only child in the family and I don't have my own kids but I have a dream. I have a dream to build my own family and have wonderful children. My father died when I was a child. I really miss him. My mother has been growing me since I was 2 years old and she taught me alone. My mother works in hospital. She has got a good job. She has been working in a hospital for a long time and she knows a lot of people. She is respected in our city. I have got a few best girl friends. I spend much of my spare time with them. They say I have a good sense of humor. I like to laugh at a good joke. I am a cheerful person so my friends do. I live in Kishkino. It is a small town. It is situated 650 km far from Moscow. I think this information will help you to know me better. I am looking forward to know about you, you job, your city. I don't have bad habits, I don't smoke. I am sure it is important for a lady not have bad habits. When gathering together with friends I can drink a glass of wine but not more. I am really keen on cooking. I usually cook fish soup, borsch, salads. You can write about your favourite dish, or maybe your cooking experience. I personally like flowers. They really make our life more beautiful-at home, outside, at work. Oh yes I have forgotten to tell you about my job. I work with children and I really like my job. I am a teacher of a foreign language at school. I teach little children English and Russian language. I think that is enough about me. I has written a really big letter. I hope you are not tired of my little letter. So what do you do? Where do you work? Please tell me about your interests. I am really looking forward to your reply. I hope my letter will not be lost with no attention. I will read your letter with pleasure and will surely reply. Ekaterina.

Another generic reply and another response from the scammer, with more photos and a video greeting — generic with no mention of the victim's name. The scammer also mentions visiting the victim's country soon, which is strange as the victim hasn't told her where he lives.

Hello Schafe ! I am very glad to get your letter. You are interested in me) And that is good news for me. I was afraid to see negative reaction from your side. I have never had friends via internet before. And that scared me. But you are a good man. I see that in your letter. That means you have found something in me and maybe want to know each other better. I wrote about my life on the whole in my first letter. You already know I live in Brutovo. It is a usual small town in Russia. But I love it so much. I love to have a walk on its tiny but comfy streets, beautiful parks among the river. You know I like to walk, together with my friends or alone. When I am outside alone I dream. Dream about future life. Where everything is good, I have a good job that brings pleasure and good income. I dream that I will meet my love. No doubt I had close relationships. But they ended with nothing behind. Many Russian men are rude and I always wanted to be loved, to feel warmth. I think everything will be alright. And what do you dream about? Do you like just to sit and dream? I like to see new films in the cinema, I also like to read. And what about you? Please tell me what films and books do you like? I am really interested in it. What do you do in your spare time. Maybe I ask too many questions. But knowing more about you is interesting for me. By the way, about my city. I think you can find it on the map easily. You can look an arrangement of my city, having passed on this link! http://www.maplandia.com/russia/vladimirskaya-oblast/suzdalskiy-rayon/brutovo/ And again shortly about myself. My favourite sports is swimming. I am good at swimming. From time to time I go to the swimming pool. My favourite colors are pink and blue. My favourite flower is a tulip. And what about you? Do you like your job? Do like what you do? I am sure that is important. It is important to love you job. Then you job will bring pleasure. Do you agree with me? In my first letter I wrote about the opportunity to visit your country. Yes, that is true. I work as a teacher. I am a young teacher and I am a successful girl)… That is not shy but anyway. I studied in the university to get this specialty. I also studied other foreign languages. My English proficiency is quite good. And I can easily learn another foreign language. I don't doubt at it. I like my job. Earlier everything was alright and the salary was worthy. But now everything changed. Maybe the economic crisis caused this. Russia was deeply influenced by it and also my job too. But I am an optimist and I believe in bright future. And recently they have offered me a new job in your country. That is very prospective and a good salary. I have thought about it much. Firstly I was afraid to go to another country alone and I denied that offer. But later I made my mind to begin a new life and I agreed with that offer. Now I am waiting for arranging on all the aspects with my job. But I don't know when exactly. Soon I will be able to go to your country and work in a school. I will teach kids Russian language. I really want to find worthy job that will bring pleasure and good income. But please let's not speak about money. I believe in bright future and every man should build his own future. Do you agree with me? What do you think about it? I want to know your opinion. I think you have understood the reason of my letter. I want to get acquainted with you. I will come to your country and will not be alone. I will know you. And maybe we will have a future where we are together. Are you against it? OK. I will end my letter for today. It is also as big as the previous. But I want to tell you so much. I hope you understand this. And I hope you will patient enough to read this big letter from an unknown girl from Russia. I am waiting for your letter Ekaterina!

The exchange continues over a number of weeks with more emails and pictures from the scammer as shown below.

Hello my dear Schafe !! I am very glad to get your letter. How are you? Is everything alright? I am alright. Today the weather is fine. The sun shines brightly. I like such weather. How is the weather by your side? I will begin my letter with a story about my family and me. I think this is important for our correspondence. I want to tell much about my life. Schafe I also ask you to write more about yourself, your life and your family. It is always interesting for me. And in this way we will know each other better. Do you agree? I have already written I live with my mom. We live in a one room apartment. But there is enough space for both of us. This is a small and comfy flat. My mother is a very kind, sweet, helpful woman. She is respected at her job. She has been always been my best friend. And we always understand each other. I love my mom very much. Unfortunately, my father passed away when I was a small girl. Schafe can you tell me about your parents. It is very interesting. My mother and I like to cook together. She taught me many recipes of dishes. I am very good at making different salads, meat dishes, soups and many others. I think my creations are very tasty. I like cooking simply because it is a creative process. But sometimes I don't have enough spare time for cooking. My work requires much time. But I am fond of my profession. I want to continue doing my job. I wrote about it to you. Now I am looking through several offers of working in schools in your country. Four schools offered me a job. But firstly I want to see them. And only then choose the best option for me. I think this is right. Do you agree? But now it is early to speak about it. I really hope to see you some day)…And you can give a good advice) Schafe. I am very glad to tell you about me again. Hope you enjoyed reading my message. I feel our correspondence is good and it will continue further. I am waiting for your answer. Your Ekaterina!

Hi my new best friend Schafe !!! How are you? How is your job? I hope everything is alright. I can confidently say you are my best friend. I feel our friendship is continuing. I see you want to communicate with me. I also want to communicate with you. I have many friends here. My attitude towards them is good and to you good too. I like you. I would say that there is some extraterrestrial force between us. And it attracts us. Don't you think so? I want to correspond with you. I want to write to you every minute. But it is impossible. You and I are busy people. I have only a couple of minutes to write you a letter. But I have an idea. If you give me your phone number I will try to call you. OK? I will wait for your phone number so I can hear your voice. This is important for me. I understand we know each other not for a very a long time. We have written only a couple of letters to each other. But I hope you will not deny me and soon I will call you and hear your voice! Well... Schafe you may think that a young and beautiful lady and still not married?! Young and beautiful) not shy)... But I think this is true). And I hope you also agree with my words?) Schafe. I have not met my ideal man but I am sure it will happen soon. I feel it. I had relationships earlier. But that was not love. I can't have relationship with a man without being loved. That is not right. Do you agree? That is the reason I am alone now. That is the reason I am looking for the real love Schafe. Please tell me about your past relationships with women. I want to know what kind of person you are. Do you understand Schafe? I will wait for your reply and your number. Yes! I am a persevering person)... Not only writing letters is important for me but also having a real conversation. I am sure you will write soon. I am waiting impatiently for your letter and will surely reply!

Ekaterina!

Hello! Hello! Hello Schafe ! How are you doing? I am ok. The weather is not very good today. There are many clouds in the sky. That makes me feel sad. But your letter makes me happier. Please tell me how is your work? Is everything alright? I am doing well. I want to tell you about one funny accident at my job. Today I hold a lecture and communicated with children. And one of the students asked me a question. Will I be always a teacher? I really did not know what to answer. Children always loved me. And they always were glad to come to my lesson. All the teachers notice this fact. Kids never are late and at that moment I heard such a question. I didn't know what to tell. Life is not a bed of roses. And from time to time you don't know what will happen tomorrow. Maybe I will work at this school or maybe not. And then I thought about you and about the opportunity to go to you. I thought about the life, job in your country. This is my chance. And I want to use this opportunity. I explained to the students that there will be other teachers during their lives and that I will not be able to stay with them all the time. I wished them more good teachers. And I think this is important. And they understood me. We continued our lesson with smiles. When the lesson was over I thought about you all the brake. And I made my mind to change my life. And I think I will change my life for the better if I go to your country to work on a new place. I want to tell you thank you. You gave me an opportunity to think about my life that one can change his own life for the better. Thank you. I think we can speak easily and then I will come to a final conclusion about my future. I am waiting for answer. Your best girlfriend Ekaterina.

Hello my Schafe ! I think you realize that this is an important decision in my life and I could not make up my mind weighing all pros and cons. I shared my ideas with my mother. I told her all about us. She smiled and understood me. My mother can always understand me. She approves of my decision. She trusts you. She thinks you are a very good and honest man. And you can show me you country and meet me. I think also so. I want to write more about my plans for the future. I will speak with my Director. They have been offering me to go to your country for a long time. And I decided to agree. And this is due to you. I will tell my Director that I agreed to work in your country. I think he will not be against it and will be glad with my decision. And this is the right decision. The Director has been advising me to go for a long time. We will arrange some points with those schools where I will possibly work. I will have to make a choice. I will come to you and we together will think about it. Will you help me with advice? Isn't it difficult for you? OK Schafe anyway now it is early to speak about it. My trip isn't planned in details yet. And now I want to think over my trip. This is a step to a new life. I want it Schafe. I will tell about all I am going to do. I wait for reply. Hope you are happy that I decided to go to you? I think you agree! Bye bye. Your Ekaterina!

Hellooooo my Schafe !!! I am very glad to see your letter and especially on such a day. Today is a very important day and I hurried to write you. I am in high spirits today! You know I decided to change my present life and the future and I made my mind to go to your country. I will work there in your country. And this is my last decision. I got up earlier today in the morning, went to school so I could speak with the director of the school before the lessons started. He was already on his working place. We spoke once again and I told him about my decision and he supported me. We spoke like we were friends. He is a good and experienced person. He picked up the phone and called the Ministry of Education. The director asked them to start the registration of all the necessary documents for me. He arranged some points so it would be possible for me to go to your country, they will make a working visa for me and an international passport. They will also book the ticket to your country, firstly to Moscow and the hotel room there. That was a long conversation. We discussed my trip, documents and about money. The Ministry of Education and our school will give money for the registration of the documents and booking the tickets. They promised that everything will be ready soon. I think everything works out and soon I will pack my luggage for the coming trip. I am very glad and happy. I believe that such a chance comes only once in a life and I should use this opportunity. I think you are also very glad that I decided to come to you! Schafe please write about the latest news, what interesting is happening in your life? I think we will see each other soon and I want to know more about your life) OK here I am coming to an end with this letter and tomorrow I will share with you with the latest news of my preparation. I think you will wait impatiently for my letter) Your

Ekaterina!

Hello Hello my Schafe !Dear I ask you inform me the full address. Also I need to know the nearest international airport to you. And as tell to me. You can meet me at the airport. In any case I shall visit you necessarily. Do not forget to write the full adress. I have great news for you today. I have spoken with my director. My preparation is going on well. He told that the Ministry of Education began the registration of all the necessary documents for the trip to you. I have got my salary and some extra bonuses, that is 550 dollars, a good sum of money. I will spend this money for my trip to you. He also told me that everything is arranged about it. They will make quickly a working visa and an international passport. I will have to go to Moscow to the embassy for getting a visa and a conversation. It will happen very soon. Tomorrow in the evening I will get on the bus and go to Moscow. I am very happy. I have so little time for the packing and the trip will be so long. But I am not afraid of difficulties. I am sure I will cope with it. Hope you are glad for me too. Will you be happy to meet me very soon?! Schafe tomorrow I will prepare for my trip. It will take a lot of time. I will have to be at school in the morning to sign all the documents, to say bye to my colleges. It was a good job and the people were nice. I worked in the best school of our town. At noon I want to meet with my friends and relatives. I hope you understand this necessity. I want to say good bye to my close relatives. I will pack the luggage in the evening and spend time with my mom, she will go with me to the railway station. Schafe I promise to write when I get to Moscow. I think I will find an internet café and will write you the day after tomorrow as soon as I get to Moscow. I miss you). Wait for my letter. I will also wait for your letter. 100000000000000 kisses!!! Ekaterina!

The pictures now stop as the scammer works their way to the eventual money request in a few emails time.

Hello my dearest Schafe ! I am very glad to read your letter. Now I can say with pleasure that I am in Moscow. I got there in the morning on the bus and stayed at the hotel. Spent some time for the rest. Now I am going to visit the embassy to have a conversation. Today I will pass it and get my documents. I found out about the internet cafe with the help of hotel workers. It is not far from the hotel and I can easily come to the internet cafe. And firstly I decided to write you a letter and only then go to the embassy. I will try to write another letter in the evening. But the best way is to have a real telephone conversation. I think I can call you and we will speak about the meeting. This or that way wait for my letter or a call. Now I will go to the embassy and then go to the airport so I can see what flights are available. I will buy the ticket at once. Wait for my call or a letter. Everything is going to be alright. I am sure in it. And very soon I will fly on the plane to you. Waiting for your letter. Yours Ekaterina!

Hello my dear Schafe ! How are you? Today the weather in Moscow is fine. How is the weather in your city? I have good news. Yesterday I visited a hospital and got a medical insurance. It took little time, it is just a formality.Give me the telephone number. I shall try to call to you. If you cannot approach to phone I shall leave the message on an answering machine. I paid some money for the insurance and in 20 minutes I got the papers. Then I went to the embassy, I should say that was not an easy journey. Moscow is a huge city. And it took 4 hours to get to the embassy! I could walk along the whole city using this time)))... So I got there and successfully passed the conversation, I got my visa and passport. I am very glad that I made all this so quickly! And now I have got all the necessary documents for my trip to you! I am very happy! I feel like starting a new life! We will meet very soon! And I am worried about it now. How will it be? I imagine our first meeting, it is so exciting. What do you feel now? How do you imagine our meeting in the airport? Please write me about it . Yesterday I had a lot of business and didn't manage to get to the airport. I want to buy tickets right now or tomorrow in the morning. I will find out about the nearest flights and will buy the ticket at once. I am so glad that everything is going well and this fact is pleasing. I hope you are glad too! Today was a hard day and I am tired. I need to go to the hotel to have some rest. I really want to come to you as soon as possible. Before going to sleep I am going to dream about our first day, I have already written to you about it).. Tomorrow is going to be a hard day too. I will write you what I find out in the airport. I will also try to call you. Wait for my call. I will call you . Wait for my letter and the call. I will also wait for your letter. With love! Yours Ekaterina!!!

Finally, the money request arrives as, in this case, the "girl" has no money to pay for her stay in Moscow.

Schafe! Hello dear! The day started very well. I was in good mood but after some hours it got worse. I will tell why. Now I am in the airport, great there is an internet cafe. I wrote that today in the morning I will go to the airport to buy the tickets so I can fly to you. I knew an approximate ticket cost. It is not so cheap but I had money to buy it. And I did not doubt. Today I will write my flight number and the exact date and the time of our meeting. As all documents too are ready. I thought that I can buy the ticket for tomorrow. But I was waited with disappointment. I could buy the ticket only for March, 23. It was the most nearest flight to you. I very much was upset to it. Because I do not know on what money I shall live till March, 23 in Moscow. I have no money to pay for hotel and meal. As to me are necessary money to pay for the Internet to contact you. I need 930 dollars. Schafe I ask to understand me. Now I am alone in this big city. I can not find such a big sum of money right now. That is impossible. I don't have that 930 dollars and I ask you to lend me these money. There is only one step till we meet each other. I hope you can help me. Please send 930 dollars. I will give them back when I get new job. I will work hard and I will earn soon. I hope you understand me right. I write this letter with tears on my face. It is a shame for me. I have never asked for help and I always relied only on myself but now I can do nothing to change this situation. I have to write this letter to you and ask for help. When I arrive I will get around 3,000 dollars. The money I will get used to the new place. Let's just say that this is my first salary. I can not get the money now. Only after I arrive I will get the money. I wait for your understanding, now I will try to call you and explain the situation. We can speak directly. I will wait for your letter. I will wait for your help, Yours Ekaterina!

After the victim confirms his willingness to help, details of how to make the payment by Western Union are sent.

Schafe! I am very glad that about understanding have concerned to my problem. You The present gentleman. You have not thrown me halfway to you. I am glad that You will help me with money. I shall give you of money as soon as I shall be arranged on Work. I can promise you these are 100 . I as have learned as you can To transfer me of quickly money. There is such system of remittances. It Refers to Western Union. You know such? It is very fast, reliable And economic system. All that you need to come it to office Western Union. Both to fill the form. And to pay money. And already through some Hours I can take away this money. Try to find this system. And To send money today or tomorrow. I shall wait from you the information about To transfer of money. That I could receive your money without problems I Should know: MTCN is a code which consists of 10 figures. Also yours Full name and surname. And your full address. I hope you all can To make quickly and correctly. I Hope we soon we shall together. I shall wait your letter. With love. Yours Ekaterina!

My data:
Russia
vladimirskaya-oblast
suzdalskiy-rayon
Zaprudnaya street, Apartment 21, house 9
601271 city Brutovo
first name: EKATERINA
last name: ARABEEVA

Bank where I got the money.
SDM-Bank: Metro Tushino 125424, Moscow, Volokolamsk highway, 73

How to avoid being scammed by Romance Scams

There are a number of things that will highlight the fact you are dealing with a scammer and not the person shown in the profile or pictures provided:

- They like to move you from the dating site to email or Yahoo/Skype/Facebook chat as quickly as possible.
- They are very quick to fall in love and declare the victim to be "the one".
- They will refer to the victim as their "wife" or "husband", even though they have never met in person.
- They will have an occupation that requires overseas travel (to give them an excuse to get stranded and have money sent to the scammer's actual country), such as contractors, the military and oil workers.

Military scammers are one of the more common forms of romance scammers and it can almost be guaranteed that if you have met someone claiming to be a member of the armed forces on a dating or social networking website you are actually dealing with a scammer. Additional things to look out for are:

- They provide lots of pictures of themselves in uniform.
- They are communicating using a free email address. Soldiers have access to official email addresses (ending .mil in the case of the US military), so they have no need to use Yahoo, Gmail or Hotmail etc. email addresses.
- They have lots of free time to chat and email – real soldiers on deployment would be too busy to spend all the time chatting to strangers and any free time they do have, they would use to communicate with their real family.
- Soldiers stationed overseas do not need to ask other people to pay for care packages, calling cards, secured phones or leave for them – all of their needs are taken care of by the military..
- The military do not communicate with soldiers immediate families, let alone Internet pen friends, any military business is carried out "in house", so random contacts on the Internet would not be contacted to arrange leave.
- Soldiers do not find large sums of money that they need help getting out of whatever country they claim to be in.

7. CHARITY SCAMS

Charity scams prey on the generosity of people who think they are helping those who are less fortunate than themselves and will take advantage of a natural disaster or tragic event, such as Hurricane Katrina, the 9/11 terrorist attacks or the devastating earthquake that hit Nepal in April 2015. As soon as an event such as these occurs, the despicable scammers will be there sending out their fake emails asking for donations for relief. Charity scammers may also claim to run orphanages in Africa and seek donations to look after the children that they claim to have under their responsibility.

Legitimate charities rarely ask for donations via email, and if they do so only to individual who have previously registered with them and agreed to be contacted in such a manner. They are much more likely to write to you by snail mail or use street collections. If there is a tragedy, legitimate charities are even less likely to email you, as they will be getting plenty of spontaneous donations without needing to request them.

If you get an email asking for money, it is always safest to start from the point of view that it is almost certainly a scam. If it asks for donations only through a money transfer service such as Western Union or Moneygram, then you can be sure that it is definitely a scam. Legitimate charities can accept donations by any number of methods, and do not depend on anonymous money transfers.

The emails below are an example of a scammer claiming to run an orphanage, the initial set of emails took place until the victim refused to pay, the individual emails after that have been sent at regular intervals to the same victim, to continue trying to get them to send money.

The initial email tries to get a small contribution as quickly as possible.

Greetings to you in Jesus Name;

I am Evangelist mike peters, I run the Happy Orphanage Home, (HOH) Nigeria. A non-governmental organization (NGO) here in Nigeria. In the facility we have 147 children. The facility has eight dormitory rooms to house the 147 children.

There are 40 staff to care for them 24 hours a day, seven days a week. Most of the children enter the Orphanage because their parents either live on the street or are deceased. The children mostly come from Nigeria, with a few being from Liberia. They come from all types of backgrounds and religions but we all live together as one family.

If it weren't for our facility, these children would have nothing.... no education, no roof over their heads, no food in their bellies. They would be forced to sell things in the market to bring in extra money for food and rent.

Many of these children in our facility have been sexually abused, starved, some even left for dead. Some of the children have physical disabilities and have been deemed "unlovable" by their own parents.

Currently we are in need of funds for foundation due to the fact that the only facility we have right now is definitely in a very bad condition. We need medication, food, clothing and recreational activities for rehabilitative purposes to boost the orphans mental abilities. However, the worse thing that we are going through now is, the fact that we are being kicked out of the facility by the Government because the roof of the building is leaking and they want us to show proof of adequate funds, which is $10,000 Dollar USD to build a newer one. On behalf of me, staffs and the orphans here in Happy Orphanage Home, we ask that you kindly come to our aid, because your help can make a significant contribution to the life of the children and the operation of the Orphanage. Please pray for Happy Orphanage Home as we look forward to hearing from you. We are excited to see how God will provide for the children that call Happy

---

Orphanage Home.

We the Happy Orphanage Home are so happy and grateful for your assistant and donations you are about to take towards helping the needy. and we plead that you please make it up to 100 so as to enable us pick it up from the bank. We pray that God almighty will bless you with whatever heart desired you wish from him. Thank you so much.

Right now our website is unavailable due to the insufficient funds to pay for subscription and we are sorry that you can't make the donations through our website.

You may be able to send $100, $250, $500, $1,000, or more! Please sow your best seed to Happy Orphanage Home.

You can make a wire transfer to us via Western Union Money Transfer (WUMT) OR Money Gram Money Order (MGMO) with this details below;

Names: Enyindah Chimele
Country: Nigeria
State; Rivers State
City; Port Harcourt
Text Question: God bless?
Text Answer: Your Family.

Send us the following details after you have made the wire transfer this week.

Amount:
Sender's name:
Money Transfer Control Number (MTCN):
Text Question:
Text Answer:
sender's Location;
Sender's Phone number;

I will be so excited to read from you. I am counting on your reply to this email.

Evang. Mike Peters
+2349095412857

When the victim expresses an interest in helping, but doesn't want to send the money by money transfer, the scammer happily provides a bank account for her to use.

Dear Geit,

How are you doing at your end? Hope all is well in the lord, please kindly send the donation to this below bank detail of our voluntary and get back to us with the payment receipt of the wire transfer. We beg of you to send the money to us today and send us the payment receipt of the wire transfer from bank.

Account Name: Anthony Alotja
Account num: 750474068
Iban code: NL87INGB0750474068
Bic code: INGBNL2A
Address: Sassenheimstraat 88-2 1059 bm - zuid Amsterdam Holland.

waiting to hear from you as soon as possible.

Evang. Mike Peter
+2349095412857

The scammer then starts sending religious passages to the victim, along with other attempts to persuade her to send some money.

Good evening,
How are you doing today and how is every body around? Are you ready for God's blessings this season of laughter? There is a next step of faith I want you to take seriously after saying the prayers above to God and you will see the greatest gift of the lord upon your life this month of March. the Lord has put all good things in place for your success and nothing can ever stop you from growing.

I WANT TO PRAY FOR YOU AND I WANT YOU TO OPEN UP YOUR HEART WHILE WE SAY THESE PRAYERS,

"And my God shall supply all your need according to His riches in glory by Christ Jesus".

Philippians 4:19

say this prayer with me.

"The Just shall live by Faith"

Habakkuk 2:4

Heavenly Father!I praise You and honor You! I thank You for being with me always and loving me with Your eternal love! You
are in control of all things and I thank You for that.O Lord! Your Scripture clearly tells that without faith I can neither please You nor receive any answer for my prayer. Please forgive me for not believing in Your love, power and goodness. Many times I've been discouraged by my circumstances and many times I have failed to trust in You. Please forgive me Lord! Your are the God of all hope and I acknowledge that nothing is too difficult for You. I am confident that You will meet all my needs as I seek to live according to Your word! Thank You Lord for helping me get over my unbelief removing all my fears and anxieties! Let me not lose heart on seeing the circumstances Lord! Strengthen my faith through which alone I can receive miracles from You Lord. You have said whatever I ask in prayer, believing, I will receive. Thank You for this promise Lord! I love You and trust in Your awesome power! I know You are with me right now to take care of my needs and I thank You for that.
In Jesus' name I pray. Amen.

God bless you.

HAPPY EASTER MY BELOVED IN CHRIST,

The death of Christ was a symbol of his greatest sacrifice, a sacrifice he made for all of us by giving up his life for the sins of humanity. Good Friday is a day of fast and abstinence which culminates by the crucifixion and death of Jesus Christ. After Judas' betrayal, he was made to wear a crown of thorns, humiliated in front pf the masses and forced to carry the cross all the way to Cavalry. After being nailed to the cross, he breathed his last and was later placed in a tomb. On the third day, he rose and ascended into heaven as the son of God. His resurrection is known as Christianity.

Thus, Easter is one of the most important festivals celebrated by Christians and the holy week thus concludes on Easter Sunday, the day Jesus Christ rose from the dead. Christians decorate churches and also arrange Easter ides to mark the day. There are also various customs that are observed on the day. Egg hunting, Easter bunny and Easter parades are traditional customs. There are also various dishes prepared on this day.

WE WISH YOU AND YOUR ENTIRE FAMILY A WONDERFUL HAPPY EASTER FROM ALL OF US AT HAPPY ORPHANAGE HOME.

Regards,
Evang. Mike Peter.

Alan Jones

Dearly beloved in Christ,

God want to use you as an instrument of his hand. The holy spirit of God will locate you this month and bless you like never before, you shall witness the blessings and love upon your life this month. Join us this month with love in your heart in helping the homeless, needy and orphans of Happy Orphanage Home in Africa with faith, hope and love.

Beloved in Christ, Happy Orphanage Home are in need of funds for renovation due to the fact that the only facility they have is definitely in a very bad condition. They need medication, food, clothing and recreational activities for rehabilitative purposes to boost the orphans mental abilities. However, the worse thing that they are going through now is, the fact that they are being kicked out of the facility by the Government because the roof of the building is leaking and they want them to show proof of adequate funds, which is $10,000 Dollar USD to build a newer one."This is the meaning of the parable. The seed is the word of God.... But as for the seed that fell on rich soil, they are the ones who, when they have heard the word, embrace it with a generous and good heart, and bear fruit through perseverance."

When you are zealous for the Lord and stand for Him, He will bless and exalt you mightily in life. God has a plan for you this month, He is willing to do all things possible for you this month. I see the divine blessings of God upon you, you are blessed you are lifted up for the bible says in Gen 26:12; Then Isaac sowed in that land, and received in the same year an hundredfold: and the LORD blessed him. The reason why many do not receive from the Lord is that they do not understand the spiritual laws concerning giving. Isaac sowed seed in the day of famine. One famine had just finished and a second just started. Many turned back and went to Egypt. But God told Isaac to sow what was left. Many Thousands had died, Livestock was almost wiped out and water was scarce. Giving is the key to success and financial breakthrough!

This is not a gimmick. It is not the latest fad. Giving is simply God's principle that has worked since the beginning of time.

Today, many of the top corporate executives I have met understand this principle, even those who aren't grounded in the Word. They are generally givers. The same goes for the best political leaders and high achievers.Success and giving go hand in hand.

Let me hasten to add that this isn't just about money. Far from it! The true secret, however, isn't just giving. It is giving according to God's plan. Look back at Psalm 96 and consider.

Proven Principles
I have seen these principles proven in my own life, over and over. Whenever you are tempted to look upon giving as a mere exercise or something you have to do, the results are always less than satisfactory. But I have found that when I give with an open, fresh heart, I always receive accordingly.

These principles of giving are so vital and far-reaching because I sense a coming harvest unlike anything we've seen before. I want you, as my partner, to be aware of the crucial times in which we live, and I want you to understand the important key to success that will allow you to participate freely in the great outpouring about to happen.

It is time to get out of debt. It is time for financial breakthrough for you and your loved ones! It is time to unleash Isaiah 48:17 in your life: "Thus saith the Lord, thy Redeemer, the Holy One of Israel, I am the Lord thy God which teacheth thee to profit, which leadeth thee by the way that thou shouldest go."

God is ready to teach you how to give, how to profit, and how to establish a powerful heritage of giving in your family. Giving is the key to success.

You may be able to send $100, $250, $500, $1,000, or more! Please sow your best seed to Happy Orphanage Home.

Now is a crucial time for Happy Orphanage Home as they continue to go through amazing open doors through your love.

Are you ready to receive God's outpouring? Give to winning souls and building His kingdom, then prepare yourself for His supernatural abundance.

I'm looking forward to hearing from you soon! Giving is the key to abundance, power, wisdom, and a strong family heritage! Send your best seed-gift today and begin to expect a financial breakthrough!

Get back to us so we can send you the payment detail to send your own contribution / donation.

For we know it is "not by might, nor by power, but by my spirit, saith the Lord of hosts" (Zechariah 4:6)....

68

God bless you from all of us @ happy orphanage home

Evang. Mike Peter
+2348161228495

BB PIN: 2BB48E31
Skype: happyorphanagehome

Greeting beloved,

Hope everything is well with you? i have been waiting to hear from you about the seed you were about to sow to the happy orphanage home. The lord has said it all, have you sow your seed to the little orphans that really needed it? If not i plead with you to leave what ever you are doing right now to sow your seed to the orphans. The lord awaits you for his blessing he promise all the way to shower on your life and he has an abundant mercies for you, he will do wonders for your life this season, sow your seed and get back to me with the payment receipt.

Pleased kindly send your donation to the below details which i sent to you and get back to me with the evidence of payment slit, payment receipt.

God bless you from all of us @ happy orphanage home

Evang. Mike Peter

+2347088409779

BB PIN: 2BB48E31
Skype: happy.orphanage.home

FB: http://www.facebook.com/happy.orphanage.home11

Greeting to you,

The Bible says the prayer of a righteous man is powerful and effective, yet something extraordinary happens when two or more agree together in prayer. If you would like someone to pray with you about a need in your life.

God Almighty will answer your prayers this month. And get back at me in t to give me the good news of testimony of what the Lord God has done for you. The best is yet to come you ain't seen nothing yet.

In Jesus' matchless name we pray

Amen.

2 Corinthians 10:12

For we dare not make ourselves of the number, or compare ourselves with some that commend themselves: but they measuring themselves by themselves, and comparing themselves among themselves, are not wise.

We beg of you to sow a seed of faith to happy orphanage home this new week and get back to us with the evidence of receipt-slit.

God bless you from all of us @ happy orphanage home

Evang. Mike Peter
+2348161228495
BB PIN: 2BB48E31
Skype: happyorphanagehome

As an example of just how callous scammers are, the email below was received a few days after Nepal was hit by an earthquake in 2015 and show just how little thought these disgusting sub-human creatures have for the suffering of others, and how they only care about finding ways to steal money from hard working individuals so that they can fund for their drug addictions, prostitutes and buy the luxury items they are too lazy to work for.

COALITION OF HELP THE DISPLACED PEOPLE
Maharajgunj Rd,
Kathmandu 44606, Nepal

Sir/Madam

May God be with you, your Organization and your Family.

We write to solicits your support for the up keep of the displaced people in the recent earth quack in our Country Nepal.

We need your help to take care of their needy, like Foods, Cloths, accommodation, health care,and so many other things.

Please what ever you can give to help will be highly welcome and appreciated by US.

May God Almighty who is the giver of things be with you and your Organization

Yours Faithfully.

Navesh Manejor.
Coordinator.

How to avoid being scammed by Charity Scams

As mentioned at the start of the chapter, legitimate charities do not send unsolicited emails requesting money. If you are a supporter of a particular charity and on their mailing list then they will write to you from a domain belonging to the charity and not a free Gmail, Yahoo or Hotmail/Outlook email address.

If you want to contribute to a cause related to a major disaster, then check the real websites of legitimate charities such as the Red Cross and ignore any emails claiming to be from them.

8. CONFERENCE SCAMS

Conference scams centre around invitations to non-existent conferences on subjects such as human trafficking, AIDS, child abuse or human rights. The scammers often tell their victims that the conference will be held in two locations, one somewhere in the Western World, such as the USA or Europe and the other somewhere in Africa.

The first email will usually be an invitation to send delegates to the conference and the victim will be asked to send details of the delegates to the conference secretariat. A reply will then be sent with fake documents showing the registration and telling them that a hotel will need to be booked for the part of the conference that is in Africa. This email will include details of the recommended hotel and ask the victim to make their booking. The hotel suggested is fake and is often no more than a free email address used by the same scammer (although some more sophisticated scammers may create a fake website for their fake hotel).

The fake hotel will respond confirming the booking and asking for payment to be sent, usually by Western Union or Moneygram, but sometimes by bank transfer. None of these methods are safe as they are all irreversible – once the money is sent, it is gone for good.

We will now take a look at an example of how conference scam plays out (insofar as we can get without sending the scammer any money). Here is the original email received

---

Dear Colleague,

The International Organization For Human Right (IOHR) is delighted to invite you to participate in our forth-coming International Conference on (Child Abuse, HIV/AIDS, Racism And Human Trafficking). These event will begins from (April 15th-18th 2014) in California, United States and (April 22nd-25th 2014) in Dakar-Senegal. I am honored to invite you to attend this events as my guest.

For more details and registration requirement, kindly contact the secretariat office via:[secretary.usa@qq.com]. You should also inform the secretariat Office that you were invited to participate by (Ms.stephanie jones) a staff member of the International Organization For Human Right (IOHR).

Note that the Organizing Committee and Our donor sponsors will take the full responsibility of all registered participants Visa processing for the United States & Senegal respectively. That will include your Round trip air tickets to both events. While delegates will only be responsible for his/her own hotel accommodation in Dakar-Senegal were the second phase of the event will be held. I do hope you can make time in your busy schedule to attend these conference and share your ideas on the above conference topics.

For more information and any further clarification concerning this event, do not hesitate to contact me through my personal e-mail: (stephaniejones814@yahoo.com).

Thanks for your kind co-operation.

Ms. stephanie jones.
International Organization For Human Right (IOHR).
Los angeles, california
United States of America.

A response from the victim gets the following reply from the scammer posing as the secretariat of the conference.

Dear Applicants,

You are welcome to participate in these forth-coming International events. The (IOHR) invites all participants across the globe to attend the International Conference on HIV/AIDS, Child Abuse, Racism And Human Trafficking taking place from (April 15th-18th 2014) in California, United State of America while the second phase will begins from (April 22nd-25th 2014) in Dakar, Senegal.

We accepted you to partake as you have been recommended by one of our staff-member. You may take this opportunity to participate in these International events. The theme of the forth-coming International Conferences is to equip participants with the strategies and policies to wage a global war against AIV/AIDS, Child Abuse, Racism & Human Trafficking.

These events is been Organized and sponsored by the International Organization For Human Right (IOHR) with the assistants of other benevolent organizations in the United States of America.

The conference organizing committee in conjunction with the donor sponsoring committee has mapped out some financial rewards to group participants that distinguished themselves in their areas of discipline. Panel of Judges has been appointed to oversee and to select participants on merit.

Our Aims and Objectives are as follows:

- to raise awareness of the current HIV/AIDS situation among the youth all over the world.
- to increase the knowledge of opportunities, challenges and obstacles for combating the HIV/AIDS epidemic in the world.
- Provide support to people with HIV/AIDS and their loved ones, as well as people with a sexual health crisis/problem.
- Provide helpline support to anyone who is worried about or potentially facing a sexual health crisis.
- to establish links of co-operation, peace and unity among the youth all over the countries.
- to carry activities on solving the problems raised in front of the Youth, and also help to fight against racism and child abuse.
- to assist the systematization, proclamation and monitoring of the information, concerning Youth issues in united state and all over the world
- To promote the projects on the development of Youth initiatives etc.

The Interested participants of the forth-coming International Conference should send the following details via email, to our Registration Desk (iohr.reg@usa.com) OR (registrationdesk@globomail.com)

1) Names exactly as in passport:
2) Passport Numbers:
3) Date of Birth:
4) Place of Birth:
5) Country of Residence:
6) Direct Contact Numbers tell/cell:
7) Profession/Sex:

Awards and Gifts will be given to participants on merit.....You are hereby advised to equip your selves and exhibit your God given talents to the fullest. We welcome Delegates, Inter-Governmental and Non-Governmental Organizations, young or old to the forth-coming International Conference.

REGISTRATION OF PARTICIPANTS: A minimum of (1-3) or maximum of (4-6) persons are expected to participate together as a group or organization to represent their Country in the forth-coming events. None of them should be less than eighteen (18) years of age and delegates must participate in both Conferences, USA/DAKAR SENEGAL.

Note Very Important: It is not necessary that one must belongs to an organization to be eligible to attend this event, he or she can also participate as an individual or a group of 1-2 members if he or she are not capable to form a group to represent a Country.

They should be in possession of their valid International Passports to enable them participate in this conferences. You are hereby required to forward the names and passport numbers of your group members to us as soon as possible, as all participants visa assistance request will be forwarded to the US Department of States Immigration for visa Authorization which shall be sent to the consular section of the US. Embassy in your country of residence for the status of your visa processing.

PLEASE TAKE PROPER NOTE OF THIS POINT: - Participants are only responsible for their own hotel booking in Senegal through the recommended hotel in Dakar for the second phase of these event. The organizing committee and the donor sponsoring committee of this event have mandated all participants to pay for their own hotel booking in order to prove to the US Department of State Visa Sector(UDSVS) that he/she will attend both events, and they do not have any intention to stay permanently in the United State after their participation in this forth-coming international conference, this is due to the past experiences in April 2009 international conference that was held here in United State, which lead to illegal immigrant to the United State of America.

All registered participants are entitled to a round trip air ticket, meals and accommodation which will be provided during their participation in the U.S.A. only.

Due to time factors of the forth-coming international events, I request that you quickly send us the requested details ASAP to enable us create your registration file and proceed further with your visa processing.

Yours Sincerely,

Mr. Thomas Cole
Secretariat Office.

International Organization For Human Right (IOHR)
400 Golden Gate Ave, San Francisco, CA 94102.
Tel: +1 (206) 888 6737
E-mail: iohr.reg@usa.com

A check on the IP address that this particular email was sent from shows that it actually originated from Senegal, rather than the USA as claimed.

> Header Analysis Quick Report
> Originating IP: 41.82.196.14
> Originating ISP: Sonatel
> City: n/a
> Country of Origin: **Senegal**
> * For a complete report on this email header goto ipTRACKERonline

A reply, sending the requested information to the "registration desk", results in the following reply from the scammer

Dear Richard Fiddler,

This is to inform you that you have been duly registered to participate in these forth-coming international events.

You are only responsible for your own hotel booking accommodation in Dakar Senegal, the conference organizing committee will be responsible for the accommodation here in the U.S. Together with the round trip air tickets which cover from your country of residence to the United State, from the United State to Dakar Senegal and from Dakar Senegal back to your country of residence. This including your visa processing to the United State.

Endeavor to furnish us with the (B) & (C) forms duly filled along with the hotel official booking confirmation receipt and a scanned copy of your international passport before the dead line date, and you should carefully follow up the instructions of the said recommended hotel management in Dakar.

DO NOTE: As soon as we receive your registration forms duly filled, together with the Hotel booking receipt, your documents will be forwarded to the Airline company for the status of your round trip air tickets.

You are advised to download the following attachments to view your registration files, and note again that delegates must participate in both phase of the conference in USA & Senegal respectively. Since you are living in the United States, you do not need to go through visa processing, but you will only require visa to Senegal upon arrival.

You are to contact the recommended hotel management in Dakar-Senegal to book room for yourself and sent us the scan copy of your (International Passport) & (B and C) forms duly filled, as you have to print it out, fill it accordingly then scan and return it back to us, by E-mail attachment, together with the (Hotel Booking Confirmation Receipt) not later than January 24th 2014.

Bellow is the contact address of the recommended hotel in Dakar Senegal were all (I.O.H.R) registered participants are to reserve their rooms and send us the requested documents before the dead lines date.

Hotel La Sillah,
Route de Aéroport International,
Rue 8099, Dakar-Senegal.
E-mail: (reservation.hotellasillah@gmail.com) /
(reservation-hotelsillah@africamail.com)
Phone: +221-77-657-6662. Fax: +221-33-860-0701

We shall be looking forward to hear from you before the dead line date, moreover the earlier you submit your requirement, the sooner you receive your entitled traveling documents.

Thanks for your co-operation,

I am wishing you a pleasant stay during your visit to United State of America.

Kind regard,

Garry Smith R.,
Registration desk,
Office +1-206-888-6737.
I.O.H.R, CA, USA.

This email also originated from Senegal.

Attached are some nice fake documents, as shown on the next three pages.

I.O.H.R

CONFERENCE ON CHILD ABUSE, HIV/AIDS & HUMAN TRAFFICKING

2014

2014 Conference Registration Form (A)

CONGRATULATION RP 2014
REGISTRATION FILE NUMBER: IOHR/ 3342546651
The file was opened with the following details:

DELEGATE REGISTRATION INFORMATION

Title: Dr ☐ Prof. ☐ Ms. ☐ Mrs. ☐ Mr. ☐

FIRST NAME & M.I.	MR RICHARD
LAST NAME:	FIDDLER
PASSPORT NUM:	1578185
DATE OF BIRTH:	23 DECEMBER 1950
PLACE OF BIRTH:	SAVILLE, OHIO USA
COUNTRY OF RES:	UNITED STATE

You have been duly registered to join the list of participants from different countries who will participate in the forthcoming International Conference on Racism and Human Trafficking.

Your documents will be forwarded to the U.S. Bureau of Immigration Affairs- U.S. Foreign Consular Department.

The processing of your documents will start soon as we receive your hotel booking confirmation from Dakar Senegal with the Global Conference Participation forms, which must be filled, signed by you, and sent to us by Email.

You are hereby required to submit the hotel reservation confirmation receipt from Dakar-Senegal, not later than February 26th 2014, to enable us forward the "B-2 Visa" support approval to the Consulate General (Visa section) at the Embassy of the United States of America in your country of residence for same day visa authorization, unless you are covered, under the U.S. Visa Waiver Permanent Program.

Your Documents will be processed here in United States before your visit to the U.S Embassy in your Country of Resident.

Same information in your Passports must be used to fill the visa form, which will be provided to you by the U.S. Bureau of immigration Affairs- U.S. Foreign Consular Department soon as all documents which includes the International conference participation registration forms, and your hotel booking confirmation receipt from Dakar Senegal, which will be forwarded to them.

We will get in touch with you soon as we receive the filled forms together with your hotel booking confirmation Receipt from Dakar, which is required to prove that you will attend both conferences.

Regards,

Berry Taylor
(REGISTRAR)

International Organization for Human Right (IOHR)
400 Golden Gate Ave, San Francisco, CA 94102
Tel +1-206-888-6737 Fax +1-516-312-4573
E-mail: registrationdesk@globomail.com

Seminar registration

I.O.H.R

CONFERENCE ON CHILD ABUSE, HIV/AIDS & HUMAN TRAFFICKING

2014

Conference Registration Form (B)

*Please read clearly and if some of these categories don't apply to you then please state by writing N/A

Name (Mr. Mrs. Miss.)

Nationality   Permanent Address:

Present Address (country of resident)   Phone Number:

In Case of Emergency Contact: Address:

Phone Number   Fax Number:

Email address:

What Languages do you speak? (In order of fluency):

Passport Number: Type of Passport:

Marital Status (circle one): Single   Married   Divorced   Separated

Name and address of group or Organization:

Group Participation file number:

Return all registration forms along with first pages of your passport information and confirmation of your hotel booking in Dakar-Senegal to the secretariat office via email   as soon as possible

International Organization for Human Right (IOHR)
400 Golden Gate Ave. San Francisco, CA 94102
Tel. +1-206-888-6737 Fax +1-516-312-4573
E-mail: registrationdesk@globomail.com

Seminar registration

I.O.H.R.
CONFERENCE ON CHILD ABUSE, HIV/AIDS & HUMAN TRAFFICKING
2014
Conference Registration Form (C)

1) Do you have relatives in the U.S.A.? Yes No   (if yes, please note their address and relationship to you) _____

_____

2) Describe experiences with culturally diverse situations: _____

PERSONAL INFORMATION

3) Religion: _____   Do you have any dietary restrictions? _____

4) Do you have allergies to certain foods? (List food) _____

_____

5) Do you smoke? Yes No Can you confine your smoking? Yes No Do you have objections to others smoking? Yes No

6) If yes, briefly describe: _____

7) Living abroad exposes you to a lifestyle that you may not be familiar with. Will you be able to adjust to unexpected situations?

_____

8) Hobbies and leisure time interests: _____

9) Have you ever been arrested or convicted of a crime? _____   If yes, please explain _____

10) How did you know of this conference? _____

International Organization for Human Right (IOHR)
400 Golden Gate Ave. San Francisco. CA 94102
Tel +1-206-888-8737 Fax +1-536-312-4573
E-mail: registrationdesk@globemail.com

Seminar registration

If the victim sends a booking enquiry to the fake hotel, they get a response similar to the below.

Dear Guest,

You should view the attached file to this email, as we advise you to make your choice and proceed with your booking payment.

We are looking forward to seeing you in our hotel for the up-coming international conference, we rest assured to offer you the best of our hotel services during your stay in hotel La Sillah.

Many thanks for your patronage & best regards.

Abdul Diouf.
Receptionist & Reservation Sector.

Hotel La Sillah.
Phone: +221-77-657-6662

Attached is the document shown on the next pages, detailing the room costs and the method of payment, which is either Western Union or Moneygram.

Route De Aéroport, BP 8099, Dakar-Senegal
Tel: +221-77-657-6662. Fax: +221-33-860-0701
Email: reservation-hotelsillah@africamail.com

Dear Guest,

We welcome you to the Hotel La Sillah; Hotel La Sillah has facilities like Swimming Pool, Lawn and Table Tennis, Billiards, Pool, Sauna, Jacuzzi, Steam and a multi - Gym. We serve the choicest of Vegetarian Indian, Chinese and Continental Asian food

Below are the available rooms and the official rate for conference participants..... All rates are in America dollars. Below are the hotel official rates for all participants.

SINGLE ROOM		DOUBLE ROOM		TRIPLE ROOM		QUAD ROOM	
Single Class	$75.00	Standard Class	$120.00	Standard Class	$170.00	Standard Class	$460.00
Business Class	$80.00	Business Class	$130.00	Business Class	$200.00	Business Class	$360.00
Premier Class	$88.00	Premier Class	$132.00	Premier Class	$220.00	Premier Class	$260.00
Club Class	$93.00	Club Class	$135.00	Club Class	$231.00	Club Class	$255.00

BOOKING PAYMENT METHOD

YOU CAN ALSO MAKE YOUR PAYMENT VIA WESTERN UNION MONEY TRANSFER OR MONEYGRAM .THESE ARE THE FASTEST MEANS OF PAYMENT FROM YOUR COUNTRY TO OUR COUNTRY AS WE CAN BE ABLE TO RECEIVED YOUR PAYMENT SAME DAY AND SEND YOUR OFFICIAL BOOKING RECEIPT.

Step 1: Make the payment.

Payment via MoneyGram
- First Name: **Ahmedu**
- Last Name: **Hassan**
- Address: 102 POINT DES ALMADIE
- City, Country: Dakar, Senegal
- Contact Phone: (+221) 77-657-6662

Payment via WESTERN UNION
- First Name: **Ahmedu**
- Last Name: **Hassan**
- Address: 102 POINT DES ALMADIE
- City, Country: Dakar, Senegal
- Contact Phone: (+221) 77-657-6662

After the payment has been made, scan and send the payment telegraphic receipt to enable us send the official letter of hotel booking confirmation to you and for forward a copy to the Conference Secretariat in the United State of America after we receive your payment.

PLEASE NOTE:

(1) We can only send you the hotel booking confirmation receipt after we receive your payment, and please let us know the type of rooms you need to enable us book the room.

(2)On receipt of your payment, we will forward the confirmation of your hotel booking for days paid for by e-mail attachment to you and a copy sent to the conference secretariat...

Please note that payment covers feeding too.

OUR HOTEL REFUNDABLE POLICY:

The organizing committee has reached an agreement with the managements of the hotel on Refund policy. Below is the reached agreement.

a) That any group or organization wishing to withdraw their participation in this conference after the payment of the hotel booking may request for refund in written to the hotel management.

b) The total payment will be refunded to the group or organization after the reduction of the bank transfer charges.

Thanks for your patronage.

Sincerely,

Abdul Diouf -BAR.

Receptionist & Reservation Sector.

Hotel La Sillah.
Route de Aéroport Inter.
Dakar BP 8099, Dakar-Senegal.
E-mail: (info_lasillahhotel@yahoo.fr) /
(reservation-hotelsillah@africamail.com)
Phone: +221-77-657-6662, Fax: +221-33-860-0701

How to avoid being scammed by Conference Scammers

As mentioned in the earlier chapters, any unsolicited email received should be viewed with scepticism, particularly when dealing with financial matters. Some other sure fire signs that you are dealing with a conference scam are:

- You would not normally be invited to such a conference.
- The conference is taking part in two locations – one in the USA and the other in a third-world country.
- As part of the registration for the conference outside the USA, you are required to book at a particular hotel.
- The hotel requests payment by Western Union/Moneygram.
- Everyone involved in the scam is using free email addresses or ones from a recently registered fake domain.

Alan Jones

9. PET SCAMS

Pet scammers prey on people who are looking for pets on the Internet – often on classifieds websites. The pets can range from popular types of puppies, such as bulldogs or Yorkies through to more exotic pets such as monkeys and wild cats. The pets will be offered at prices much lower than such a pet would realistically cost or to be donated free to a good home. All the victim has to do is pay for the shipping of the pet, which as usual will be requested through Western Union or Moneygram.

The scammers will often rely on pictures stolen from legitimate breeders to show the animals that they have for sale, and may even use a fake website pretending to be a breeder.

If the victim pays the initial shipping fee to the fake shipper, then the scammer will try and get more money from them for things such as payment for a crate for the shipping, or fees that have been incurred due to unexpected customs charges or special handling fees. The scammer will continue to request more money until the victim either runs out of money or realizes they are being scammed.

The following is a set of emails from a pet scammer up until the point where the initial shipping payment is requested to be paid to someone in Cameroon by money transfer. Here is the initial response after answering a random classified advert.

---

good day Mike Hunt and nice to know that you are looking for
puppies Mike Hunt
my names are evangelist rollings and i have a male and a female
Pomeranian puppies that was given to me as a present since i am a
lover of pets and due to my evangelical work i do move from place to
place to carry out my evangelical mission so i do not have time to
look after the puppies.
i do not want to sell the puppies because i am a lover of pets and i
do not believe in selling pets so all i want is a loving and caring
home for them.
since you want the puppies for charity home i will give my support by
letting you have them
i use to call the puppies with a pet name of Lilly and rexie. Lilly is
the female and rexie is the male

Gender: Male and female
Age: 11 weeks of age.
Champion Bloodline: Yes
Champion Sir / Dam,
Temperament: curious and very friendly.
Health Problems: No
Living conditions: everybody
Preparation: Preparation moderate.
Trained and house trained and potty trained.
State of health: good health, veterinary
checked, registered and confirmed health guarantee.
Sociability: well socialized with children and pets.

> before i continue i will like to ask you some few questions
> where exactly are you coming from......?
> can you be able to take both Lilly and rexie ..?
> will be able to take good care of them....?
> i will wait to read from you soon with urgent reply so that i know
> your next step
> regards and stay bless with happy Sunday

Attached are a few stolen images of puppies, as shown below.

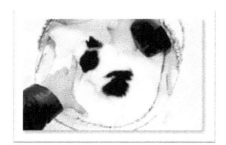  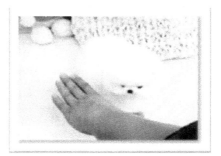

A reply gets the following response

good day mike and how are you doing to day hope you are doing good
as for me am doing fine and the puppies are also doing good
i am presently in Ireland because i was called two days ago to
Ireland to carry out an evangelism there since i always move from
place to place to carry out my evangelism. so i am not always stable
and i traveled with rexie and lilly to Ireland since there is no one
to look after them and these is really really stressful for me and
the puppies. so i just want the best for them that is why i want to
give to them to someone that can really take good of them and to
adopt them.
i could have asked that you come pick them up here but that will be
more of an expenditure and also waste of time and it will also be very
stressful for you since i am not stable. so the best i can do is just
to send them to you through a pet transportation agency that i know
of which can bring the puppies to your address in where ever you are
in Birmingham because they are are very fast, safer reliable and more
to that the puppies will be well insured with them during delivery
so if you will be interested in taking the puppies you will only have
to pay for the transportation cost of the puppies and also for me to
make the transfer of ownership papers so that the puppies documents
can legally be change to your name.
all the process will cost you just 150 pounds for the transportation
fee, transfer of ownership papers,i will personally carry out the
process today since am not too busy and then register the puppies for
delivery at the agency , you should not border about the registration
because i will pay for it
i will need your full information so that i can start with the process
your full names......?
full delivery address....?
post code in your location.....?
your telephone number......?
these are all the information i will be needing so that i can start
with the process immediately and register the puppies for delivery.
once i am done with all the process and register the puppies for
delivery i will contact you to let you and give you the details of
the delivery agency i use i registering the puppies.
i shall wait for your response
regards and stay bless

Providing the personal details that are requested will result in the below emails from the "seller" and fake shipping company being received.

good day mr mike and i am very sorry for the late reply to your mail
 actually i could register the puppies yesterday for delivery because
before i could finish making the transfer of ownership papers i was
very tired and the agency had closed for the day
i am just coming from the delivery agency to register rexie and lilly
to be delivered today to the address you gave to me
i register them at UK PETS TRANSPORTATION bceuase they are very
reliable and more to that they are very fast. i register the puppies
with the original copie of the documents along the chnage of ownership
papers they will be contacting you soon to confirm your delivery address and
also to tell when they will be bringing the puppies to your address
today
 please do update me when they contact you i shall be waiting to read from you soon
 regardcs and stay bless

UK PETS TRANSPORTATION

 ## REGIONAL PET AIR CARGO

UK PETS TRANSPORTATION SERVICE

Ireland to Birmingaham-England

UK PETS TRANSPORTATION shipping Express

Email:::(petani)

Welcome to UK PETS TRANSPORTATION Service , the relocating pets

best friend since 1977. The relationship of pets and people is a treasured one, as evidenced by the love shown with the

children and their pets in the above photos; and is recognized as the human-animal bond. As you contemplate moving

your family pet by air as you relocate, you want the best for your Animal transport service holds the welfare and safety of

your family pet as our primary consideration. Whether your pet is an experienced flyer or a first time flyer, Air Animal's

pet move specialists, pet owners themselves, understand the relationship you have with your pet and will only provide the

best pet moving service for your family pet both, nationwide & worldwide as you relocate..

Dear Client,

Welcome to our notification services by mail.

Welcome to Professional Pet Transportation service, the relocating pets best friend since 1978. We are working in the collaboration with the Continental and Delta airways. The relationship of pets and people is a treasured one, as evidenced by the love shown with the children and their pets; and is recognized as the human-animal bond. As you contemplate moving your family pet by air as you relocate, you want the best for your pet. ANIMALS TRANSPORT holds the welfare and safety of your family pet as our primary consideration. Whether your pet is an experienced flier or a first time flier, Air pet move specialists, pet owners themselves, understand the relationship you have with your pet and will only provide the best pet moving service for your family pet both, nationwide & worldwide as you relocate

We do take care of the following operations:

. Reservation of flight for pets.

. Insure that all vaccines and health papers are updated.

. Take care of your pets during the flight.

. Take care of your pet's delivery at your home from the airport.

We are professional pet movers responsible for the relocation of pets to their new families. When your contract is with us, you are assigned a PERSONAL PET MOVE COUNSELOR who will work with you to arrange the fastest, most direct flight for your pet. We work with your relocation schedule to ensure as smooth as possible.

Information on the Transportation of your MALE AND FEMALE POMERANIAN PUPPIES :(REXIE AND LILLY).

Dear Client,

We here by inform you that we are in possession of your Male and female pomeranian puppies with rexie and lilly in Delivery Cage Numbers 013 From Mr meilla rollings here at the UK pets transportation Anchorage AK 99513 to be transported and delivered to you using the following address.:

BELOW ARE YOUR DELIVERY DETAILS WHICH WE ARE TO GET YOUR PUPPIES DELIVERED TO .

URGENTLY: DELIVERY ADDRESS TO BE CONFIRMED.

RECEIVERS FULL NAMES	**MICLEAL HUNT**
DESTINATION/COUNTRY	**ENGLAND**
DELIVERY ADDRESS	**23 Felching Drive, Shirley**
STATE/CITY	**Birmingaham**
ZIP CODE	**B1 5ED**
CONTACT NUMBER	------------------
DESTINATION AIRPORT	**BIRMINGAHAM AIRPORT**

 PUPPIES Description;

Breed...................................Pomeranian puppies.

puppies ID....................EU70732 47630/11ES.

Model of Cage:................. 5790AC AF-12 5791AC

puppies Documents.............Vet Certificate,Shot Records, Birth Certificate, Feeding Manual And Microchip

Sensor Manual.

Others.. .... .Pet Toys, Pet Crate, First Aid And Microchip Sensor,Blanket,bowls.

INFORMATION OF YOUR PARCEL

Health Documents	Valid
Adoption Papers	Valid
Delivery Fee Payments	Pending...
Shipping Details	Valid

These Puppies will come with all necessary papers needed, but as the our delivery policy demands, The Anchorage Düsseldorf, Ak veterinarian must conduct another test to be sure of The health status. The tests were conducted and the results were positive. The Health Papers and USDA Certs were accurate and the Puppies are free from QUARANTINE. The test results indicated that the Puppies are free from all diseases that may attack other animals (Horses, Birds, Cats etc.). The experienced pets moving specialists at **uk pets transportation Delivery Express**, the IATA Air Cargo Agency(A.C.A) will handle your puppies delivery with confidence, professionalism, and trust. **Pet Animal Delivery Express**, NO TRANQUILIZER rule is designed for the safety and welfare of your pomeranian puppies during airline cargo transport. uk pets transportation registered with the USDA as an Intermediate Handler, is governed by the rules, regulations and mandates of the Animal Welfare Act, the AWA and the Federal Law governing scheduled airline air cargo shipments.

The Puppies is now ready for delivery, but it should be noted that this process cannot be carried out unless the delivery fee (150 pounds) **is completely paid to register for for transportation and delivery. The Puppies** will come alongside with two of our pets carriers.

The payment is to be done to Air Animal's developed 3rd party Pets Delivery Service to the moving & relocation industry in our Sub-branch Office and Account Department in Cameroon because we receive all payments for International Deliveries through a third party who makes sure the kitten is safely delivered before payment is sent over to us. We will need you to pay the money as soon as possible, so we can board the puppies on to morning's deliveries to your location which will be leaving to your location at approx in an hours time and will be delivered at your address as stated above within 3-6 hours.When the puppies reaches your location, the delivery agents will call/will have your male and Female pomeranian puppies (rexie and lilly) delivered to your address as given to us by the Sender Mr meilla rollings .

YOU ARE REQUESTED TO PAY THE TOTAL FUND THROUGH MONEY TRANSFER-MONEY GRAM TRANSFER..AVAILABLE IN ANY OF YOUR LOCATIONS

NOTE: You will be using the details, of our director of budget partition and control, who is presently, at our HEAD QUARTER IN Cameroon who are specialize in these kind of transaction. You have to make the payment immediately so that we can have time to make arrangements and proceed with delivery.

The details of our director (MONEY GRAM account details), you will need to use in making the payment Below. Just copy the details on a piece of paper and take it to any Western Union store and make the payment so we can proceed with shipment.

PAYMENT ADDRESS BELOW.

THIS SHOULD BE RESPECTED!!

PAYMENT ADDRESS

NAME OF CASHIER (RECEIVER) :ABEY HENDRIECKS AYUK
AMOUNT.: 150 pounds
CITY/STATE:LIMBE
DESTINATION/COUNTRY:CAMEROON
TEST QUESTION.: WHEN?
TEST ANSWER.:SOON

The payment should be done as soon as possible so that the puppies can be home delivered to you on time tonight. If the fee is not provided the puppies will not be dispatched from our detention and will spend more on daily feeding until the Cameroon branch manager confirms the payment of the 150 pounds

Kindly email us with the MONEY GRAM Transfer Money Transfer Control Number (MTCN #) & the **Sender's full names Name** and a scan copy of the MONEY GRAM Receipt as soon as the payment is done. Immediately the payment is confirmed then the Delivery Tracking Number as well as the flight receipt to ensure a 100% assurance for the transaction will be sent to you.

Thanks

Testimonials
"savanna kittens arrived safely in scotland Sunday evening." A BIG thanks to you and the Regional Animal & pets Service Team. I'm very happy and impressed with the service'. Again, thanks a lot for an outstanding door-to-door hassle-free service!

&nb sp;

REGIONAL ANIMAL AIRWAYS CARGO'S DELIVERIES

UK

Below is a further email received when the victim did not send the money or respond.

DEAR CLIENT
WE ARE TO INFORM YOU THAT WE SEND YOU A MAIL NOTIFICATION REGARDING THE DELIVERY OF YOUR MALE AND FEMALE POMERANIAN PUPPIES TO HERE AT OUR IN IRELAND REGISTERED BY ONE MR MEILLA ROLLINGS TO BE DELIVERED TO YOUR ADDRESS AT BIRMINGHAM AND WE HAVE ALREADY PUT THE PUPPIES IN THEIR VARIOUS DELIVERY CAGES WAITING TO BE DELIVERED
THE MAIL WE SEND TO YOU IS FOR YOU TO CONFIRM YOUR EMAIL ADDRESS WHERE WE SHALL BE MAKING THE DELIVERY AND ALSO TO MAKE THE AVAILABLE PAYMENT OF 150 POUNDS FOR THE DELIVERY FLIGHT ACTIVATION TICKETS OF THE PUPPIES USING OUR BRANCH HEAD OFFICE IN CHARGE OF ALL OUR INTERNATIONAL TRANSACTION AND WHO IN CHARGE OF FLIGHT DELIVERIES OF PETS REGISTERED AT OUR AGENCY
WE CANNOT PROCEED WITH THE DELIVERY TO YOUR DELIVERY ADDRESS BECAUSE WE HAVE NOT CONFIRM PAYMENT FOR THE FLIGHT DELIVERY AND ONCE WE CONFIRM THE PAYMENT WE WILL ACTIVATE THE FLIGHT TICKET OF THE PUPPIES FOR FLIGHT TICKET ACTIVATION TAKES JUST AN HOUR
SO KINDLY COPY THE PAYMENT INFORMATION WE SEND TO YOU AND MAKE THE PAYMENT WITHIN ANY MONEY GRAM TRANSFER MONEY TRANSFER STORE IN YOUR LOCATION
ONCE YOU MAKE THE PAYMENT DO SCAN TO US A COPY OF THE PAYMENT RECEIPT FOR CONFIRMATION AND TO ENABLE US HAVE ENOUGH TIME TO PROCEED WIT THE DELIVERY
WE SHALL BE WAITING TO CONFIRM THE PAYMENT
THANKS FOR USING OUR SERVICE
UK PETS TRANSPORTATION

I have not sent money to the scammers, so I cannot show what this particular scammer would have done next to get even more money from his victim, however there are various tactics they will use as show in the below emails.

Refundable insurance

Here the scammer is asking the victim to pay for insurance that will be refunded

---

PETS INSURANCE DEPT

DEAR CLIENT,
WE WISH TO INFORM YOU THAT WE HAVE RECEIVED AND CONFIRMED A PAYMENT FOR THE VACCINE AND AIR CONDITION CRATE OF YOUR PUPPY

The Insurance Department of our service wishes to bring to your knowledge, that after the check up prior to delivery of your Akita Puppy, we discovered not all rules and regulations were met for the puppy to be transported and delivered. Full details on this follow in the subsequent paragraphs.
1. Following the International Animal Transportation Association (IATA) ' Rules and Regulations on Pets Transportation on section 12 sub paragraph 2, ".... the life of all animals being commercially transported from One State to another throughout Unites State and out of United State must be fully Insured by the insurance department of the company in charge of the flight and delivery at the State of Origin against any unforeseen eventualities".
2. Following a compromise between the United State Aviation Complaint Commission and the Financial Commission of the INTERNATIONAL ANIMAL TRANSPORTATION BOARD (IATA) , it was concluded that---------- "..the life of all pets being COMMERCIALLY transported throughout the U.S and out of U.S, Should be insured and this insurance fee should vary from one animal to another depending on Financial Value of the Animal".------------------
From the above, the Life Insurance fee you were supposed to pay for your Puppy is $3800.00 and your puppy can

---

commercially and privately travel through its life time through U.S and out of U.S, with no restrictions.

Due to a good number of complaints by clients to the INTERNATIONAL ANIMAL TRANSPORTATION BOARD (IATA) about this Insurance Scheme, the Management of International Animal transportation board in collaboration with the U.S Financial commission, we came out with a Partial Refundable Animal Life Insurance Scheme, which provides for the following:
* You could use our Partial Insurance Scheme to Insure your Puppy's Life for 1/2 the cost of the full Insurance fund (financial value).
* After the insurance fee is paid, the company in charge of the flight and delivery of the animals, must provide a fully refundable receipt to be signed by the customer, which will entitle the client to a full refunds of the money paid for insurance cash upon delivery.

*The insurance fee paid by the client, must be fully refunded cash upon delivery of puppy or any other method deemed suitable by the client, but this should take a maximum of 24 hours.
*If anything should happen to the puppy during delivery after this insurance fees have been paid for, the company shall be fully reliable for all expenses and extra compensation and the company shall stand a chance of being taking legally to court by the customer in question.

From the above rules and regulations, we come to a conclusion that the delivery cannot proceed except the fully refundable insurance fee is paid for and you will have to pay an extra $10 for extra pet feeding and care. This extra is because Akita puppies need more care and quality feeding than other animals ..

* This means you will have to pay the sum of $2200,00 which is 1/3 the initial value for your puppy and $10.00 for our services all this while the puppy has been with us, which gives you a total of $2210.00 of which $2200.00 will be refunded to you when your Puppy is delivered to you at your home address by our agent, Which is responsible for the delivery to you at your home address details which we have registered.

So we are expecting the sum of $2210 from you in which $2200 will be refunded to you (in cash or any other method of payment you prefer) when the puppy are delivered to you at your home address registered in our database. As soon as you go through this we do expect you to go and make the payment of the $2210 and get back to us with the payment details as soon as possible.
You are expected to make the total payment to I.A.T SHIPPERS International head office, they are responsible for the refundable insurance fees, once you get that done you are to e-mail the full payment details to us for confirmation, after confirmation we shall issue a receipt which shall entitle you to $2210 when your puppy are delivered, you will have to print, sign and scan this receipt and send to us immediately and keep a copy as a record and authorization for you to collect your money back when the puppy are delivered.
N.B: You are expected to make the payment via WESTERN UNION

INFORMATION TO USE AT THE WESTERN UNION:

PAYMENT ADDRESS

NAMES:.............. KELLY VINCENT
COUNTRY:.........................CAMEROON
ZIP CODE:............................00237
STATE:...............LITTORAL
CITY:............DOUALA
TEST QUESTION..........How Soon
ANSWER...............Now
We hereby apologize if this has caused any minor complications, but still remind you that everything we do, is to ensure the safety of your pet.

We count on your understanding and prompt action.

(YOU CAN E-MAIL US FOR ANY CORRECTIONS OR NOTIFICATIONS)

Shipping Crate required

WELCOME TO UNIQUE PETS TRANSPORTERS
THE LEADER OF PETS RELOCATION.
THIS IS A CONFIRMATION E-MAIL

HOW CAN WE HELP YOU?
We are specialists in the relocation of your pets by air. An International run business, with more than 20 years of experience in airfreight and the movement of live animals.
We have expert knowledge in flying animals, having been involved in moving everything from police dogs to parrots, tortoises to a tiger, and not forgetting our beloved domestic cats and dogs.
We acknowledge your desire for the best and provide you with a service second to none.

AUTO REGULATORY CRATE NEEDED:
Dear Client xxxxxxxx,
We wish to inform you that the payment of the transportation cost has been confirmed. The flight ticket has been activated. we have also process and aproved the transfer of ownership document.

We wish to inform you that, your kittens are ready to leave to your address. The kittens can not leave because we noticed that your kittens have no crate. All pets are supposed to be transported in a crate. The kittens can only leave when a crate is provided.

CONFIRM THE DELIVERY ADDRESS;
FULL NAMES: xxxxxxxxxxxx
HOUSE ADDRESS: xxxxxxxx
CITY: xxxxxxxxx
POSTAL CODE: xxxxxxxxxx
CONTACT NUMBER: xxxxxxxxx
FULL NAMES: xxxxxxxxx
HOUSE ADDRESS: xxxxxxxxx
POSTAL CODE: xxxxxxxx
Please, ensure the above delivery address is correct, in case of any error, notify us immediately.

WE CAN PROVIDE CRATE AT OUR AGENCY
1) We offer crates to pets without crates. We collect a refundable amount for the crate provided.
2) We do sell crates to pets without crates. We do collect the amount of the crate.

CRATE TO BE PROVIDED:

If you are not buying our crate, You are to make a refundable deposit of $ 365 . immediately your kittens are delivered to you, you will be given the sum of $ 360, the $ 5 is for using our crate. The money will be given back to you by our delivery agents.

PAYMENT ADDRESS
DIRECTOR'S NAME: CLARKE ANDERSON
COUNTRY: USA
STATE: VIRGINIA
CITY: RICHMOND
POSTAL CODE: 23219
AMOUNT: $ 365
TEST QUESTION: FROM
TEST ANSWER: SENDER

You have to make the payment using Money Gram as you did with the first payment.

If you are not buying the crate. Once, the money is paid, You will be given back $ 360 at your home today.

IMMEDIATELY YOU COMPLETE THE PAYMENT. SEND US THE 8 DIGIT MTCN. SENDER'S NAME. TEST QUESTION AND ANSWER. ALSO SEND A SCANNED COPY OF THE PAYMENT RECEIPT TO FACILITATE THE CONFIRMATION OF PAYMENT.

Visit a Money Gram ® Agent location near you to send the money.

USA Safe Hands - Safe Journey

Independent Pet and Animal Transportation Association
We are number one in the world of transporting animals around the globe with our qualified surgeons
An International Trade Association of animal handlers, pet moving providers, kennel operators, veterinarians and others who are dedicated to the care and welfare of pets and small animals during transport locally . . . Nationwide . . . Worldwide. Also provides a comprehensive list of approved shippers.

How to avoid being scammed by Pet Scammers

If you are involved with a pet scammer, it is probably because you are looking for a pet on a classifieds site. The vast majority of pet adverts on such sites are fake and placed by scammers. Some sure signs of scam adverts are:

- The scammer is vague about their location until you tell them yours, when they will then tell you that they are over the other side of the country or overseas.
- The pet is a popular breed (Bulldogs, Pomeranians, etc.), but is being given away just for the cost of shipping.
- The "seller" recommends a pet transport company.
- The seller/transporter requests payment by Western Union/Moneygram.
- There is **any mention whatsoever** of Cameroon – Cameroon is the centre of the pet scam "business", so if you see mention of payments being sent there or companies based there then it is guaranteed to be a scam.

The best advice if you are buying a pet is to buy locally and actually view the animal before handing over any money. Not only will you avoid scams such as the one described above, but you will be able to ensure the animal is healthy and comes from a good home/breeder.

10. EMPLOYMENT SCAMS

Employment scams target those looking for jobs and the scammers often get their victims details from job sites that hold CVs, although some will just mass mail in the same way other scammers do.

There are a number of different types of employment scam, ranging from the simple scam designed to steal a small amount of money from the victim in the form of a payment for a security check, through to scams involving victims receiving stolen goods or payments from other scam victims.

Visa scams

In this scam, the scammer targets victims from third world countries, who might be looking to work overseas (often in hotel or farming jobs, but sometimes in jobs in engineering) and make them pay for a visa or work permit. The emails will often turn up with a long list of vacancies and ask the victim to send his CV or resume. The example below is a series of emails sent to a victim who responded to a job email in Canada.

The first email was mass mailed to numerous people with the guise of being an employment agency looking for staff for a company in Canada

---

Dear Sir/Madam,

We are currently recruiting workers for the post of Fish Packing job Requirement in Canada.Please let us know if you have unskilled and skilled workers for the following position.

Job description:

Type of Job - Fish Packer,

Responsibilities: Fish packing, fish cleaning, fish packing for delivery to customers and export.

TERMS AND CONDITIONS:

1. Accommodation   - Provided.
2. Ticket   - Provided (Employer pays 50%).
3. Medical   - Provided.
4. Feeding   - Provided
5. Medical Insurance   - Provided
6. Transportation   - Provided.
7. Working hours   - 8a.m-4p.m [Mon-Sat]
8. Vacation   - 28.5 days every year
9. Salary   - Ca$20 per hour
10. Contract   - 2 years.
11. Extra time   - Ca$22per hour
12. Insurance & Pension - According to Quebec Labor laws.
13. Other Benefits   - Family status, group benefit and other fringe benefits.

Other terms according to Quebec labor laws.

Thanks & Regards

Mr. Brown Jackson

A response from the victim asking if she would be suitable, gets the following reply from the scammer.

> Kindly send your CV's to enable us forward it to the employed for processing.
>
> MANAGEMENT.

The victim sends her CV and after a few days is told that she is being offered the job (with no form of interview)

> Dear Sweet Vigina,
>
> Bubler Industries has employed you in it's company. these letter of intent is to inform you that we have successfully secured your employment letter from your employer. kindly sign the contract letter and mail it back to us for further processing.
>
> MANAGEMENT

Attached is a contract for the victim to sign, as shown on the next page. The victim signs and returns the contract and is finally told of the fees required and introduced to a new email address to pay them

> Sweet Vigina,
>
> We are in receipt of your mail and have received your signed Employment Contract letter.
>
> This is what next you have to do:
>
> 1. Appointed Worker(s) is expected to sign and return the Employment Contract Letter immediately
>
> 2. Appointed worker(s) will pay for Administrative Charge which enables the processing of their document to obtain their work permit visa which we guarantee you as 100% certainty.
>
> The statistics of the Administrative fee is below:
>
> a. Visa Application Fee: $150
> b. Representative Fee: $600
> c. CAQ (Certificate of Acceptance of Quebec): $199
>
> So each candidate / worker is expected to pay the sum of $949
>
> You are to contact the Administrative Processor Unit for information on how to send the processing fee with the below details:
>
> NAME: ANITA WILSON
> EMAIL: canadaprocessingunit@hotmail.com
>
> Once again Congratulation. Waiting to hear from you
>
> MANAGEMENT

Buhler Manufacturing
1260 Clarence Ave, Winnipeg, MB
Telephone: +16073171120
Email: info.buhlerindustriescompanys@gmail.com

May 23rd, 2015.

Employment Contract Letter

Dear Sweet vagina,

We are delighted that you have agreed to join our industry in the important position as a food processor. The purpose of this letter is to confirm our mutual agreement with respect to the terms of your employment.

Work schedule and hours of service: You will have one day off per week, usually Sunday. You understand that by the virtue of the nature of the position, there will be occasions when scheduling changes will be necessary to accommodate our schedule. Your services may be required on holidays. The nature of this position together with the variability of our needs for service can sometimes cause need for your services beyond the general scope of this agreement.

Duties: You will have primary responsibility for all aspects of the management of the inside of the industry as we direct.

Compensation: Your starting salary will be CAD20 per hour and additional CAD22 for extra hour. Your starting date will be Monday 15th, June 2015. This contract would be renewable in two (2) years.

Benefits: You will be provided medical benefits, free accommodation, transportation and other fringe benefits. Your eligibility for such benefits is subject to the provisions of our 'employee benefit plan' with respect to waiting periods etc.

Vacation: After the first eight (8) months of employment, you are eligible for 28.5 days paid vacation and thereafter you may plan to take up to a week of paid leave for each completed eight (8) month period. You taking vacation leave is naturally contingent upon a schedule which is mutually acceptable to both yourself and to us. Vacation time cannot be accumulated beyond four (4) weeks of total earned vacation time.

Other Terms: Food/Accommodation/Medical/Air Ticket provided to employee.

Performance Appraisals: At four (4) months, eight (8) months and annually thereafter.

We expect you to reflect my high ethical and legal standards at all times whether on or off. If this 'Letter of Agreement' accurately reflects your understanding of our relations and is completely acceptable to you. Please sign and return a copy of this letter. If you have any questions concerning this agreement. Kindly get back to us.

Todd Trueman, Director
Human Resources, Buhler Industries Inc.

⦿ *I have read the foregoing and understand and accept the stated terms and conditions*

_____

Sweet vagina [Employee].

Contacting the "Administrative Processor Unit", gets the details to send the fee (a mule in the USA whose details have been redacted here)

Sweet Vigina,

Thank you for your quick respond, The statistics of the Administrative fee is below:

a. Visa Application Fee: $150
b. Representative Fee: $600
c. CAQ (Certificate of Acceptance of Quebec): $199

So each candidate / worker is expected to pay the sum of $949.

You are to send the processing fee via Western Union to my secretary with this below information:

Receiver Name: Ixxxxx Sxxxxx
Address: Chicago illinois USA
Text Question: Processing
Answer: Fee
Amount: $949 only.

You are to get back to us immediately with the payment receipt-slip and the MTCN so we can process your work permit visa.

Regards
Anita Wilson
Processing Unit

Money mule scam

In this scam, the scammer will recruit his victim to receive payments from victims of other scams and forward them on to the scammer, less the mule's commission. The payments may be received into the victims bank account, they may be asked to collect Western Union or Moneygram transfers sent in their name or even receive payments sent as money orders through the mail. Again, the victim will potentially be facing a criminal investigation and charges for money laundering. An example of the Money mule scam, where the victim is asked to receive Western Union payments can be seen below in the cheque printing scam, which develops into a money mule scam.

Here is an example of a fake company website, that is really just a shell to look like a legitimate eCommerce business that needs representatives to handle its payment processing and the job description given to the victims who will be receiving money into their bank accounts.

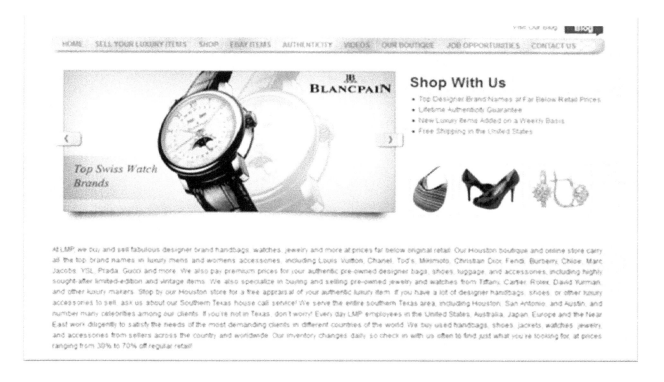

The scammers will use legitimate job websites to look for job hunters and then write to them detailing the position that they have available.

> LMP Company opens a employment of Administrative Assistant. We are an affiliate of main international goods distributor so the offered position will be connected with sales customer support for arrangements held in Australia.
>
> We have open both, full and part-time employments with flexible time:
> - you will be paid up to 3500 AUD per month plus bonuses for the partial post;
> - for full-time post - 5500 AUD monthly plus bonuses.
>
> As an Administrative Assistant you will provide all the necessary service to our sales department; purchase orders and other reports handling; keep the data of all the arrangements and payments; communicate with our clients in America, Eastern Europe and Asia.
>
> We have a probation period, during which you will be trained and guided. This period is paid. Your training is held online, but additional support will be provided also to you via phone.
>
> Conditions:
> - computer with access to the Internet;
> - basic Excel skills the software must be pre-installed;
> - good communication skills and positive motivation.
>
> To have more information about, please answer to us back.
>
> CV will be a plus for our HR team.
> Thank you!
> LMP Team.

Victims who respond will be sent a mail asking them to complete an application form.

> Dear _____,
>
> We would like to offer position of Administrative Assistant at our company. Please, find more information about us and this position below.
>
> LMP is a leading distributor of finest designer goods. Currently it is one of the most important specializing in online sales. With more than 5 years of experience in the designer goods industry. We offer a continuous renovation in our collections, following the latest trends in each country and season, thus satisfying the demand of clients. We always keep in mind that prices are an important factor when it comes to sales.
>
> We are looking for a responsible person in Australia who will be ready to incur all necessary activities. Our candidate should be highly motivated. We believe that the experience is not the most important thing. The key to success is a fresh look and bold ideas!
>
> The main duties of Administrative Assistant:
>
> - Helping Entity's Sales Department as a special projects support
> - Data entry and other functions as specified in the instruction
> - Running reports for all completed deals and wire transfers
> - Providing overall administrative maintenance such as making of letters, processing purchase orders and transaction reports etc.
> - Emailing correspondence every day
>
> Hours: Full-time or part-time schedule possible. Your schedule can be irregular. For a part time variant - you will spend 3 hours per day average, from Monday to Friday.

Salary: Essential pay for a part time job is 840AUD on a weekly basis
plus 5 percent commission. Full-time job pay is 1300AUD on a weekly basis plus commission.

You will be on Probation period for your first month.

I'm sending you Application Form and short presentation of LMP(you can find it attached to this email). You can find full job description in the brochure(pages: 5,6,7). Please read it carefully, complete and send it back to me via email or by fax +1-832-209-8015. If you have any questions, please feel free to ask.

Thank you,
Daisy Hicks

In many cases, the applicants will be offered a job with no interview, or at most an interview conducted over over an Instant Messenger such as Yahoo Messenger. They will then receive an email offering them the job for a trial period.

Dear XXX,

We have received your Application Form and would like to consider you for the position of administrative assistant/sales support. Please find more information about our company and this position below.

LMP is a leading distributor of top designer goods. Currently it is one of the most important specializing in online sales. At LMP, we buy and sell fabulous designer brand handbags, watches, jewelry and more at prices far below original retail. The items are sold through established websites such as amazon, eBay, yahoo, and more. Our Houston boutique and online store carry all the top brand names in luxury men's and women's accessories, including Louis Vuitton, Chanel, Tod's, Mikimoto, Christian Dior, Fendi, Burberry, Chloe, Marc Jacobs, YSL, Prada, Gucci and more. We also pay premium prices for your authentic pre-owned designer bags, shoes, luggage, and accessories, including highly sought-after limited-edition and vintage items. We also specialize in buying and selling pre-owned jewelry and watches from Tiffany, Cartier, Rolex, David Yurman, and other makers.

We are looking for a responsible person who will be ready to incur all necessary activities. Our candidate should be highly motivated. We believe that the experience is not the most important thing. The key to success is a fresh look and bold ideas!

The main duties of Administrative Assistant:

• Incorporating effective priorities for the virtual office function
• Administer day-to-day financial responsibilities for clients
• Reporting online daily
• Preparing brief summary reports, and weekly financial reports

Salary: Essential pay for a part time job is 840AUD on a weekly basis plus 5 commission. Full-time job pay is 1300AUD on a weekly basis plus 5 commission.

Office: This position is a home-based one, means you`ll get in contact with other Company`s employees online. For the test period our supervisors will provide you assistance online.

You will be on Probation period for your first month. The probation period begins from the moment of incorporation.

I'm sending you the Agreement(you can find it attached to this email).
Please read it carefully, sign it, scan and send it back to me via
email or by fax +1-832-247-4472. If you have any questions, please feel free to ask.

Thank you,
Grace Madsen

And an agreement to sign.

TRIAL PERIOD AGREEMENT
BETWEEN: [EMPLOYEE NAME] (the "Employee"), an individual with his main
address at:
[COMPLETE ADDRESS]

AND: LMP (the "Company"), an entity organized and existing under the laws
of the US with its head office located at:
1410 Woodhead Street, Houston, TX 77019

RECITALS

In consideration of the covenants and agreements herein contained and the moneys to be paid hereunder, the Company hereby employs the Employee and the Employee hereby agrees to perform services as an employee of the Company, on an "at will" basis, upon the following terms and conditions:

1. Subject of the Agreement
1.1. According to the present Agreement the Company hereby engages the Employee and the Employee is obliged to perform the services set forth herein. The Employee hereby accepts such engagement and undersigns to act to the interests of the Company while the present Agreement is in force and to receive compensation for his services.

1.2. The services provided to the Company in sense of the present Agreement are understood as professional activity of the Employee consisting of a complex of transactions set out in the Exhibit A, attached to this Core Agreement. Exhibit A represents the integral part of the Agreement and contains the principles and values governing the relationship between the Company and the Employee. The Employee takes the responsibility to provide the Company with the estimate, which is later attached as Exhibit A of the present Agreement. The Exhibit A shall define the Employee's duties, term of engagement, compensation and provisions for payment thereof.

2. General provisions

2.1. The provisions of the Agreement may be negotiated and amended in writing from time to time, or supplemented with subsequent estimates for services to be rendered by the Employee and agreed to by the Company. No modification or amendment to this Agreement shall be valid unless made in writing and signed by duly authorized representatives of both Parties All changes, supplements and appendices to the present Agreement are the integral part of the present Agreement.

2.2. The Employee provides services in strict conformity with Exhibit A with the purpose of receiving the greatest possible profit. The Exhibit A is adjusted and signed by the Parties along with signing of the present Agreement.

2.3. Section headings do not completely and accurately reflect the content of the present Agreement and therefore shall not be considered a part of this Agreement.

2.4. This Agreement and the Prior Agreement contains the entire understanding of the Parties with respect to the matters contained herein and supersedes all previous negotiations, agreements and commitments related thereto. There are no promises, covenants or undertakings between the Parties other than those expressly set forth herein and in the Prior Agreement. In the event of any conflicts between this Agreement and the Prior Agreement, this Agreement shall prevail.

2.5. Neither Party shall be liable for any delay or nonperformance of any provision of this Agreement. If any provision of this Agreement, or any portion thereof, is held to be invalid and unenforceable, then the remainder of this Agreement shall nevertheless remain non-cancelable in full force and effect.

3. Expenses and dues

3.1. All expenses or dues, which the Employee has paid (or should pay in the future) at execution of the obligations under the present Agreement, are subject to compensation at the expense of the Company, at a rate of actual expenses.

3.2. The Company undertakes to reimburse all reasonable and approved out-of-pocket expenses which are incurred in connection with the performance of the duties hereunder during the term of this Agreement except for the expenses for the time spent by the Employee in traveling to and from Company facilities.

3.3. The above-stated expenses and the dues shall be reflected in Exhibit A.

4. Employee's reports

4.1. The accountability of the Employee consists of monthly project plans, progress reports and a final results report, provided to the Company. On request from the Company the Employee shall be ready to present to the Company reports summarizing all activities conduced by Employee to date. A comprehensive final results report shall be due at the conclusion of the project and shall be submitted to the Company in a confidential written report at such time.

4.2. The results report shall be presented in such form and contain such information and data as is reasonably requested by the Company. In case the Company has not signed the results report and also has not presented the motived refusal, the report is deemed accepted by the Company.

5. Privacy statement

5.1. Any information transferred from one Party to another in the framework of the present Agreement, is confidential and is not subject to disclosure to the third parties without the written agreement of the Parties, except for cases stipulated hereto.

5.2. The Employee, by signing this Agreement, expressly grants to the Company for all copyrightable material, any and all inventions, discoveries, developments and innovations conceived by the Employee during this engagement relative to the duties under this Agreement shall be the exclusive property of the Company.

5.3. Any and all inventions, discoveries, developments and innovations conceived by the Employee prior to the term of this Agreement and utilized by him in rendering duties to the Company are hereby licensed to the Company for use in its operations and for an infinite duration. This license is non-exclusive, and may be assigned without the Employee's prior written approval by the Company to a wholly owned subsidiary of the Company.

5.4. The Employee limits a circle of the employees admitted to the Company information, to the number of the employees necessary for present Agreement execution.

5.5. The Employee undertakes not to disclose the information about operations, accounts and essential elements of the Company for the third parties, except for the cases, when the disclosure of such information is directly authorized by the Company or follows the necessity of execution of the present Agreement.

5.6. The Employee is cognizant, that the system of the accounts utilized by the Employee is extremely internal system. No record which has been designated as confidential, or is the subject of a pending application of confidentiality, shall be disclosed by the Employee.

5.7. The Company and the Employee shall identify preexisting confidential or proprietary items to be delivered under this Agreement as follows. The Employee and the Company agree that during this Agreement, it is possible that the Employee may develop additional data or information that the Employee considers to be protectable as confidential information. The Employee acknowledges that during the engagement he will have access to and become acquainted with various trade secrets, inventions, innovations, processes, information, records and specifications owned or licensed by the Company and/or used by the Company in connection with the operation of its business including, without limitation, the Company's business and product processes, methods, customer lists, accounts and procedures.

5.8. All files, records, documents, blueprints, specifications, information, letters, notes, media lists, original artwork/creative, notebooks, and similar items relating to the business of the Company, whether prepared by the Employee or otherwise coming into his possession, shall remain the exclusive property of the Company.

5.9. The Employee shall not retain any copies of the foregoing without the Company's prior written permission. Upon the expiration or earlier termination of this Agreement, or whenever requested by the Company, the Employee shall immediately deliver to the Company all such files, records, documents, specifications, information, and other items in his possession or under his control.

5.10. The Employee undertakes to do not distribute the information, which becomes known to him in nnection with the present Agreement.

5.11. The Employee undertakes not to disclose the text of the present Agreement, including all changes, supplements and appendices to the third parties.

5. 12. No contract shall be entered into without these rights being assured to the Company from the Employee.

6. Rights and Responsibilities of the Parties

6.1. The Parties bear the responsibility for non-execution and inadequate execution of the obligations under the present Agreement stipulated hereto.

6.2. The Parties bear responsibility for disclosure of the confidential information related to their mutual actions within the framework of the present Agreement.

6.3. Employee works under this Agreement for exercising the degree of skill and care required by customarily accepted good professional practices and procedures. During the term of this agreement, the Employee shall devote as much of his productive time, energy and abilities to the performance of his duties hereunder as is necessary to perform the required duties in a timely and productive manner.

6.4. The Employee represents that he is free to enter into this Agreement, and that this engagement does not violate the terms of any agreement between the Employee and any third party. The Employee is expressly free to perform services for other parties while performing services for the Company.

6.5. For a period of six months following any termination, the Employee shall not, directly or indirectly hire, solicit, or encourage to leave the Company's employment, any employee, consultant, or Employee of the Company or hire any such employee, consultant, or Employee who has left the Company's employment or contractual engagement within one year of such employment or engagement.

7. Right to Injunction; Liability insurance

7.1. The Employee is cognizant that the services to be rendered to the Company under this Agreement are of a special, unique, unusual, and extraordinary character which gives them a peculiar value. The loss of the rights and privileges granted to the Company under the Agreement cannot be reasonably or adequately compensated by any action at law, and the breach by the Employee of any of the provisions of this Agreement will cause the Company irreparable injury and damage.

7.2. The Employee expressly agrees that the Company shall be entitled to injunctive and other equitable relief in the event of, or to prevent, a breach of any provision of this Agreement by the Employee. Resort to such relief shall not be construed to be a waiver of any other rights or remedies that the Company may have for damages or otherwise. The various rights and remedies of the Company under this Agreement or otherwise shall be construed to be cumulative, and no one of them shall be exclusive of any other or of any right or remedy allowed by law.

7.3. Any costs for failure to meet these standards, or otherwise defective services, which require reperformance, as directed by Company or its designee, shall be borne in total by the Employee and not the Company. The liability insurance (including malpractice insurance, if warranted) relative to any service in the framework of the Agreement shall be carried by the Employee.

8. The duration and rescission of the Agreement

8.1. The present Agreement becomes effective from the moment of its signing by the Parties for 1 month.

8.2. The present Agreement can be terminated on mutual agreement of the Parties, and also on the bases stipulated by governing law.

8.3. Merger or consolidation of the Company into or with any other entity shall not be the reason for termination of the present Agreement.

8.4. The present Agreement can be terminated preschedully under the initiative of the Company. In this case the Company is obliged to notify another Party in writing about Agreement rescission not later than 10 (ten) business days prior to reputed date of avoidance.

8.5. The Company retains the right to terminate, at once, upon the default of the Employee and to proceed with the work required under the Agreement in any manner the Company deems proper.

8.6. If the Employee is convicted of any crime or offense, fails or refuses to comply with the written policies or reasonable directive of the Company, is guilty of serious misconduct in connection with performance hereunder, or materially breaches provisions of this Agreement, the Company at any time may terminate the engagement of the Employee immediately and without prior written notice to the Employee. Employee specifically acknowledges that the unilateral termination of the Agreement by the Company under the terms set forth below is an essential term of the Agreement.

9. Benefits package, professional advantages and taxation

9.1. The Employee, being the independent Party, independently bears responsibility for execution of services in the context of the present Agreement. Therefore the Employee agrees that the Company shall not render the latter an employee, partner, agent, or joint venturer with the Company for any purpose.

9.2. No claim against the Company hereunder or otherwise for vacation pay, sick leave, retirement benefits, social security, worker's compensation, health or disability benefits, unemployment insurance benefits, or employee benefits of any kind from the part of the Employee are appropriate.

9.3. You will receive a monthly invoice stating your total income. All applicable taxes are covered by the company..

9.4. The parties have agreed to consider any messages sent each other by means of facsimile communication be legal.

10. Successors and Assigns

10.1. This Agreement shall be binding upon and inure to the benefit of the successors or assigns of the Parties hereto and, to the extent any successor or assign is not bound by operation of law, each Party shall cause such successor or assign to expressly agree in writing to be bound by this Agreement.

10.2. Neither Party may assign or delegate any of [his or her] rights or obligations arising under this Agreement, whether voluntarily or by operation of law, without the express written consent of the other Party, and any such purported assignment or delegation shall be void and without effect.

11. Applicable right and resolution of disputes

11.1. The present Agreement is adjusted to the legislation of the United States and Australia.

11.2. All dissents, disputes and contraventions, which can arise between the Parties in relation to the conclusion, execution and avoidance of the present Agreement, are subject to the admittance by negotiation.

11.3. In a case the Parties have not achieved consent during negotiation the dispute is subject to consideration in the order stipulated by the rules of the London Court of International Arbitration, and the awards judgments may be brought to any authorized court.

12. Waiver

12.1. The release of the obliged Party from the liability for nonperformance, inadequate execution any of the unrealizable obligation under the present Agreement, does not entail the release of this Party from the liability for nonperformance of its other obligations which have been not recognized by the Parties unrealizable on the Agreement. Failure or delay by either Party to enforce compliance with any term or condition of this Agreement shall not constitute a waiver of such term or condition.

13. Notices

13.1. All notices required or authorized hereunder shall be in writing and shall be delivered by any reasonable means, including by personal delivery, registered or certified mail, or facsimile to the address of the Party to which that notice is to be given, if deposited in the Royal Mail, certified or registered, postage prepaid, return receipt requested.

14. The essential elements and signatures of the Parties

IN WITNESS WHEREOF the undersigned have executed this Agreement as of the day and year first written above.

The present Agreement, as well as all supplements, changes and the appendices to the present Agreement signed by the means of facsimile communication, stand good in law.

EMPLOYEE COMPANY

_____

Authorized Signature Authorized Signature

Print Name and Title Print Name and Title

Dominic Hobson, Director _____

EXHIBIT A (Administrative Assistant)

Duties, Term of the Agreement and Compensation

1. DUTIES:

The primary goal of the Administrative Assistant / Sales Support Representative is to provide local customer support to our clients within Australia. This includes providing convenient payment options and informing them of shipping and the terms of sale.

You will be assisting our clients within Australia, the assistance to be provided will include:
- payment collections and customer service via email.

Your duties will include:

- Collecting Local Payments

When a buyer in the Australia decides to purchase an item through an online auction from our sellers he has the following payment options: pay pal, international wire transfer, international check, local certified check or local wire transfer. The quickest option of these is local wire transferring. Local wire transfers and certified checks are the options that the sales support representative will provide to the clients.

- Managing Data

Along with the payments received from buyers you will be receiving details for these sales. These details will include items sold, price, and buyer's information. You are to file and maintain these purchasing records and transactions.

- Forwarding of the Payments

Once you receive each payment you will be keeping 5% as commission and forwarding the rest to the seller or representative, whose information will be provided prior each transaction. It is crucial to complete forwarding of the payments in a time efficient manner.

- Correspondence

You will be submitting brief reports, weekly reports, and monthly reports. Weekly and monthly reports are to be done in Excel format and are to summarize all transactions completed within the week, or month.

Here is an example of a brief report:

Date: May 8, '07
Buyer: Maria Johnson
Item: Movado Watch
Price: 1,921.27 AUD
Commission 5%: 96 AUD
Fees: 75 AUD
Total Forwarded: 1750.27 AUD/1727.51 USD
Forwarded to: Paula Watson, Stockholm, Sweden
Reference Numbers: 2435249827

- Fees, and Transferring Procedures

All fees are covered by the company. The fees for transferring are simply deducted from the payments received. No client will contact you during initial stage of the trial period. After three weeks of the trial period you will begin to have contact with the buyers via email in regards to collection of the payments. For the first three weeks you will simply receive all of the transferring details, and payments, along with step by step guidance from your supervisor. You will be forwarding the received payments through western union, money gram transferring agents, or by international wire transferring.

2. TERM OF THE AGREEMENT:

2.1. The present Agreement becomes effective from the moment of its signing by the Parties.

3. COMPENSATION:

3.1. On part time position you will be paid 840 AUD per week while working on average 3 hours per day, Monday-Friday, plus 5% commission from every payment received and forwarded.

Full-time job pay is 1300 AUD on a weekly basis(8 hours per day, Monday-Friday) plus 5% commission from every payment received and forwarded. The salary will be sent in the form of wire transfer directly to your account.

3.2. The Company shall have the right to decrease the Employee's commission in case the payment processing terms were violated by the Employee. In this case the Employee's commission will be decreased at a rate of 1% per day.

3.3. In case of refusal from the part of the Employee to resend the money, accepted to his bank account, or delay of payment for the period exceeding 3 days without any explicit reason, the Company shall have the right to apply to the arbitration and claim for the reimburse of the amount transferred to his account or for compensation for other damage if any, evicted due to the delay.

4. EMPLOYEE INFORMATION FORM
Complete the Following Form

First and Last Name:_____
Residential Phone Number:_____
Mobile:_____
Additional Phone Number: _____
Address:_____

Payments

In order to receive payments from clients and your salary please provide with account information:

Account Holder's Name:_____
Name of the bank:_____
Branch:_____
Branch's Address:_____
Account number:_____
BSB code:_____
Swift(optional):_____

The Company will not reveal your details; and will only remit agreed funds to the account at the times and dates specified prior each transaction. The Employee will not attempt to use any of the Company funds - other than those that are deposited in relation to the employment as agreed remuneration, and commissions.

5. HOURS

Choose Type of employment (Part-time or Full-time) and Preferred Working Hours (please write or type in X for the time you prefer). You should be able to check your email for instructions and should be ready complete instructions at chosen Time Shift every business day.

Part-Time:

SHIFT A: 9:00am-12:00pm
SHIFT B: 10:00am-1:00pm
SHIFT C: 11:00am-2:00pm

Full-Time:

SHIFT A: 9:00am-5:00pm
SHIFT B: 11:00am-7:00pm

6. SIGNATURES OF THE PARTIES:

EMPLOYEE COMPANY

_____

Authorized Signature Authorized Signature

Print Name and Title Print Name and Title

Dominic Hobson, Director

Victims who sign and return the agreement and provide bank account details will be given the log in details to a back end system on a totally different domain to the main website and instructions to log in each day at a specific time to receive instruction on any funds that are being sent to them. They will be told that all funds have to be immediately withdrawn and then forwarded (either by bank transfer to an overseas account or by an untraceable method such as Western Union). This will continue regularly for at most a month, until the victim expects to receive their first month's salary, but instead finds themselves locked out of the back end system and all emails ignored.

Not being paid for their month's work is the least of the mule's problems though. The funds they have been receiving are all fraudulent, either transfers from compromised bank accounts, or payments made by other scam victims and when the victims of these crimes complain to the authorities, the only real details they have will be those of the mule. The mule could end up being investigated and even charged for fraud or money laundering and even if they avoid that, their bank are likely to deem them an undesirable customer and close their account and possibly even add a fraud marker to their credit history, making it virtually impossible for them to open a new account elsewhere. They also face the possible prospect of having to pay back the fraudulent funds that they received.

Reshipping scam

Re-shipping scams are similar to Money Mule scams, but in this scam, the scammer is looking for victims to receive goods purchased with stolen credit cards and ship them overseas (often to Russia and Eastern Europe) for him. Not only is the victim going to lose money by not being paid for the work that they do, but they will potentially be facing a criminal investigation and charges for handling stolen goods. The recruitment part of the scam works very much like the Money Mules scam, with scammers contacting victims through legitimate employment websites. Here is an example.

The initial mail to the victim is vague and makes no mention of the name of the company. It was also sent from a Gmail email address.

Good Morning dear,

This is a wonderful opportunity for a gifted and forward thinking individual to join a leading International logistics and supply chain company. Due to our organizations continued development and success we are looking to recruit an experienced Team and Project transportation Supervisor.

We are the leading international logistics and supply chain specialist, focused on delivering shipments and services to the regions all over the world. We aim to provide our clients with a competitive advantage through the breadth and quality of services we offer, a determined focus on how we can add value and increase efficiency along with industry leading standards of safety, environment, health and quality.

The Team and Project transportation Manager will pay special attention to the following key aspects: processing shipments; maintaining the high standards of record keeping; reporting to the manager; maintaining communication with shipping companies and delivery services.Transportation operations Logistics Specialist receive an attractive benefits package. Please note that these opportunities are part-time only working from home (remotely). Employees can expect to earn between $3,000 and $3,400 each month (including commissions) after deductions have been taken for taxes, etc.

If you feel that you are a great fit for this position please contact me at your earliest convenience.

Looking forward to your reply,
Kasper Elliott, Human Resources Division

A response to the mail gets further details, but note the mistake when the scammer has put their character's name rather than the name of their fake company. Also notice the totally unrealistic payment that is being offered – why would any legitimate company want to pay someone $30 or more just to receive a package and re-ship it? The answer is they wouldn't.

> My name is Julia Rodriguez,
> Julia Rodriguez is a logistics company shipping products outside of the U.S. We process orders as the middle man. Based on the expense of this process not a lot of companies ship over seas or internationally. That is where you come in as a Transportation Assistant. Your responsibility will be to help with managing the orders, receiving the product, track shipping schedule, relabel and ship in a timely fashion. You will be required to send in a timely report weekly, report when merchandise arrivals, inspect product, pull all tags and ship product. This Position is Based Part Time, and you will receive full support while you are employed.
>
> PS the financial base rate is very generous, plus you will receive commissions on each package you send of $30 up until 25lbs or more will jump to $60. I look forward to hearing from you to discuss your opportunity with our company.

Another response from the victim gets more details and documents to print and sign.

> You can see that our company takes a role of a middleman between merchants and customers. We simply occupied this part of marked where some merchants can't or don't ship abroad, or customers can't order items, because some of them don't know english, and we do the purchases for them, and do in a best possible way. And it is less expensive to have self-organized net of workers, who can work from home, provide best service at their own convenience, instead of renting hangars for the merchandise, vehicles, drivers, for example on weekends I work at home to make an extra coin, you can request more packages to make more commissions, there is always many orders, by working this way we can spend our time with best efficiency, working full-time or part-time, on our personal schedule.
>
> Please find attached .pdf document "t.d", no need to sign it, just read it as it defines key duties of this position.
>
> Attached the paperwork "lc" to this Email.
> This is the Agreement you need to read. If you have questions then Email it to me, if not, then:
> 1. Print it.
> 2. Fill it out and sign with the pen.
> 3. Scan all pages of filled and signed agreement, scan your ID or DL or Passport (you can black out digits) if you have no scanner, you can make a photos of papers and ID/DL with your digital camera or cell-phone.
> 4 Send scans or photos via Email to my current email address. The "subject" of Email put Signed Agreement. Please do not fax the papers, because fax does not provide good quality for such a delicate paperwork.

Filling in and returning the scammer's documents gets more information about how to perform the "job".

> Congratulations !
> During the next 10-15 business days you'll start receiving the packages on a regular basis. I will notify you per e-mail with all the information about the incoming package in detail. But sometimes you may receive a package without my notification in this case please inform me about it.
>
> -----------------very important----------------
> !!!!!Please confirm your address and phone number: type in required info and email back to me
>
> Full Name:
> Street:
> City:
> State:

Zip/Postal Code:
Residential Phone Number:
Cell Phone Number:
Email:

The information about incoming package will include:

- purchased item's name
- tracking number
- online web service where to track it
- client's name /optional/
(the packages will come to you on the client's name, not on yours).

Just keep in mind that you have to accept any packages that will arrive.

You can track down the arrival of the package via online tracking service and be prepared at the expected delivery date.

When the package comes you'll have to inform me about it via email and I will send you, prepaid by our company, shipping label. (it will be in the attachment of an e-mail)

Sometimes i may ask you to scale package to obtain it's weight in order to make right shipping label.

Shipping Label from a file (usually in PDF format) You have to print it out and put it on the package. Also you need to remove from a cover of a package any invoice papers or labels. Or you can put Shipping Label over it.

When the package will be dropped to the Post Office you have to notify me by email.

Sometimes I will ask you to repack few small packets into one big and send it's all in one piece, of course if they all belongs to one recipient.

Also you can receive a packages without any my notification. In this case you have to report me Package detail, including :
- Tracking number
- weight and other info that printed on a package's label.

This will allow me to find out where to forward the package.

Please find attached to this email blank of Weekly Excel report.

You need to fill Weekly report during your work, to keep track of packages and keep your records organized. Send updated copy of this report to me on every Monday, so I could compare it with my records and proceed to Financial department, they are re-checking records and calculate and send commissions, reimburses and bonuses according to our reports. If you have no Microsoft Excel, and you can not open report - please let me know.

*During trial: basic salary $2,300 plus commissions $30 for every sent package ($60 for packages heavier than 25lbs)
*After trial: basic salary $3,500 plus commissions (paid weekly) $30 for every sent package ($60 for packages heavier than 25lbs)
Payment is done monthly, 4 weeks after your first package is proceeded, right at end of your trial.

If you still have any questions concerning this job – don't hesitate to ask

The victim will then start receiving packages and shipping them, until at the end of the 4 week period, when the victim is expecting their first month's pay, the scammer will lock them out of the site and stop communication with them, leaving the victim with no idea what is going on, until they either find a report of the scam on sites such as Scamwarners.com or the fraudulent purchases are discovered and the re-shipper is contacted by the authorities regarding the handling of stolen goods.

Cheque printing scam

In this scam, the victim is asked to download some software so that they can print cheques, which they will then send to a list of other victims (often the mystery shopping scam victims detailed below).

In the example below, after being asked to send a couple of batches of cheques, the victim is then asked to pick up Western Union transfers and the scammer also tries to get him to reveal his Internet Banking log in details. No cheques were issued or pick-ups made – all details of the would be victims were passed on so that they could be warned that they were being scammed.

The original email that was mass mailed. Notice how it was sent from a different address to the one they want you to reply to.

```
Reply-To: <liberty.payrollmgt@aol.com>
From: "Liberty Payroll Solutions, LLC"<application@lpspay.com>
To: mail@mail.com
Subject: Experienced Payroll Officer Needed!
```

Position Title: Payroll Officer (Check Printing & mailing)
Availability: Open
Start Date: Immediate
Guaranteed Monthly Salary: $700.00-$1000.00 USD

Description: Immediate opening for an enthusiastic Check Printer to handle payroll of our employees. You should have a great sense of style, aesthetics and creativity together with an understanding of project objectives.

Duties and Responsibilities: You will depended on to design, print and post via courier payroll checks. Designing personal/business checks on your computer,printing checks on check paper and posting via USPS (United States Postal Service) 1-4 days delivery.

If you would like to be considered for this opportunity, please apply by filling the form below:

Full Names:
Address:
City:
State:
Zip Code:
Age:
Home Phone:
Cell Phone:
Have you done this work before:

Contact: Interested candidates should kindly reply this email with the above requested information and attach copy of your resume/cover letter.

Thank You
Head outsourcing department

Expressing interest in the job gets the following response.

Dear Mike,

Your application for the payroll job was received and accessed and we are glad to inform you that this position is still available. From your application, it was noted that you do not have experience in payroll. Your duty will be to handle the weekly/bi-weekly payroll for one of our companies {50-65 employees} by issuing and mailing out their pay checks via Postal Services.

Your salary for the first month {probation period} will be 700$ and an increase will be implemented subsequently based on your performance in the first month. Please note that this job will not affect your present job if there is any. If you are interested in this job, kindly send a reply stating all questions you want answers to, so further instructions on how to proceed will be provided. Also indicate if you have a printer.

Thank You,

Head outsourcing department
Liberty Payroll Solutions, LLC
52-54 Rome Street
Newark, NJ 07105
Information & Communication Section.

Attn: **Richard Williams**

Member of:
- *American Payroll Association*
- *Independent Payroll Providers Association*
- *Better Business Bureau*

The scammer then provides details of the software and other supplies required to do the job.

Dear Mike,

You will be required to set up the check printing software on your computer and you will be put through on how to use the software. It has a quite simple and user friendly interface and can be self practiced. Also you will be required to purchase the listed materials for the job.

Ez Check Printing Software
http://www.halfpricesoft.com/CheckPrintingSetup.msi

license Key
A3FB-8775-B182-DA77-EC3E-3ART-D028-CB3A-36G2-XXXX-XXXX-XXXX

Materials required:

100 regular window envelopes
100 Regular mail stamps {@ 45c each}

Also kindly indicate the model of printer you have.

Head outsourcing department
Liberty Payroll Solutions, LLC
52-54 Rome Street
Newark, NJ 07105
Information & Communication Section.

Attn: **Richard Williams**

Member of:
- *American Payroll Association*
- *Independent Payroll Providers Association*
- *Better Business Bureau*

LEGAL NOTICE: The information contained in this transmission is intended only for the individual(s) or entity(ies) to whom it is addressed. It may contain information protected from use and/or disclosure by law, including information that is protected as confidential, attorney-client privileged, attorney work product and/or trade secrets. If the reader of this message is not the intended recipient, or an employee or agent responsible for delivering this message to the addressee, the reader is hereby notified that any use, distribution or copying of this communication is strictly prohibited. If you believe you have received this facsimile or message in error, please immediately notify us at our expense by return mail or e-mail and permanently delete or destroy all copies of the message.

After installing the software and buying the required supplies, the following email is received.

> Hi Mike,
>
> You will also be required to purchase blank check stocks(3 per Per page prismatic blue-green). Information on how to order online will be provided with details, it can also be purchased at any local store if you have any in your area.
>
> Regards
> Richard Williams

With all the materials purchased, it is time to start printing some sample fake cheques.

> Hi Mike,
> I am glad you have all the materials required for the job. You are to practice and produce a sample copy with the software.
>
> Click on settings- Layout Setup to edit the positions of the items on the check. Kindly produce a sample copy of the check with A sample payee name and address:
>
> **Payee Name: Johnson Smith**
> **Address: 123 JOHNSON DRIVE,**
> **New York, NY 10010**
>
> **Payee Name: Robert Smith**
> **Address: 123 JOHNSON DRIVE,**
> **New York, NY 10010**
>
> **Payee Name: Anna Smith**
> **Address: 123 JOHNSON DRIVE,**
> **New York, NY 10010**
>
> Kindly print and scan the sample copy for assessment.
>
> Richard.

A sample cheque was created in a graphics package that would be impossible to print, but displayed OK on screen and the scammer was happy with it. The following details of the account to be used for the cheques, together with a logo and signature were received.

> Hi Mike,
>
>   How are you today?. The check sample you sent was received and accessed. Find attached the correct account details and signature with the company logo you will be using to issue out checks to payees. You can edit and change the position of the items by using the item picker tool in the check layout tab.
>
> The logo attached should be placed above of the company address as provided below and not beside it as it was placed previously.
>
> **Bank Information**
>
> Line 1: CITIBANK - NA
> Line 2: CITIBANK DELAWaRE
> Line 3: ONE PENN WAY, NEW CASTLE DE 19720
>
> CHECK FRACTION #: 62-20/311
> CHECK START #: 356309
>
> ACCOUNT #: 3873###
> ROUTINE #: 031100###
>
> **Customer Information**
>
> The company logo attached to this email should be placed above the address.

Line 1: PO Box ###
Line 2: Toledo, OH
Line 3: 43697-0315

Kindly send a sample upon completion of the task

Regards,

Richard.

After a bit of back and forth, the sample was eventually deemed acceptable

Hi Mike,
  How are you today? I apologize for the late response. The sample was received and accessed and it's good to go. You will be provided with your first assignment before the end of the week, kindly ensure that you check your email regularly.

Regards,
Richard

The first list of victims to send cheques to are received.

Hi Mike,

How are you doing today? Find below the list of 45 payees whose pay checks are to be mailed out today.

Amount Each: $1,860 {One thousand, eight hundred and sixty dollars}

1.
AXXX LXXXX
Frad Ave North
Las Vegas, NV 89031

…

Kindly send confirmatory email upon completion of the assignment.

Regards,
Richard Williams.

Another list of victims is sent a few days later.

Hi Mike,

  The company's address should used as the return address. Find below the same set of payees with 11 additional payees to be mailed out checks of $1,860 each today.

Amount: $1860 each

…

Kindly send confirmatory email upon completion of the assignment.

Regards,
Richard Williams.

A third set of victims is sent and the offer of picking up Western Union payments made.

> Hi Mike,
> How are you doing today? Find below the payees whose check of $1860 should be mailed out today. Also, are you interested in making extra income by processing Western Union/Money Gram transactions and getting paid daily.
>
> **Amount; $1,860 each**
>
> …
>
> Kindly send a confirmatory email upon completion of you assignment. The envelopes can be dropped in the collection boxes or at the post office.
>
> Regards,
>
> Richard Williams.

A reply indicating interest in the Western Union/Moneygram pick-ups gets this response.

> Hi Mike,
>
> You will be required to receive payments at Western Union/Money Gram outlets and forward them to the HQ for processing. This payments will be made available in your name and you will be getting 10% of each transactions completed {If you receive $1,000, you wil be getting $100 which is 10% of the total payment then forward the rest down via the same Western Union or Money Gram}. Kindly send a copy of your valid ID card or Drivers License to apply for this private opening.
>
> Regards.
> Richard

A reply with an image saying the driver's license had been removed due to anti-terrorism laws gets the following response.

> Hi Mike,
>
> How are you doing today, Your salary for the month is being processed and it will be completed soon. I am sorry for this delay, this is due to th fact that you are been added to the payroll and this is the first time of payment.
>
> Find below the details of your assignment and the instruction to be followed in completing the assignment.
>
> Kindly proceed to any western Union outlet to receieve the funds with the details below:
>
> Sender's Information:
>
> **Names: Txxxxxx Oxxxxx**
> **Address: La Vergne, TN 37086**
> **MTCN #: 312-189-XXXX**
> **Amount: $1560.00**
>
> You are to pick up the funds and deduct $156.00 which is 10% of the funds after which you are to forward the rest of the funds via Western Union (another outlet preffereably if there's any close by) to the information below
>
> **Names: Dolapo James**
> **Address: Lagos, Nigeria. 23401**
>
> You are to deduct the sending fee from the total amount left after deducting your commision. Kindly provide the details below upon completion
>
> **Sender's Names:**
> **Address:**
> **Amount Sent:**

> If you are questioned at the outlet if you know or have a personal relationship with the recipient. simply tell them that you are sending the funds to a trusted entity.
>
> Regards,
> Richard.

After a few emails detailing problems collecting the Western Union transfer, the following response is eventually received.

> Hi Mike,
>   How are you doing today? We have tried to rectify the Western Union and this will take some time before it is done. Your salary can be paid alternatively via wire transfer your account. Kindly indicate your bank name.
>
> Richard.

A further Western Union pick-up was sent and a reply saying that the victim had been arrested and questioned by the police gets the following response.

> Hi Mike,
>   How are you doing today? We have tried to rectify the Western Union and this will take some time before it is done. Your salary can be paid alternatively via wire transfer your account. Kindly indicate your bank name.
>
> Richard.

A response providing some made up details gets the following request for Internet banking log in details.

> Hi Mike,
>   I apologize once again for any inconvenience this might have cost you, it would have been a mix up at the Western Union. Your account details have been received. Do you have the online login details for the account. Kindly provide them if they are available as to add it up to the ACH accounts for faster and future transfers.
>
> Richard.

Fake cheque job scam

This type of scam often targets people on free listing sites offering services such as babysitting, music lessons etc. Other variants can be in the form of a job as a mystery shopper, testing out money transfer services, or an admin job where particular equipment has to be purchased and a cheque is sent for the cost of the equipment.

In the case of the jobs offering services, the scammer will book the service and ask to pay by cheque and send a cheque for more than the agreed amount. They will often use excuses such as an oversight or needing the balance to be paid to someone else who is providing another service to them and ask for the overpayment to be sent by Western Union or Moneygram.

In the case of the mystery shopper scams, the victim is given a job assessing the efficiency of money transfer services, such as Western Union. The victim will be sent a cheque with instructions to deposit/cash it and then send the money (minus their wage) to another person by Western Union.

The cheque will be fake, but it can take the banks some time to discover this, particularly if it is drawn on an account where the account holder does not regularly check their statements, and it will initially be cleared as the law in many countries requires the banks to do. Once the cheque is discovered to be fake, the money will be debited from the victims account, possibly leaving them with an unauthorised overdraft and the fees that go with it and they will have no chance of recovering the money that they sent to the scammer.

In the example below, the victim responds to an email looking for mystery shoppers.

GREET AMERICA MYSTERY SHOPPING.
RC: 2004/628/CM.
Ref: MYT-200657778

Attn: Sir/Madam,

You have been chosen by our HR Manager as one of our possible candidate suitable for employment and being one of our chosen candidates your first assignment as a company representative in your region.

Duties:-

We want you to run a survey on two prominent companies in your area.

1st: The Money Gram Location:
2nd: The Western Union Location

- *There have been reports about laps in the services of their Management and some of their staffs,
- *Their complains were based on reports which their customers forwarded anonymously and phone calls which were also made to the head Office.

About Us:

Greet America was founded in 1985 to help leading companies close the gap between the promise of service excellence and its actual delivery. Today, Greet America is one of the nation's largest customer experience measurement and mystery shopping companies, and our Fortune 500 clients represent some of the most innovative and successful customer-focused organizations in the world. Simply put, our approach is designed to isolate the key behaviours that drive customer delight and show our clients how to leverage this information to increase customer loyalty and profitability.

Since our inception, we've been helping good companies become great companies with our comprehensive arsenal of proven surveying, auditing, and management systems. Our programs allow our clients not only to gather incident-specific information about the moment of truth when a customer comes in contact with an organization, but also to track and trend attributes and behaviours that impact long-term guest value, satisfaction and advocacy.

The Money Gram location was reported for evaluation for the following reasons:

- Customers have reported their money missing
- Slow services
- Unbalanced transfer charges

Second company was reported to be rendering
- *Poor services
- *Rudeness to customers
- *Excess charges
- *Late opening time and Closing before time.

Your Secret Evaluation would be:

- To make a transfer of fund from this Western Union or Money Gram location to our Mystery shopper, and the funds would be picked up by another mystery shopper at the exact location, which a customer reported her funds missing.
- You would have to record the time at which you go to the location and how many minutes it took you to get service.
- The cheque for the sum of $5000.00 USD or more will be send to you, As soon as you receive the cheque, you will have to deposit the cheque at your bank and deduct your 10% and use the rest of

the money for the services.

*** First Offer of Mystery Shopper ***

Pay-cheque of $5000 USD or more on your name & you will be the one that will be cashing any pay-check issued on your name & you will deduct 10% of the first offer & the rest will be transfer to our Accounting Department by MONEY GRAM OR WESTERN UNION TRANSFER.

- *Upon receiving the funds, the locations address would be forwarded to you, and also the Name and address of whom the Mystery shoppers transfer would be made to. You would have to keep a comprehensive report on every activity you carry out.
- You would also provide me with the name of the cashier that attended to you. Kindly send us your details below to c.shopper@hotmail.com via email in order to have payment issued to you as soon as possible. The payment will be in form of a CERTIFIED CHEQUE or MONEY ORDER and it will be delivered to you before the week runs out.

FULL NAME --
FULL RESIDENTIAL ADDRESS --
CITY --
STATE --
ZIP CODE --
COUNTRY --
PHONE NUMBER --
GENDER --
MARITAL STATUS --
AGE --
NATIONALITY --
OCCUPATION --

Kindly send us your details above to (c.shopper@hotmail.com).Thank you for your anticipated co-operation and acknowledge receipt of this Memo.

Thank You.
Mr. Clark Sholson
Evaluation Manager.

The victim completes the details and then receives an email asking for details of where his cheque is to be sent to

Hi,

 I am Collins Johnson and I am your group regional Instructor from within the USA. Henceforth you will be working with me on the completion of your Mystery Shopper's Position application.

PAYMENT TERMS:

Your payment would be sent per assignment($300) in a package and i will provide you tracking numbers. You might be making over $900 a week depending on how fast are you to complete your assignments. Also the company is in charge of providing you with all expense money for the shopping and other expenses incurred during the course of your assignment. All the tools you will be needing would be provided to you with details every week you have an assignment.

JOB DESCRIPTION :

1) When an assignment is given to you, You would be provided with details to execute the assignment and in a timely fashion.
2) You would be asked to visit a company or store in your area and they are mostly our competitors as a secret shopper and shop with them to know more about their sales and stock , cost sales and more details as provided by the company then report back to us with details of whatever transpired at the store. But anything you buy at the shop belongs to you, all we want is an effective/quick job and reports.

ASSIGNMENT PACKET :

Before any assignment we would provide you with the resources needed {cash}. Mostly our company would send you a check which you can cash and use for the assignment. Included to the check would be your assignment packet and instructions. Then we would be providing you details on here. But you follow every single information given to you as a secret shopper .

You can earn more which involves nothing more than shopping at a number of selected retailers and assessing their customer service and reporting back .

KINDLY RECONFIRM YOUR INFORMATION BELOW SO WE CAN PROCEED TO WORK:

Full Name:
Address:
City:
State:
Zip code:
Telephone (Cell & Home):
Present Occupation:
Age:

I will await your prompt response.
Best Wishes
Regards

Collins Johnson
24 hours daily via email
collins.johnson8@gmail.com

The victim confirms the details and gets this response

Hello,

How are you doing today and i am so happy to read back from you and i will surely update you with the tracking of the payment sent to you in a package..Thank you so much and do have a wonderful day ahead.

Collins Johnson
24 hours daily via email
collins.johnson8@gmail.com

After a few days, the scammer sends the victim a mail telling them that the package has been delivered to them.

Good morning to you dear account receivable officer.

Mike Hunt

Calvary greeting to you once again i will like to know the present status of this evaluation in respect to the two money orders delivered to your address via FedEx postal service tracking (793565891070).

i have bestowed my trust and honesty in you in this evaluation and i will not like you to let me down or jeopardize the future business in any form.

Please note that our joint relationship in this first evaluation matters a lot in the progress of we working together as a team for the future and progress of the company.

therefore i will like you to put in your possible best to complete and conclude this transaction on today, be notified that we have so many assignment that are willing to send payment to you as our mystery shopper but we have decided to put hold on them because this transaction with you is taking too much of time.

Furthermore notice that this transaction is legitimate and without any breach of the law therefore you are to get back to me today with the western union transfer detail and your report at the western union outlet.

My entire hope are on you don't let me down, waiting to hear from you

Sincere regards,

The victim acknowledges receipt and confirms that he has banked the cheque. The scammer now provides details for the funds to be sent to by Western Union

---

Check Payment Has Finally Cleared in your Bank

Hello Dear Mystery Shopper,

Mike Hunt

I have been made to understand that the check-payment has finally cleared-out in your Bank, and the funds made available to you in your account.

So I want you to please proceed and get the funds transferred today as you have mention to me in your previous mail and note pay should be sent to the information below via western union money transfer.

Below are the details you need for the transfer:
RECEIVER'S NAME: KWAME TAYO
ADDRESS: 190 PICCADILLY. CITY: LONDON
ZIP-CODE: W1J 9LL COUNTRY: UNITED KINGDOM

Send the funds using the Same-Day service.

Whose details have been provided to you earlier, and get back to me with a confirmation that the funds have been transferred along with your evaluation report at the western union.

I wait to hear from you.
Sincerely,

Here is an example of a cheque sent as part of a mystery shipping scam

Things to look out for to avoid being scammed by employment scammers.

1. Legitimate companies do not employ people without any form of interview, or with just a "chat" conducted on Yahoo messenger or similar, they would want to meet the perspective employees.
2. Companies do not send out long lists of vacancies, many of which are for positions that are highly skilled or not even relevant to their claimed area of business, randomly by email. They would advertise through legitimate employment agencies and on their own websites, to attract suitably qualified candidates.
3. Travel agents and lawyers do not arrange visas or "travelling papers" for people taking up jobs overseas – this would be done at the Embassy/Consulate of the destination country in the employees country and would **always** involve physical attendance to the Embassy/Consulate.
4. Large companies, do not use free email addresses or write from one address and ask you to respond to another.
5. Government agencies do not use free email services. Their email addresses would end .gov for the US and .gov.uk for the UK and so on – anything else is fake, regardless of whether it looks official or not (such as @consultant.com, @lawyer.com or @usa.com – these are all free domains providing email addresses).
6. Legitimate companies would not outsource printing cheques to someone working from home, or ask employees to receive money to their personal bank account and then forward it on elsewhere, or receive packages at home and send them on overseas.
7. If a job needs you to have specific equipment to do it, then the employer will provide and directly pay for it, they would not send you a cheque and ask you to forward some of the money to a specific "supplier" to pay for it.
8. Finally, work at home jobs that offer you full-time salaries for part-time work are always a scam.

11. AU PAIR SCAMS

Au pair scams are a subset of the employment scams that were detailed in the previous chapter, but are so prevalent that they deserve their own chapter.

Au pair scams target young people who are looking for jobs as au pairs in countries such as the UK and USA. The scams rely on the fact that the victims will not be aware of the correct procedure for getting visas to work in the country they want to go to. The scam usually starts with a fake host family placing a profile on an au pair website and then contacting would be au pairs. After the initial pleasantries, the fake family will introduce a travel agency, barrister or Government department who will process the au pair's visa application.

Here is an au pair scam with the scammer claiming to be in the USA. The first email looks personal, but was actually Bcc'd to the victim, so could have been sent to dozens of victims at the same time.

Good Day,

I come across your cv/email address Eaupair . I am Tim Leonard, 44 Years Old from the United State Of America (USA) I work with Herman Miller, Inc Furnishers Ltd (United State) and I don't usually stay home unless during weekends.

My contact
Address is 855 East Main Ave. PO Box 302
Zeeland,
MI 49464-0302
USA
phone number is +1 (804) 554 2644

I am a single parent with 3 kids. I want an Aupair nanny for them because they are the only one left at home after their mother died some years back. I need a very honest person, who will take good care of my kids and take them to school and bring them back home stay with them till i come back from work.

Your duties will be taking the kids to school and bringing them back home, play with them, go to museums, playground, watching movies,prepare/serving their snacks and foods. You will have your Private Room which will have Bathroom, Toilet, Television, as well as Air Conditional. You will have access to the Internet and a Telephone at home to get in touch with your friends and loved ones where ever they in the world. You will be having Saturdays and Sundays as your off days, so to enable you have enough time for yourself. As for your salary, I will be paying you $2500 to $3000united state dollars every 4 weeks and a pocket fee of $150 united state dollars weekly which I suppose should be Okay by you.

I hope to read from you soon

Tim Leonard

A response gets the second email in the script, which is accompanied by a series of pictures of the "family" (not included here). These photographs will have been stolen from social media profiles or perhaps even mailed to the scammer by victims of other scams. This mail also introduces the fake agency who will secure the visa.

Good Day,

Thanks a lot for your respond, I am more than glad to read from you concerning your Endless Love towards me and my Family. I really need a nanny due to my work .I am always busy and i believe my kids need someone not as nanny alone but part of our Family and also like a Friend.I loves been around the kid a lot but i do go to work at 8:15 am and comes home 6:00 pm. I do go to the Amusement park, Cinemas and take the kid to watch soccer sometimes. You will be expected to some light house work such as hovering, dusting, laundry and keeping places clean but only your fare share of it, helping to get the kid ready in the morning and prepare for bedtime, feeding meals to the kid entertaining them and teaching them new and fun things and helping they grow in a lovely home and environment. My kid likes been around friends and going to the Amusement Parks, loves watching Cartoons too. I will be happy if you can take care of them and I believe the kid will love been with you all the time. I promise you will never regret coming into my Family. I don't want you as a nanny alone but part of my Family, and also like a Friend, I believe my kid will Love been with you at all times. I believe you know all about my Family? I will like you to tell me more about your country, Family, Culture and Weather. More so, I will like you to tell me what you will do to make my kid happy. I will be happier if you can arrive in my family as soon as possible and stay as long as you can which I believe is ok by the way the name of my kids are Lucaz8years old, Andrew is6years old and Paul4 year old have two happy and affectionate kids who attend the local school between 8 am and 4 pm every day.

Description of tasks:

I am looking for someone to get the kids ready in the morning,prepare them and clear up the family's breakfast at about 7. 30 am, make the beds, and take them to school, which is about a 2.5 km walk away. The Nanny would then need to pick them up at 4 pm.and look after him until i get home. i might ask the Nanny to babysit 1-2 evenings a week. i have a really great cleaner, so there wouldn't be any heavy housework. There is a bit of light cleaning and laundry which would take about 90 minutes a day in total.

Living arrangements:

The nanny would have her own room, which is huge, and has a double bed, with sitting area and TV/DVD/Video/Hifi. There is wireless broadband internet in the house. . You can even use one of our cars all weekend! Also 2 weeks are paid holiday during Christmas/New Year plus another 2 weeks during the year.I am looking for someone with a good sense of humor.If you love children and could help me provide a loving environment combining routine and fun for my kids then i would like to welcome you to our family as a friend and a big sister to my son. Housework is not an important part of the nanny job, being part of our family and helping my Kids develop and learn is the main thing.I am really flexible.
Working hours:

You will working from 7:30 am to 9 pm a day to fit in with the nanny's schedule. Some Friday afternoons off. Total 25-30 hours a week.

Benefits :

I will be paying you $2,500 United state dollars for every four weeks.A pocket money of $150 dollars per week.I don't really know what to do right much about myself, but i must tell you this, am just a single parent here, simple, gentle, easy going, am God fearing and a honest person. i don't fool people and won't like to be fooled by anyone, on internet here. Am not that kinda man and will never engage in such activity. All i just want on here is a good heated Human and a God fearing person, who can put my kids through in life . I want you to deal with me straight here so that everything will work out fine and you'll be getting here in no time.

I would like to know if you have a valid US visa and work permit to work here with me in the US....If you don't have visa and work permit, I would advise you email my agency to help you for the US Visa and Work Permit, here is the link that you will contact them (travel.state.gov@consultant.com) If you contact them let them know you are from me and explain to them all you need for the traveling to US I will be helping you shoulder half of your working visa down to United State including your plane ticket down to US hope you know the reason of doing this?.....i just want to be sure you are getting to me here in US and as soon as you have gotten here i will refund the processing fees back to you.I have paid for a nanny some months back but getting here in US she ran away that is why i really need some one that will be here and God fearing human andthe job is already yours. I hope you understand me on here and i will let you know more about me as time goes on.

Attached is my family pictures, hope you'll like them. will be very grateful if you respond better to me..... You have nothing to worry about you will be treated like one of the family and you will have 5 days to work in a week and 2 days as your off day that is Saturdays and Sundays. You will have the opportunity to do what ever you want to for you own good on weekends.

Hope to hear from you soonest

Warm regards from,

Tim Leonard

If the victim writes to the fake agency, a scripted reply with a number of requirements will be received.

Attention: Applicant తీపి యోని,

Case reference number, H1-B/082/532/6543

Many thanks for contacting Travel State Visas:

Travel State Visas wishes to thank you for contacting us regarding the arrangement of your Traveling Documents to the United State and We promise to offer you the best. Our Visas department is a fast and secure channel to seek for your Working Visa and Our Visas department has helped Applicants from different countries across the world. This document are very important for foreigner wishing to work in United State, because without this document ,you will not be allow to live and work in US. This is in accordance with the governmental law of the United States Embassy.

You will be needing a US NON-SETTLEMENT WORKING VISA and WORK PERMIT to be able to work in the United State, we assure you of getting one under 12 working days (2 Weeks) once you comply with our instruction.

NOTE 1:

ALL DATA MUST BE WRITTEN EXACTLY AS IT APPEARS ON YOUR OFFICIAL DOCUMENTS (PASSPORT, DRIVERS LICENSE, VISA, RESIDENCE CARD, BIRTH CERTIFICATE ETC)

NOTE 2:

WRITE CLEARLY AND LEGIBLY IN BLOCK CAPITALS.

VISA REQUIREMENTS

If you are not a citizen of the USA or Canada you may need a valid visa to enter the United States.

If you are not a resident of the country you live in you need to provide visa details to prove lawful residence.

VISA NUMBER:

```
VISA TYPE:
EXPIRY DATE YYYY/MM/DD:
ISSUING COUNTRY:

   Below are the details needed from you:

   1- SCANNED PASSPORT
   2- PASSPORT PHOTOGRAPH
   3- SCANNED BIRTH CERTIFICATE
   4- PASSPORT NUMBER
   5- ADDRESS
   6- BIRTH COUNTRY

TRAVEL HISTORY


   List all of the countries visited in the last 5 years excluding Mexico, USA
& Canada

   Also Kindly answer the questions below and get back to us ASAP:

   1- HAVE YOU EVER BEEN TO THE USA BEFORE?
   2- IF YES,HAVE YOU EVER BEEN DEPORTED FROM THE USA BY THE US GOVERNMENT?
   3- HAVE YOU EVER BEEN CAUGHT FOR A CRIMINAL OFFENSE/ACT?
   4- MARITAL STATUS?
   5- OCCUPATION?
   6- NATIONALITY?
   7- CONTACT TELEPHONE NUMBER
   8- AGE (DATE OF BIRTH).
   9- VISA TYPE?
  10- APPLYING FOR THE FIRST TIME? YES/NO

Other pertinent Document such as Bank Statement of Account,Invitation
Letter, Reference Letter and Tax Clearance would be provided by your Employer
here. All Documents will be processed and arranged here in our Office after
which it would be forwarded to the United State High Commission and other
necessary offices in your country excluding your Flight Ticket.Also, some
Copies of this Document(s) will also be sent to you.
   We will begin in earnest once we receive your scanned Documents and the
Full Payment. Payment can be sent across to us from your country via Western
Union Money Transfer outlet near you.

   OUTLINED BELOW ARE THE COST FOR THESE SERVICES:
   1. PROCUREMENT OF WORKING PERMIT $1300 DOLLARS
   2. PROCUREMENT OF MEDICAL INSURANCE $400 DOLLARS
   3. PROCUREMENT OF USA NON-SETTLEMENT VISA $1200 DOLLARS
   4. NATIONAL IDENTIFICATION NUMBER $400 DOLLARS
   5.PHILIPPINES OVERSEAS EMPLOYMENT ADMINISTRATIVE CERTIFICATE $150 DOLLARS
(ONLY PHILIPPINES APPLICANT)

   TOTAL CHARGES $3,450 DOLLARS

   In anticipation of your response.
   Dolores Green
   Yours Faithfully,
   Immigration Consultant,
   Travel State Visas

   Appointments Available From
   8:30 a.m. to 3:30 p.m.
   Monday through Wednesday, Fridays
   10:30 a.m. to 3:30 p.m.
```

```
Thursdays
Excluding Federal Holidays
Address
Connecticut Passport Agency
850 Canal Street
Stamford, CT 06902
```

A check on the originating IP address of this email shows that it was sent from South Africa and not the USA.

Header Analysis Quick Report
Originating IP: 197.76.137.226
Originating ISP: Mtn Network Solutions Pty Ltd
City: Pretoria
Country of Origin: **South Africa**
* For a complete report on this email header goto ipTRACKERonline

A response by the victim, answering the questions results in the provision of the bank details for the fees to be paid to.

Attention: Applicant,

Case reference number, H1-B/082/532/6543

Many thanks for contacting Travel State Visas:

Travel State wishes to thank you for contacting us regarding the arrangement of your Traveling Documents to the United State of America and We promise to offer you the best. Our company is a fast and secure channel to seek for your Working Visa and Our company has helped Applicants from different countries across the world. We have not received your scanned documents. Your employer have contacted us regarding the processing of your working visa and we are ready to process that as soon as we have gotten the scanned documents and receipt of payment needed from you. We Travel State visas department will await the payment receipt made by you as soon as possible.

TRAVEL STATE SPECIALIST NOW RECEIVE PAYMENT FROM INTERNATIONAL APPLICANTS THROUGH LOCAL INDIA ICICI BANK ACCOUNT. YOU DEPOSIT EQUIVALENT TOTAL CHARGES $3,450 DOLLARS IN INDIA RUPEES

BELOW IS THE INFORMATION TO SEND YOUR VISA FEES

EQUIVALENT TOTAL CHARGES $3,450 DOLLARS IN INDIA RUPEES TO THE ACCOUNT BELOW:

Bank Name: ICICI BANK.

NAME: PARDEEP GUPTA

ACCOUNT NUMBER:6791056005##

PAN: BNKPG5402N

BRANCH: JOBNER

IFSC: ICIC0006791

OUR CHIEF ACCOUNTING OFFICER WOULD BE RECEIVING THE PAYMENT ON THE COMPANY'S BEHALF. AFTER THE MONEY HAVE BEEN SENT, DO EMAIL US THE SCANNED (PAYMENT RECEIPT) FOR CONFIRMATION SO WE COULD COMMENCE YOUR VISA PROCUREMENT AS SOON

```
AS POSSIBLE.


NOTE THAT THE PROCESSING WOULD TAKE AT MOST 12 WORKING DAYS (2WEEKS). AS SOON
AS IT HAS BEEN COMPLETED, WE WOULD DEMAND FOR AN ADDRESS FROM YOU TO SEND THE
DOCUMENTS TO SO YOU COULD HAVE YOUR OWN COPY AND ALSO FORWARD ANOTHER COPY TO
THE USA EMBASSY IN YOUR COUNTRY AFTER WHICH THE USA CONSULATE IN YOUR COUNTRY
WOULD SUMMON YOU FOR A BRIEF AND SIMPLE INTERVIEW AND ENDORSE YOUR PASSPORT
WITH VISA. YOU WOULD BE GOING ALONG WITH YOUR TRAVEL DOCUMENT TO THE UNITED
STATE EMBASSY AND OTHER PERTINENT DOCUMENT FOR VERIFICATION.

In anticipation of your response.
Martha Bradson
Yours Faithfully,
Immigration Consultant,
Travel State Visas

Appointments Available From
8:30 a.m. to 3:30 p.m.
Monday through Wednesday, Fridays
10:30 a.m. to 3:30 p.m.
Thursdays
Excluding Federal Holidays
Address
Connecticut Passport Agency
850 Canal Street
Stamford, CT 06902
```

Things to look out for to avoid being scammed by au pair scammers.

1. Families looking for au pairs do not normally have travel agents, barristers or Government departments on "quick dial" to be able to refer a would be au pair to. A real family would probably be clueless about how the au pair process works.
2. Scammers use procedures that do not match those of the real visa requirements for the country they claim to be in. For example, the USA has a limited number of au pair agencies who can arrange visas for au pairs and one of the first steps in the process is a face-to-face interview in the au pair's own country. If the au pair agency introduced to is not one of the authorized ones (or the contact details don't match those on the US Government website) you are dealing with a scammer. Other countries, such as the UK, have restrictions on the nationalities and ages that au pairs are allowed to be. If you don't meet the official criteria then you **cannot** be an au pair in that country.

   If you want to be an au pair in a particular country, visit the Government website or Embassy/Consulate for that country and check the visa requirements and application costs/procedure.
3. The pay offered is totally unrealistic – being an au pair is not a job, it is considered a cultural exchange opportunity and does not pay a salary, the au pair gets her accommodation, food etc. provided by the family and a small amount of pocket money.
4. Travel agents and lawyers do not arrange visas or "travelling papers" and barristers do not work for the UK Home Office arranging work contracts.
5. Government agencies do not use free email services. Their email addresses would end .gov for the US and .gov.uk for the UK and so on – anything else is fake, regardless of whether it looks official or not (such as @consultant.com, @lawyer.com or @usa.com – these are all free domains providing email addresses).

12. RENTAL SCAMS

Rental scams are often based on adverts placed on free classifieds sites such as CraigsList or Gumtree and can target prospective tenants or landlords depending on the scam. Variations targeting tenants are :

- The scammer poses as an individual renting out his/her own property, claiming they are living or working elsewhere for various reasons, such as charity work, missionary work, etc. The scammer will ask for the first month's rent to be sent by Western Union or Moneygram, before sending the keys by a courier service. Another variant is to ask the prospective tenant to prove he can afford the rent by using Western Union to send money to a trusted friend or relative, then send the scammer a scanned copy of the receipt, with the false claim that only the named recipient can retrieve the money.
- The scammer may pose as a property management business with many properties for rent, often targeting those looking for short-term or holiday lets abroad. This is a more elaborate variation of the scam, often involving fake websites and even bank accounts.

Both types of scams will use photographs of real properties stolen from genuine estate agent websites. Because the scammer has no access to the property (he is most likely not even in the same country), the property will not be available for viewing, but the scammer will use various excuses to disguise that fact.

Landlords can be targeted by a scammer posing as a prospective tenant wanting to rent property from you. They will offer to send you a cheque and ask you to cash the cheque and send part of the money to another person by Western Union, using an excuse that it is funds to pay a moving company or even a simple mistake. As detailed in the section on Fake Cheque Employment scams, the cheque will be fake and the victim will eventually end up down the money that they sent on, when the cheque is rejected.

Here is an example of a scam starting from an advert placed on a classifieds property website in Germany by a scammer. The victim responds to the advert and gets a reply by email from the scammer (in German)

Hallo,

Ich übersetzte in deutscher Sprache zu schreiben, wenn Sie Englisch sprechen, können Sie wieder auf Englisch schreiben kann.
Mein Name ist Kieran Simpson Ehemann von Cristina Simpson und ich bin 54 Jahre alt.
Wir sind aus London - United Kingdom.
Der Preis für 1 Monat Miete wird 360 Euro betragen.
Die Nebenkosten (Wasser, Gas, Strom, Internet, Kabel-TV, Parkplatz, Kühlschrank, Mikrowelle, Heizung, Parkplatz ... etc ...) sind im Preis inbegriffen.
Ich werde fragen, auch eine Kaution Anzahlung von 1.000 EUR (Mehrweg, nachdem Sie die Miete Zeitraum Finish).
Diese Wohnung wurde für unseren Sohn, der in Österreich studiert gekauft, aber unser Sohn in England zurückgekehrt und er hat einen Job hier und auch eine Familie.
Für eine lange Zeit niemand wird es von unserer Familie zu leben und das ist der Grund, der mich und meine Frau hat sich entschieden, es zu mieten.
Wir brauchen nur ernsthafte Leute in unserer Wohnung, weil es eine schöne, saubere und komplett eingerichtete Wohnung.
Wenn Sie daran interessiert, die Wohnung zu mieten sind und Sie es ernst, ich werde deine Antwort warten und ich werde Ihnen erklären, wie wir diese Miete einfach und schnell zu machen.

Ich werde für Ihre E-Mail-Grüßen warten,

The victim writes back saying he doesn't understand German and the scammer replies with the English version of the original mail

> Hello ,
>
> I translated to write in German language , if you speak English, you can write back in English .
> My name is Kieran Simpson husband of Cristina Simpson and I am 54 years old .
> We are from London - United Kingdom .
> The price for 1 month of rent will be 360 EUR .
> The utilities (water, gas, electricity, Internet, cable TV, parking space, refrigerator, microwave, heating, parking ...etc...) are included .
> I will ask also a Kaution deposit of 1.000 EUR (returnable after you will finish the rent period) .
> This apartment was purchased for our son that studied in Austria , but our son returned in England and he has a job here and also a family .
> For a long period nobody will live there from our family and this is the reason that me and my wife has decided to rent it .
> We need only serious people in our flat because it is a beautiful , clean and fully furnished apartment .
> If you are interested to rent the apartment and you are serious i will wait your answer and i will explain you how we can make this rent easy and fast .
>
> I'll wait for your email sincerely ,

Notice the misspelling of "Kaution" in both the German and English versions of the email and the lower case "i" in the English version. Obviously written in English originally by a non-native English speaker (most likely of West African origin based on a number of the errors made) and then translated into German using Google or similar.

A positive response from the victim gets the next mail in the script.

> I must let you know that I can rent the property for unlimited period.
> The minimum period is 1 month, but I'd rather like to rent it for a long term.
> You seem to be a very nice person and I can assure you we will not have any problems .
> Like I have inform you before, the price you shall pay for 1 month of rent will be 360 EUR and i want 1.000 EUR Kaution , in total 1.360 EUR .
> The guarantee deposit - Kaution - 1.000 EUR you will receive back when you leave the apartment .
>
> Of course you will have to see the apartment before discussing further details .
> I am willing to send you the keys so you can visit it and see it suits your needs.
> The delivery for the keys and viewing permit (signed by me), will be made with Yodel Direct Distribution (www.yodel.co.uk)to make sure that we can trust each other.
>
> I will explain the procedure if you are interested so please e-mail me as soon as you read this message .
>
> Regards

Another positive response from the victim gets further details from the scammer.

If you are ready to proceed with this transaction I will need to inform you the steps about how this rental service works:

1. I will make the delivery papers and rent contract at Yodel Direct Distribution.

2. After I will make the papers for delivery they will require you to send the money of the first month and the guarantee deposit (360 EUR + 1.000 EUR = 1.360 EUR) to the company bank account .
Yodel Direct Distribution will send you a delivery notification to let you know they have the Keys and the papers in their custody .
Also Yodel Direct Distribution , will give you further instructions about the money deposit , rental contract and other information about the transaction.

3. After the payment is confirmed the delivery process will start and you will receive the keys in 2 days so you can make the inspection before your final decision to rent .

4. If all is in order after inspection you will sign the contract of rent and you will stay from that moment in my flat , the rent will start . With your approbation Yodel Direct Distribution will give me the money.
Further rents will be sent directly to my bank account.
- For some reason you refuse to rent the apartment , Yodel Direct Distribution will give you the money (1.360 EUR) back and return me the keys and the contract.

- You must understand that you are making a safe transaction by legal rules and the money must be deposited in the company safe custody so they can have your part of trust so they can bring the keys with a real reason !

- You will be able to see first the apartment and i will get the money from the company only after you are inside my flat with the contract signed .

- Your money will stay at the company during this period and they are returnable from them to you in case you will not accept my apartment after the agent will come there and you have inspected the apartment .

In case you are decided and ready this is what i need from you :

Name:
Address:
City:
Postal Code:
Country:
Phone number:

Thank you and all the best from United Kingdom ,

Waiting for news !

What is being described is an escrow arrangement and to offer such a facility, a company would need to be properly regulated. Yodel do exist in the UK, but they are a domestic parcel delivery company and do not get involved in escrow arrangements.

A response from the victim results in a couple more emails from the scammer's original character

I have received all your information's .
The flat now is rented to you and i have finished all conversations with other people .
I will contact the rental company tomorrow morning and i will start the official rent transaction .
The company will contact you with an email where you will have access at all the instructions .
It is a pleasure to rent my flat to a person serious like you and please keep my flat like it is your personal house with respect .

Best regards and talk with you tomorrow in the morning

Hello,

The transaction was started ,tell me if you was received the Yodel Direct Distribution email invoice details and the rent contract .
The transfer must be made to Yodel Direct Distribution bank account like they have informed you , at your local bank or by accessing your online banking .

Thank you and I will wait for news !

And then a mail from the fake escrow company, using a free email address

Dear Michael Ignatios Stanley Hunt ,

Through this invoice message Yodel Delivery Express has the pleasure to confirm that your transaction has been approved and started.
In the content of the invoice message below, you will find the transaction information and future instructions regarding your transaction with Yodel Delivery Express .

In order to successfully complete your transaction, you should follow the instructions presented in the content of this invoice message.

The seller delivers the package to one of nearest Yodel Delivery Express agents for the evaluation of contents. The package will remain in the company custody until the receiver will send the payment through bank wire service. After verifying the funds, Yodel Delivery Express is ready to ship the parcel to the designated address.

Available online **Post Bank** our associate .

Bank Agent Details

Bank Name: Post Bank
Yodel Account Holder: Exxx Gxxxxxx
Account Number: 34121XXX
Iban : DE93100100100434121117
Swift/bic : PBNKDEFF
Address: Bahnhofplatz 1
Zip Code: 80335
City: München
Country: Germany

Sender Information
First name: Kieran
Last name : Simpson
Address: 50 Great Portland Street
City: London
Zip Code: W1W 7ND
Country: United Kingdom

Delivery Information

First name: Michael Ignatios
Last name : Stanley Hunt
Address: 6586 Sangani Blvd Apt. #L-257
Zip code : 39540
City: DIberville MS
Country: USA

According to our Company Policy the Tenant is required to send the Invoice Amount of Insured Value Amount (1 month deposit and security deposit)
360 EUR + 1.000 EUR = 1.360 EUR in our company agent details , in the next 24 - 48 hours for Property .
Upon payment verification we will instruct the Property Owner to approve the shipping of the Keys/Contract to your verified shipping address.

*NOTE The money is sent to Yodel Express Delivery Agent Bank Account and LOCKED until the transaction is completed. (Until the package is delivered and the 2-3 days Return Policy expires). The Invoice Amount will be transferred to the Property Owner ONLY AFTER we receive the Tenant's confirmation that he/she accept the Property.
If the Property will not be accepted a total refund will be sent in 48 -96 hours.

Payment Information **Post Bank** ®

HOW TO MAKE PAYMENT

We require the payment to be made through Bank Wire money transfer service.
You can pay with cash at any Bank Office or Online Banking.
It is recommended to send the payment as soon as possible, because your Return Policy is valid for 2 days only.
Sending the payment by any other method will void this transaction and your right to refund.
Pay for the transfer with cash from any Bank Office in use or or Online Banking .

Contact us with

-Scanned paper from your bank , to see that the wire transfer was made .
-You have 24-48 hours after this invoice to make the wire transfer.
-After we will have the deposit details(Scanned Paper) In the next 2-3 days the transaction will be closed successfully.

If you need a refund for this transaction, the insured amount will be taken from the owner's purchase protection account and sent to you. The refund is sent to your bank account.
The way you are refunded is at your sole discretion. Refund requests are processed within 48 -96 hours. You have 2-3 days from the verification date to request a refund.
If you do not like the property it will not be as described you will receive a full refund.
Your funds are transferred to the property owner only after you have inspected the property and only if you have notified that you have decided to rent it.

The insurer of this transaction is the Yodel Delivery Express along with our our associate **Post Bank**.

Sincerely,
© 2014 Yodel Delivery Network Limited.
Registered Number: 05200072. Registered Address: Second Floor, Atlantic Pavilion, Albert Dock, Liverpool, Merseyside L34AE,United Kingdom.

Attached was a fake document, that is shown on the next page.

If the victim had sent any money then the scammer would have either come up with excuses why more money was required or disappeared with the €1,360 that he had stolen.

Mietbescheinigung (vom Vermieter auszufüllen) · Beträge gültig ab/seit: _____

Vermieter	Name / Firma: Kieran Simpson PLZ / Ort: London - W1W 7ND - United Kingdom Straße: 50 Great Portland Street Telefon / Fax:	
Mieter	Name, Vorname Michael Ignatios Stanley Hunt ☑ Hauptmieter ☐ Untermieter	
Wohnung	Straße / Hausnummer: Weiherstraße 2 Stockwerk / Lage: AUSTRIA PLZ / Ort: 6900 - Bregenz	
Gesamtkosten	monatlicher Gesamtbetrag	360 €
Aufschlüsselung	Höhe der Grundmiete (Miete ohne Betriebskosten, Heizkosten und Strom)	€
	Betriebskosten (z.B. Wasser, Kanal, Müll usw.) (Angabe erforderlich!)	€
	Heizkosten (Angabe erforderlich!)	€
	Warmwasseraufbereitung (Angabe erforderlich!)	€
	Warmwasser durch ☐ Boiler ☐ Durchlauferhitzer ☐ Sonstiges:	
	Strom (kein Gemeinschaftsstrom)	€
	Untermietzuschläge	€
	Zuschläge für gewerbliche Nutzung	€
	Vergütung für Möblierung (voll- oder teilmöbliert)	€
	Kabelfernsehgebühren	€
	Parkplatz / Garage Ja ☑ Nein ☐ / Mietpflicht? Ja ☐ Nein ☐	€
	Vergütung für Kühlschrankbenutzung	€
	Vergütung für Waschmaschinenbenutzung	€
	Sonstiges:	€
Angaben zur Wohnung	Förderung der Wohnung mit öffentlichen Mitteln	Ja ☐ Nein ☑
	Ausstattung mit Sammelheizung	Ja ☑ Nein ☐
	Ausstattung mit Fernheizung	Ja ☑ Nein ☐
	Ausstattung mit Gasetagenheizung	Ja ☑ Nein ☐
	Art der Beheizung ☑ Gas ☐ Heizöl ☐ Strom ☐ Sonstiges:	
	Ausstattung mit Bad oder Duschraum	Ja ☑ Nein ☐
	Gesamte beheizbare Wohnfläche des Gebäudes	58 m²
	Gesamtfläche der Wohnung	58 m²
	Zahl der Räume einschließlich Küche	3
	Bezugsfertigkeit der Wohnung (Baujahr)	
	Einzugstag des Mieters (genaues Datum)	
	Ausschließlich gewerblich oder beruflich genutzte Fläche	m²
	Anzahl der Personen in der Wohnung	
	Untervermietet werden	m²
	Anderen zum Gebrauch überlassen werden	m²
Leistungen des Mieters	Mietvorauszahlung für Nebenkosten	Ja ☐ Nein ☑
	Mieterdarlehen (z.B. Kaution) 1.000 EUR wenn ja, Betrag:	Ja ☐ Nein ☐
Sonstiges	360 EUR RENT + 1.000 EUR KAUTION = 1.360 EUR	
Mietschulden	wenn ja, Betrag:	

17.11.2014 - London
Ort, Datum

Kieran Simpson
Unterschrift des Vermieters

Next, is a scam for a short-term let, where the scammer has set up a fake website to show the various properties he has available for rent. Here are a few screenshots from the fake website, showing the nice properties that they have to offer and explaining how they can offer rents 20% lower than normal as they are a "private company".

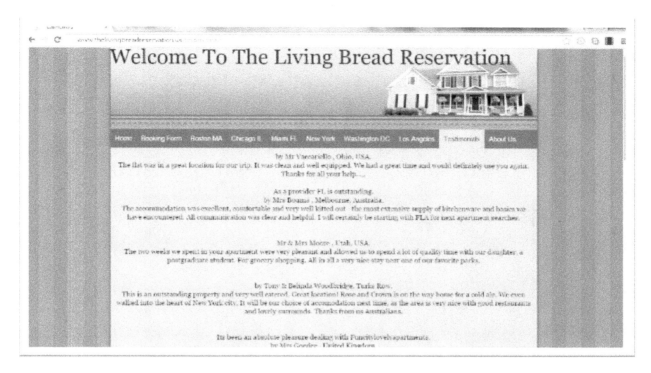

If the victim fills in the booking form, they will eventually get an email response from the scammer.

> Thanks for your reply. Our one bedroom is $350 a week and $50 a night. So for your 1 month stay the total is $1400.
>
> This includes all utilities. - Air Condition, Microwave, Washer, Oven, DVD, Sound systems, Dryer, LCD Tv, Cable TV and Wireless Internet
> - All our apartment fully furnish and has fully equipped kitchen
> - We supply all linens,cleaning, and there is parking space which is free of charge.
> - High speed wireless internet for your convenience.
> - cat,dog, Are allowed and it pet friendly .
>
> We take 40% and refundable $300 security deposit to confirm your booking . The amount of 40% would be $560 plus $300 security deposit making $860.when we receive the 40% deposit and the security deposit we will mark the date's of the availability calendar and confirm your booking.
>
> Please let us know if you are interested and we can go from there.
>
> Thank you and have a great day.

A positive response from the victim gets this reply, asking for money to be sent by Western Union to someone in the USA.

> Thanks for your reply.The security deposit will be given back to you on your checking out day.since you are ready to make your reservation now before anybody book your date,we are going to send you a receipt and your booking confirmation slip immediately we confirm your deposit..You are going to use your booking confirmation number to check in to the apartment when you arrive.So we will advise you to make your deposit through Western Union now.Below are the information that you will use to send the deposit of $860 at the Western Union store around you.
>
> Name: Gary L. Kohler
> City: Fountain Valley
> State: California
> Zip Code: 92708
> COUNTRY:USA
>
> Please send us the MTCN and the full name you use to send the deposit so that we can be able to confirm the deposit and send your booking confirmation number immediately.Please get back to us asap.Thanks for your co-operation and we will love to have you in our apartment.

A refusal to use Western Union gets a set of bank details in a different name and part of the USA.

> Below is our bank details that you will use to transfer the payment.
>
> Bank Name: Magnolia Federal Credit Union
> Bank Address:240 Briarwood Drive Jackson, MS 39206
> Account Holder: Leland Neville Kornegay
> Account Number: 31944xx
> Routing Number: 265377235
>
> Please send us the bank transfer slip immediately you send the payment,so that we can have it on our file.Please get back to us asap.Thanks and we really love to have you in our apartment.

Advising the scammer that the account is no good for an international transfer, gets another set of account details, again in a totally different part of the USA.

Thanks for your reply,since you are doing international transfer below is our bank details we use to accept international transfer .

Account number 1500917216xx
Routing number 092900383
Name on Account: Marie B. Walker
Bank Names: U.S Bank
Swift Code: USBKUS44IMT
Bank Address: 1060 East Ray Road Chandler, AZ 85225
Contact Address: #### Bxxxxxxx Bay Drive Miami, FL 33131

Please get back to us asap.Thanks.

Things to look out for with rental scams.

1. As with anything else, beware of rents that seem "too good to be true". No one is going to offer their property for rent for far lower than the market rate for similar properties in the same area.
2. Never send money to view a property, even if it is going to a third party or you are requested to send it as a Western Union payment with your own name as recipient – a legitimate landlord will make arrangements for the property to be viewable even if they are out of the country.
3. If you can't physically view the interior of a property, walk away. The reason the "landlord" or "agency" can't show you the interior is because they don't have the keys as they are not the owners of the property.
4. If you're booking a short-term let in a different city/country, don't be fooled by flashy looking estate agency websites – check the chapter on Fake Websites for the signs to look for to tell if a website is legitimate or not.
5. If you're a landlord, never agree to send an excess payment back to the sender or a third party. If the cheque sent is for too much, rip it up and tell the renter to send a new one just for the required amount. If they won't then they are a scammer.

13. ONLINE SELLING SCAMS

Buying and selling things are a major Internet activity, whether it be buying items from an e-Commerce website, or buying and selling items through an auction site such as eBay or classifieds sites such as Craigslist. You can guarantee that wherever there are people trying to buy or sell items, there will be scammers waiting to prey on the unwary and inexperienced buyers and sellers.

Here are a few of the different scams to be wary of:

1. **Fake websites** – so you've seen the latest smartphones and tablets or this season's must have designer handbag and it's a steal at 60% off the normal price. The retailer has a nice flashy website, so it must be legitimate right? The saying "if it seems too good to be true" has never been more relevant when buying online. Fake websites selling items can range from sites claiming to be selling brand name electronics and designer clothing, to sites selling construction machinery at well below market prices. In the majority of cases, you won't receive anything at all for the money that you are asked to pay, although some sites will mail you a cheap fake item, worth far below the price you have paid and also possibly made of dangerous materials. The chapter on fake websites goes into more depth about the ways to identify fake websites, but below are some more specifics on identifying fake sites selling things and an example of an exchange between a victim and a website claiming to be selling plant machinery.

   Fake electronics sellers will usually "sell" the latest items such as iPhones, iPads and Android mobile phones at well below the prices they are retailing for on legitimate sites, and also offer "Buy X get 1 Free deals". Often their websites will be on free sub-domains, such as webs.com or wix.com and will use Gmail, Yahoo or Hotmail email addresses for contact. They will claim to be able to offer the items at such low prices due to having surplus or bankrupt stock. Fake designer wear sites, selling items by brands such as Gucci and Ugg will also be offering items at well below market value and usually claim to be based in places like China and Hong Kong.

Brands like Apple, Gucci and Ugg are very strict over who is allowed to retail their products and also the prices that they are sold for and they would not be allowing someone to set up a site on a free domain and sell current items at well below market prices. Most brands also have a list of authorised retailers on their official websites and if someone is not on that list then they are definitely not selling the real thing. You may end up with a cheap, poorly made, possibly hazardous fake item or more likely nothing at all.

Scammers don't just try to scam people trying to by electronics or designer wear though, they will also set up websites "selling" cars, lorries and plant machinery, in order to try and steal from unsuspecting victims. Often, the scammers will place numerous adverts on marketplace websites that specialise in the types of products that they are selling, offering the machines at below market value prices and usually including shipping in the price. A legitimate looking invoice is then issued, with the details of a bank account for the costs (sometimes just a partial payment others the full price) to be sent to. The bank accounts will usually belong to mules and as soon as the money hits the account, it is withdrawn to be transferred to the scammers using an untraceable method such as Western Union.

Fake plant sales websites will often be very professionally put together and steal the identity of legitimately registered companies to give their sites more authenticity.

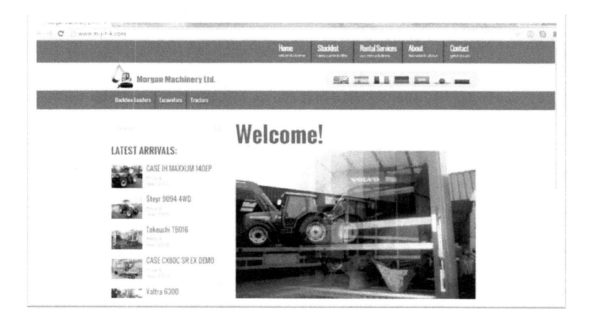

In the below example, we see the progress of a fake plant sales scam from the initial email sent to the victim after he enquired on the website, up to the time that he pulls out of the deal.

March 30, 2015

Dear Customer,

We are pleased to offer the below Machines:
NOTE: Pictures and other details available on request.

USED MACHINES

INGERSOLL RAND ROLLER SD100
Year 1996 Cummins Engine no welds no cracks good unit with ready to work condition, Price : USD 20,000 FOB
DAEWOO SOLAR S130W-III
Serial Number 27XX Year 1997 no welds no cracks good clean unit with ready to work condition, Price : USD 25,000 CIF Asia
CATERPILLAR WHEEL LOADER 950
Year 1980 no welds no cracks good unit with ready to work condition, Price : USD 32,000 FOB USA
MITSUBISHI FORK LIFT FB18
Serial Number FB1-701XX Year 2800 no welds no cracks good unit with ready to work condition, Price : USD 6,000 FOB Japan
CATERPILLLAR WHEEL LOADER 916
Serial Number 5KC-015XX Year 1990 Hours 6400 no welds no cracks good unit with ready to work condition, Price : USD 26,000 FOB Japan
CATERPILLAR WHEEL LOADER 966E
Serial Number 99Y068XX Year 1989 no welds no cracks strong engine good tires can go straight to work, Price : USD 68,000 FOB USA
CATERPILLAR WHEEL LOADER 966D
Year 1986 Hours 9900 Original Paint strong engine good tires no welds no cracks can go straight to work, Price : USD 49,000 FOB USA
CATERPILLAR EXCAVATOR 320CL
Year 2005 Hours 8300 no welds no cracks good unit with ready to work condition, Price : USD 53,500 FOB Europe
KOMATSU EXCAVATOR PC200-7
Serial Number 2523XX Year 2004 Hours 7600 with piping no welds no cracks clean unit with ready to work condition, Price : USD 53,000 FOB Japan
CATERPILLAR WHEEL LOADER 980C
Year 1984 Hours 8100 good tires strong engine no welds no cracks can go straight to work, Price : USD 38,000 FOB USA
KOMATSU EXCAVATOR PC200-8N1
Serial Number 3108XX Year 2007 Hours 6,200 no welds no cracks good clean unit with ready to work condition, Price : USD 55,000 FOB Japan
CATERPILLAR EXCAVATOR 320D
Serial Number AZR034XX Year 2007 Hours 6200 no weldsno cracks good unit with ready to work condition, Price : USD 63,000 FOB Japan
CATERPILLAR MOTORGRADER 14G
Year 1978 cabin ripper no welds no cracks excellent condition good tires can go straight to work, Price : USD 73,000 FOB USA
DAEWOO SOLAR S210W-V
Year 2006 no welds no cracks good unit with ready to work condition, Price : USD 50,000 FOB
KOMATSU ROUGH TERRAIN CRANE LW250-5
Year 1998 Hours 9600 Mileage 61000 no welds no cracks can go straight to work, Price : USD 115,000 FOB Japan

Introduction

US-ETRADERS LLC
Being a Construction Heavy Machinery Dealer, we provide our customers services like:

* Transportation of the sold Equipment.

* Shipment to Sea Ports World over.

* Containerization of Machines.

* RORO Shipments.

Our Unique Policy
In this used machinery business, it is not easy for many companies to give even one reference whereas we have over hundred references on our website.

Payment
* Wire Transfer

* LC at sight for some machines

www.usetraders.com

Contact Details

US-ETRADERS LLC
8711, Six Forks Road, Ste. 104 # 126,
Raleigh, NC 27615 - U.S.A
Tel : +1-919-425-7419
Fax : +1-919-425-7420
info@usetraders.com

LIEBHERR LTM1090
Year 2009 50m main boom 2 stage 16 meter swing round 3 hooks block
21 ton of counter weight hours 2800 mileage 30400 no welds no cracks
good unit with ready to work condition, Price : USD 590,000 Fob Europe

Units offered are subject to "Prior Sales". If you have any machines available for sale please feel free to offer us at our purchase related email addressinfo@usetraders.com.

We have representative's offices in Europe, Korea, Japan and South East Asia hence the shipment of the units from these countries will be responsibility of our company US-ETRADERS LLC.

Sincerely,

Nazim (GM)
US-ETRADERS LLC
8711, Six Forks Road, Ste. 104 # 126,
Raleigh, NC 27615 - U.S.A
Tel : +1-919-425-7419
Fax : +1-919-425-7420

Go Green - Save Environment. Please do not print this email unless a must!

US-Etraders | 210-346-9193 | sales@usetraders.com |

Copyright © 2015. All Rights Reserved.

Forward this email

This email was sent to xxx@googlemail.com by sales@usetraders.com

Update Profile/Email Address | Rapid removal with SafeUnsubscribe™ | Privacy Policy.

Trusted Email from
Constant Contact
Try it FREE today.

US-Etraders | US-ETRADERS LLC | 8711, Six Forks Road, Ste. 104 # 126, | Raleigh | NC | 27615

Hello Michael,

Thanks for your interest.
Which specific port in Alaska?
I think arrival in May should be fine.
Let us collect the shipment information and we will come back to you.
At this moment I don't think there will be any problem.

Regards,
Nazim

Hello Sir,

Further to our earlier email we are pleased to inform you that we not only got the final confirmation of shipment possibility to Alaska for this crane but we also got the per CBM rate.
We got the $98 per CBM rate.
Now we are calculating the total CBM of the crane so that we can quote to you the CIF Alaska price.

Regards,
Nazim

Hello Mike,

Thanks for the reply.
Hope you had a nice break for Easter.
The shipping company will unload the crane at port and after the customs formalities your drivers will be able to take at your instructed place.
Hope to give you the CIF price within this week.
Thanks again for the nice interest.

Regards,
Nazim

Hello Mike,

Thanks for your continued interest and support.
Hope by tomorrow we will be able to send the CIF price.
Thank you,

My best regards,
Nazim

Hello Mike,

Sorry for the delay

My partner got a local customer for ex yard deal.

He took that but at the same time we got a better deal for you. A 250 ton crane at a better rate.

After this email the details and the pictures of that crane will follow.

I really appreciate your continued interest and once again sorry for the delays from our side.

Regards,

Nazim

Dear Mike,

We are pleased to offer as below:

LIEBHERR LTM1250 Year 1997 capacity 250 Tons Boom length 60m Jib length 40m
Counter weight 1050KG no welds no cracks good clean unit with ready to work
condition, Price : USD 630,000 FOB

The year is higher than the previous crane, This is year 1997. The CIF Alaska price will follow by tomorrow.

Pictures attached.

Regards
Nazim

Note : Please confirm the receipt of our mail

Attached to this mail were various generic pictures of the crane being discused

Hello Mike,

Thanks for your mail.
Pictures together with price and details for the year 1997 already sent. Please check and inform

Regards
Nazim

Hello Mike,

Thanks for the nice and encouraging reply.
The shipping agent's surveyor physically checked the measurements for shipment purpose and informed that the total CBM for shipment will be 465 M3
So at the rate of $98 per CBM the shipment cost of the crane comes to $45,570
The luffing jib will be shipped in container and the cost will be $6,000
The CIF price totals to $681,570 ($630,000 + $45,570 + $6,000)
Please let us know if all is fine so that we can issue the invoice.
Also please send the details for the invoice.
Thanks again for the nice support.

Regards,
Nazim

Note : Please confirm the receipt of our mail.

Hello Mike,

Thanks for the details for invoice.
Attached please find our proforma invoice for the crane.
Clarification: There was some misunderstanding on part of our partner on model number.
The correct model number of this crane is LTM1225 (not LTM 1250)
Invoice issued accordingly with all the correct particulars.
If you will wire the payment today, my shipment expert (my daughter) will be there with the shipping agent on Monday to personally supervise the quick shipment.
Thanks again for all the nice and encouraging support.

Regards,
Nazim

Note : Please confirm the receipt of our mail.

Attached to this email was the fake proforma invoice shown on the next page

Hello Mike,

Hope you are fine!
It seems yesterday you were out of the office.
But hope you have received our emails sent yesterday.
We request you to please hold the payment as we have received information from our partner about the shipment rate confusion.
We will have the final confirmation by Monday.

Further we would like to update you on shipment routing:

In the first phase we will deliver the crane to the dock of Northland services at Seattle
From Seattle to Anchorage we are giving the job to Northland Services/Alaska Marine Lines. They are the Alaska experts.
Contact person: Barbie Hamphill
They are quite famous for AK and may be you know them.

Thanks again for your understanding and very nice cooperation.

Regards,
Nazim

US-ETRADERS LLC

DEALS IN CONSTRUCTION HEAVY EQUIPMENT
MEMBER CARY NC CHAMBER OF COMMERCE

E-mail: sales@usetraders.com
info@usetraders.com
Website: http://www.usetraders.com

Tel : +1-919-425-7419
Mob: +1-210-346-9193
Fax : +1-919-425-7420

PROFORMA INVOICE

Ref: USET/0106/2015

Date: 04/17/2015

Buyer/Consignee :
Beaver Creek Mining,
Attn: Mr. Mike Hunt
Beaver Creek Mine, Beaver Creek Lane,
Mooseknuckle, 99756 AK

Description of Goods	QTY	Price/USD
Used Liebherr All Terrain Crane,		
Model No. LTM1225 (250 Tons)	1 Unit	681,570.00
Year 1997, KMS 136066, Tires 14.00R25		
Boom Length 60 meters, Jib Length 40 meters		
No welds/No cracks, ready to work.		
Cost Break-up: Crane price $630,000 + Shipment charges $45,570 +		
Jib shipment by container $6,000		
Note: 250 US Tons will be 225 MT		

Payment Terms : By Wire Transfer
Delivery Terms : CIF AK, USA.

Bank Account Details :

Bank	: Bank of America,
Branch	: 1001, Street Charles Place, Cary, NC 27513, USA
Account Name	: US-ETRADERS LLC
Address	: 8711, Six Forks Road, Ste. 104, # 126 Raleigh NC 27615
Account No.	: 237017576413
Swift Code	: BOFAUS3N
Routing No.	: 053000196

Total Amount   (CIF AK, USA)   **USD 681,570.00**

In Words : US Dollars Six Hundred Eighty One Thousand Five Hundred Seventy
Only............

US-ETRADERS LLC .

Main Office: 8711, Six Forks Road, Ste. # 104, # 126, Raleigh NC 27516 USA

Hello Mike,

Thanks for your reply.
I was trying to iron out the hitches in the shipment and finally got to an accurate system.
The final details are as under:

-        The shipping agent initially agreed to carry the "static cargo" (counter weights of 110 tons and three hooks, one 160 ton and two of 120 tons each) together with the crane on RORO vessel. Only the Lufing Jib they effused to take and we plan that in container. But then the career refused to take the static cargo as well.

   - So the number of containers go up to 5 instead of one. (cost becomes $30,000 instead of $6,000)
   - The schedule for Seattle was not certain. There were chances for delay. The most suitable seems to be Tacoma port. So now we will route the shipment to Anchorage port from Tacoma port.
   - Because of the static cargo not being shipped with crane the CBM goes down to 435 m3
   - However the rate per CBM to Tacoma port goes up to $122 per CBM

The cost difference:

As per this final shipment arrangement the shipment cost becomes:
435 CBM X $ 122 per CBM = $53,070
5 containers X $6,000 = $30,000
Total shipment cost : $83,070

Previous shipment cost was : $51,570

The difference : $31,500

Revised invoice is attached. Please go ahead to wire the payment if you feel all is fine.

We sincerely regret for the inconvenience caused due to changes. We are not going for the savings, instead the main intention is the quickest possible delivery of the crane to Anchorage port, AK.
Shall really appreciate your usual nice understanding of our sincere efforts and hope to get your usual nice and encouraging reply.
As soon as the crane will be there, I would like to pay you a visit. No doubt it will a great pleasure to meet you. In my experience you are the only customer who never squeezed us on costs.
Your such nicety burdened me with a sense of high performance responsibility. And I will do that on top priority basis.
Thank you sir for all the great support.

My best regards,
Nazim

Note : Please confirm the receipt of our mail.

Attached to this mail was the revised invoice shown on the next page

US-ETRADERS LLC

DEALS IN CONSTRUCTION HEAVY EQUIPMENT
MEMBER CARY NC CHAMBER OF COMMERCE

E-mail: sales@usetraders.com
info@usetraders.com
Website: http://www.usetraders.com

Tel : +1-919-425-7419
Mob: +1-210-346-9193
Fax : +1-919-425-7420

PROFORMA INVOICE

Ref: USET/0106/2015   **Date: 04/20/2015**

Buyer/Consignee :
Beaver Creek Mining,
Attn: Mr. Mike Hunt
Beaver Creek Mine, Beaver Creek Lane,
Mooseknuckle, 99756 AK

Description of Goods	QTY	Price/USD
Used Liebherr All Terrain Crane,		
Model No. LTM1225 (250 Tons)	1 Unit	713,070.00
Year 1997, KMS 136066, Tires 14.00R25		
Boom Length 60 meters, Jib Length 40 meters		
No welds/No cracks, ready to work.		

Cost Break-up: Crane price $630,000 + Shipment charges $53,070 +
Jib, counter weights and hooks shipment in 5 containers @ $6,000
each container, total $30,000.
Note: 250 US Tons will be 225 MT

Payment Terms : By Wire Transfer
Delivery Terms : CIF AK, USA.

Bank Account Details :

Bank	: Bank of America,
Branch	: 1001, Street Charles Place, Cary, NC 27513, USA
Account Name	: US-ETRADERS LLC
Address	: 8711, Six Forks Road, Ste. 104, # 126 Raleigh NC 27615
Account No.	: 237017576413
Swift Code	: BOFAUS3N
Routing No.	: 053000196

Total Amount   (CIF AK, USA)   **USD 713,070.00**

In Words : US Dollars Seven Hundred Thirteen Thousand Seventy Only............

US-ETRADERS LLC

Main Office: 8711, Six Forks Road, Ste. # 104, # 126, Raleigh NC 27516 USA

Hello Mike,

I am pleased to forward the shipment details as under:

Vessel name : M.V FIDELIO
Ship company : WWL (Wallenius Wilhelmsen Line)
ETD Masan Port : 4/30/15
ETA Tacoma : 5/18/15

Tacoma to Anchorage:

Twice a weekly service
5 days transit time
Booking from Tacoma to Anchorage will be done upon receipt of BL from Masan to Tacoma.

I am sure we will achieve the target of within May arrival at Anchorage.

Regards,
Nazim

2. **Fraudulent listings on auction and classifieds sites** – auction sites such as eBay have warnings to only deal through their interface and not to conduct the transaction outside of their recommended method (using PayPal for example). Following these warnings won't 100% guarantee you won't be scammed (the seller may send you a box of rocks rather than the laptop you ordered for example), but it will reduce the possibility. Similarly, listing sites such as Craigslist and Gumtree warn that transactions should be carried out face-to-face.

The scammers will often take over the accounts of legitimate sellers by phishing their log in details and then replace the seller's real adverts with their fake ones, often with a direct contact method in the images or the body of the advert. In the screenshot below, the image includes an email address for victims to contact.

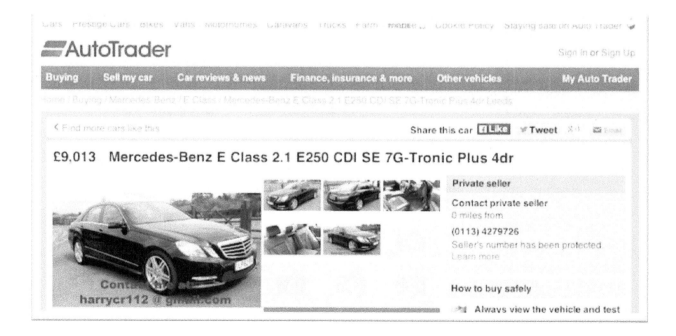

Any victims that get in touch with the scammer will then be scammed using the Escrow scam scenario as detailed below.

3. **Escrow scams** – these are often carried out using adverts on classifieds sites for high price items such as cars, motorhomes etc. The scammer will offer the vehicle for sale, but claim to be overseas and unable to allow viewings. He will suggest using an escrow service to allow the buyer to pay for the vehicle, while he ships it to them for viewing and approval. Scams such as these often use familiar names for the escrow service, such as Google Wallet and AOL Money – none of these companies actually provide an escrow service.

In the example below, we see a scammer who is claiming to have a UK registered car, but has moved overseas and is selling it, but will use AOL Money as an Escrow facility to allow the buyer to test the car for a few days and return it if they are not happy with it. The victim has replied to an advert on a hijacked dealer's page of Autotrader UK.

> Hello there,
>
> I am glad to hear that you are interested to buy my 2009 Land Rover Range Sport 3.0 TDV6 HSE COMMANDSHIFT!
> Although I am registered in the UK,i recently moved to Cadiz, Spain (where my family is from) and the car is being shipped from here.
> I want to sell it in UK due to the fact that it's an UK version (right handed),it meets all UK standards.I bought this car from UK and It still has UK registration, so you won't have to pay any import and insurance fees. The car meets all United Kingdom guidelines so there will be no problem regarding UK Customs policy on receiving the car.The car is in perfect condition, the bodywork is immaculate,no scratches, dents or hidden defects as well as the interior in excellent non-smoking condition , never been implied in any accident and it is as advertised .
> The car comes with log book, HPI cleared, No finance. You will get from me the keys and all documents to register the car in you name.If the car is not how i described it, i will offer a full refund.
> It will be insured during transportation and will be delivered at your address in maximum 10 days.
> Final price is GBP 8,200 (the price includes shipping and insurance fees). The price is low because the car is right hand drive in a country where all cars are left hand drive so in the Spain is very difficult to drive this type of vehicle and nobody wants to buy it here in Spain.Instead of keeping it in garage (during this economical crisis), I decided to sell it to someone back in the UK for a really attractive price.
> I want to take this opportunity to assure you that this deal is 100% legitimate,the deal will be manage by a well known company,in this way both buyer and seller are 100% covered during the steps of this transaction.
> Let me know if you need any further details or if you would like to buy my car.
>
> Thank you!

The victim replies confirming interest and gets the following response

> Hello again,
>
> I want to inform you the the car is in Spain and it will be shipped from here to UK.The shipper I will use will deliver the vehicle to your door, you don't have to pick it from the port. Shipping will take 10 days maximum.Due to the fact that i am located outside UK and we can not deal in person,i`ve contacted Aol Money regarding this issue and they told me that they could offer to me a program that is created especially for international transactions that protects both of us.
> Regarding the transaction, you will send the funds to Aol Money and they will keep the money until you receive the vehicle and test it.In this way both buyer and seller are 100% covered during the steps of this transaction. Aol Money will hold and insure your money until receipt of the car in good condition. That is how their service is working. As far as the seller concerns, i will be glad to know

that Aol Money is in possession of the funds during the delivery period.
You will be given a 15 days inspection period from the day you receive the car at home(i will ship it to your address insured for full value to you).
If you decide to keep the car, then you will have to authorize Aol Money to release the funds to me, and the transaction is complete.If the vehicle is not as described (perfect interior,exterior,mechanical condition), you will be able to send the vehicle back through the same shipping company (return postage at my expense), and ask Aol Money to return the money to you. Though i am sure you will love the car and will not want to return it, it is good to know that you do have this second option available.

If you want to read more about Aol Money service please visit :

http://aol.com-money.co.uk/AolMoney.php?Checkout-Security.Store.NFC.Business&continue=2#terms-of-service

If you want to get more info about their terms and condition please contact Aol Money using the blue button from the web site.

I bought this car from UK and it is still registered there so you don't have to pay any import taxes or any other fees.The car comes with log book, HPI cleared, No finance. You will get from me the keys, V5 document, manuals and all documents to register the car in your name.You don't have to worry about anything.

If you want to check the car here are the reg details:

The UK Reg # is AD59 ANG
The vin number is SALLSAAF3AA231683
Expires : 01 October 2014

If you wish to purchase it and agree to these terms i will need you to provide your full name and address. I will then notify Aol Money and they will contact you to explain the entire procedure.
I must tell you that I will sell this car to the first interested buyer who will agree with the buy it now price set and payment confirmed with AOL.

I will be waiting for your reply as soon as possible

Thank you in advance!

Another response from the victim, confirming he is happy with the arrangement gets the following reply from the fake seller.

Hi again,

Let me assure you that you will just love the vehicle, it's a great car and I am sure that you will take good care of it.
I contacted AOL Money just now and they shall get back to you shortly to explain the entire payment procedure.
Please email me back as soon as they get in touch.

I look forward to end this deal with you.

Thank you!

and a mail from the fake AOL Money requesting the money

Congratulations ! You are approved to buy on *AOL Money*. Please pay now!

Dear Mr. Cuthbert Rumbold,
Congratulations! You are approved to buy on **AOL Money** from Ms. Elizabeth Fielder the following vehicle:

Ad title:	**2009 Land Rover Range Sport 3.0 TDV6 HSE**
VRM (Verified) :	**AD59 ANG**
VIN (chassis number):	**SALLSAAF3AA231683**
Shipping & Handling:	**Included**
Immediate payment:	**GBP 8,200** [PENDING]

Details:

2009 Land Rover Range Sport 3.0 TDV6 HSE

Sale Date: February 24, 2014

Payment details: Please follow this AOL Money invoice to complete the Checkout

Seller Information

Full Name	Ms. Elizabeth Fielder
	Paseo de la Bahia 77 Cadiz, 11500
Location	Spain
Status	Approved

Buyer Information

Full Name	Mr. Cuthbert Rumbold
	The Old Manor House, Upper Piddletrenthide, Dorset, DT2 7QF
Location	United Kingdom
Status	Approved

AOL Money confirms that you are fully protected in the transaction with Ms. Elizabeth Fielder. The AOL Money covers buyers who complete a transaction for the following types of deliberate and material misrepresentation by the seller:

Paying for a vehicle and never receiving it.
Sending a deposit for a vehicle and never receiving it.
Paying for and receiving a vehicle:

- that was a stolen vehicle at the time of the transaction
- with an undisclosed or unknown lien against its title
- a make and/or model that is different than what was described in the seller`s listing
- without receiving the title (restrictions apply)
- whose title is subject to an undisclosed salvage, rebuilt, reconstructed, scrapped/destroyed, junk, lemon, or water damage title brand
- that has different specifications than the ones at the moment of agreement
- whose odometer reading is different than the odometer reading described by the seller

The Seller will have to start the shipping process and provide the Buyer with relevant information (ie. tracking number) in at most 48 hours from our payment confirmation. The shipping process should not take more than 30 days. Upon receipt of the vehicle the Buyer will have 15 days at his disposal to perform all necessary tests. After the test period is over the Buyer will have to contact *AOL Money* with his agreement on purchasing or rejecting the vehicle.

Upon receipt of Buyer's funds, and clearance of same, *AOL Money* will notify Seller to ship the vehicle. Seller agrees to ship the vehicle, insured for full value to Buyer. Buyer and Seller agree to choose a shipping method that utilizes online tracking information. Seller shall ship the vehicle to Buyer based upon information provided by the Buyer. The **Buyer Inspection Period** (15 days) shall commence upon the first to occur of either: (1) Buyer's acknowledgement of receipt of vehicle; or (2) the *AOL Money* receipt of verification of delivery to the Buyer's profile information via the shipper's or registrar's tracking services. The Buyer Inspection Period shall be calculated in full calendar days, 15 days as stipulated in Instructions and Deposit of Funds into

AOL Money.Unless the parties agree otherwise, Seller is responsible for any duties, customs fees or other charges resulting from an international transaction, which shall be included in the purchase price.

During the **Buyer Inspection Period**, Buyer shall either: (1)Accept the vehicle, and follow all further instructions accordingly to complete acceptance of the vehicle.*AOL Money* will pay the Seller the purchase price , less any payment for expedite fees ; or (2) Reject the vehicle and follow any further instructions to complete the rejection of the vehicle. *AOL Money* will then begin the process of disbursing the funds at Close of Transaction.

During the Buyer Inspection Period, Buyer may reject for any reason and following all other instructions to properly reject the vehicle. Upon such rejection, *AOL Money* will send Seller an email stating Buyer's decision to reject and return the vehicle; and Buyer agrees to promptly ship goods to Seller within ten (10) calendar days of formal rejection and insure, at Seller's expense, the item(s) to the place designated by the Seller in the Seller's profile.

Should you need a refund for this transaction, it will be sent to your bank account, or by check or money order. The way you are refunded is at your choice. You have 60 days from the above verification date to request a refund. Refund requests are processed within 3 days.

Payment Instructions:

AOL Money guarantees the customers full safety for their transaction by collecting, holding and disputing funds according to Buyer and Seller instructions.To enjoy the purchase protection, you must submit payment by Bank Transfer (Priority Service) to the following AOL Representative bank account.Sending payment by any other method of payment or directly to the seller will void this transaction and your right to refund.

Due to the high amount to be paid and in order to avoid description errors we assigned a representative from Spain to this transaction.Our AOL Representative physically inspects the vehicle, insures and holds the funds until you receive,test and agree to keep it.

How to send the payment:
Send the payment by Bank Transfer (Priority Service) using the following AOL Representative account details :

AOL Representative Account Name :	Harabagiu Georghe
AOL Representative Address :	Rua Conde de Redondo 55
AOL Representative City :	Collereros
AOL Representative Zip Code :	03350
AOL Representative Country :	Spain
Beneficiary Bank Name :	BANCO SANTANDER
Beneficiary Bank IBAN :	ES13 00494215532314050821
Beneficiary Bank Account Number :	00494215532314050821
Beneficiary Bank Swift Code :	BSCHESMMXXX
Beneficiary Bank Address :	Avenida del Carmen 45
Beneficiary Bank City :	Collereros
Beneficiary Bank Zip Code :	03350
Beneficiary Bank Country :	Spain

How to complete and confirm payment :

1. The payment must be sent by bank transfer to the bank account of our AOL Representative.
2. After payment is complete send us the receipt from your bank by FAX or by e-mail.
3. E-mail us the serial numbers of the payment receipt document.
4. Fax the payment receipt to our fax number: **(+44) 208 711 2466**

*** Once the bank transfer clears and our AOL Representative confirms payment, we will instruct the seller to start the shipping process. We will hold the funds until you send us your confirmation that you are satisfied with the product you received. As soon as we receive your confirmation we will release payment to the seller.

If you need assistance with your purchase, please don't hesitate to contact us:

Regards,

AOL Money Department

AOL Inc.

4. **Scams targeting sellers** – these can take one of two forms, depending on whether the item you are selling is desirable to the scammer or not. If you are selling something that the scammer wants or thinks that he can make a profit on by selling local to where he is then he may ask you to actually ship the item, but in most cases the scam will take the form of an overpayment scam, with the payment being sent to the seller either by cheque (which will be fake) or a fake PayPal invoice.

In the first form, the scammer will probably use a fake PayPal (or perhaps bank) email to fool the victim into thinking that they've been paid, but that the payment is on hold until they arrange the shipping and provide the tracking ID. In the second form, the scammer will tell the victim that he has his own shipper who will pick up the item and will include the payment for the shipping in with the payment for the item and ask for the money to be sent by Western Union/Moneygram. This may be done using a fake cheque or a fake PayPal bank email similar to above, but with the payment being put on hold until the overpayment has been sent to the shipper. For more information of the cheque version of an overpayment scam, see the section on Fake Cheque scams in the Employment Scams chapter as it works the same way.

Scams like this will often start with a text message or email from the scammer expressing interest in the "item" (without specifying what they are interested in) and requesting a mail to confirm if it is available.

In this example, a text message was received by the seller asking them to contact the scammer on an email address. Here is the initial text message

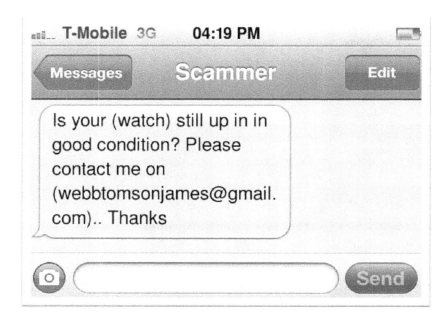

A response from the victim gets a scripted email reply

Good to hear back from you.I will be glad to buy it from you, this what i have been looking for to buy,but i will not be able to come and see it in your place Note that i will be responsible for shipping and handling.My shipping/pickup company will come to your location for the pick up because i will not be able to come and see it due to my work,please provide me with the address where it will be picked up so that i can forward it to the shipping company to calculate the cost of pick up for me.i'll be waiting for the address where the item is so i can send it to my shipping / pick up company for the calculation of there fees and i'm sure they will get back to me soon. So about the payment i will like the payment to be made via paypal online secure payment . So i want you to get back to me with your verified PayPal Account Email Address And your full Name Please include your email address in your reply for effective contact,So that i can Deposit the funds now and if you don't have one you can get one done at www.paypal.com and with that i can have a good transaction.
1.Am ok with the asking price
2.Your PayPal Full Name
3.Your Paypal E-mail address.
4. Your phone number.
Best Regards.

The victim replies giving the requested details and gets the following response

I need to inform you about a slight change with the pick up arrangements received an email from my pick agent he said he won't come for the pick up unless i pay him the agent commission fee first in order to be able to schedule a pick up time and date, the Courier Agency Head Quarters is in China and all commission payment made for pick up from anywhere in the world is sent to their Head Quarters and the only form of payment they accept is Western Union Money Transfer.

I will now include the $950.00 CAD they charged to pick it up and take it home (1st Class Cargo) to the payments i will send through PayPal..

After receiving the confirmation email from PayPal after i have made the payments to you and received the whole money, I will need you to send the $950.00 CAD to my pick up agent address via Western Union Money Transfer and will include an additional fee of $50 as western union charges when sending money..

The western union money transfer can be made at any post office or any western union outlet around you. I will be making the payments of $2,250.00 CAD to you shortly and will email you as soon as am done.

Get back to me As soon as possible.

The victim replies, confirming that he is happy with the arrangement and gets the following response from the scammer's initial email address

> I have just completed the payment and i expected PayPal to have notified you to this effect check your mail folders (inbox,spam and junk mail) i sent $2,250 in all.i added $1,000 but $950 will be sent to my agent in China through western union at post office,the extra $50 is to cover the western union fee. PayPal said they will not release the fund until you email them the western union details for verification,and also to enable my pick up agent to come for pick up and inspection.Here is the agent's details where the money will be sent.
> First name: Yalin
> Surname: Wang
> Address: Jiangxi gongzi.jintai lu
> City:Ji'an   State:Jiangxi
> Zip:343900
> Country: China.
> Please get the necessary details sent to PayPal (Money Transfer Control Number)MTCN and senders name and address used to send the $950 so that they can release the whole fund into your account.Please get back to me once done

and these 2 responses from a fake PayPal email address

You've got new funds from Webbtomson James

Transaction Overview

Summary of this payment

Transaction ID	9TQ95072YQ3810695P
Transaction STATUS	**PENDING**
Sent To	XXX@googlemail.com
Sent From	webbtomsonjames@gmail.com
Date	Oct-05- 2015
Amount	$1,250.00 CAD
Shipping Charges	$950.00 CAD
Estimated Western Union Charges	$50.00 CAD
Total	$2,250.00 CAD

To receive this payment, locate the nearest Western Union Office in your area Find Agent Location to proceed with the payment of the Pick-Up Agent Fee.

Issues with this transaction

To complete this Transaction you are required to send an upfront sum of $950.00 CAD meant for the Pick up fee to the Shipping Agent's Information given below via Western Union Money Transfer and get back to us with the Transaction Details which you will be provided with after the money has been sent, Inclusive of the MTCN [Money Transfer Control Number], Sender's Name and Address used to process the transfer and the Receipt given to you. As soon as you provide these Information for Verification we will credit a Total Sum of $2,250.00 CAD to your PayPal account.

Agent's
  Info:

> **First name: Yalin**
> **Surname: Wang**
> **Address: Jiangxi gongzi.jintai lu**
> **City:Ji'an**
> **State:Jiangxi**
> **Zip:343900**
> **China.**

Address
 Status: Confirmed

Please, understand that this is a security measure intended to help protect both the Buyer and the Seller.We apologize for the inconvenience that has caused you.

This payment has been deducted from the buyer's account and has been "APPROVED" but will not be credited into your account until the MTCN is sent to us for verification, so as to secure both the buyer and the seller.

Click Here to locate nearest Western Union Agent in your area or send money online.

Questions Please contact PayPal® on paypaservicecustomercare@consultant.com concerning this Transaction.

Help Center   Safety Advice

Please Note: As this transaction was done via our e-mail payments service, any inquiries and necessary information should be sent to us by directly replying to this message because of the status of this transaction, it has not been passed on to our customer care phone service section,and all inquiries should be directed back to this e-mail as it is the being monitored for this transaction.

This payment was issued to your account through our online payment service and monitored by our fund verification team.

Email: ? Questions? Go to the Help Center PayPal Customer Care at: paypaservicecustomercare@consultant.com.

PayPal Email ID PP307

Submit the information received from Western Union for Verification and Accreditation of your PayPal account.

David Marcus
President
PayPal, Inc.

Dear Michael Hunt ,

Status: Pending●

This email confirms that a payment confirmation e-mail you recently received as regards a payments of **$2,250.00 CAD** sent to you by **Webbtomson James** is Originated from PayPal® Service, and as soon as you have e-mailed the necessary western union details for a transferred sum of **$950.00CAD** to the address you were provided with the in the payment confirmation e-mail sent to you earlier, a sum of **$2,250.00 CAD** will be credited into your account.

The transfer can be done via Western Union Money Transfer Post Office. Click this link for nearest **western union office** section at your post office.

Your Account will be credited accordingly upon the receipt of details requested . It should either be sent in JPG format or send type details as: Sender's Name; Receiver's Name; MTCN; Amount Sent.

Please, understand that this is a security measure to help protect both the Buyer and the Seller. Therefore, we apologize for the inconvenience that we may have caused you.

Help Center: For any inquiries, you can contact our customer care service by replying directly to this e-mail directly, as this transaction was done via e-mail, all inquiries should be directed to this e-mail address only and any inquiries about this transaction directed to our phone service section will be returned as null and void.

Safety Advice
This transaction is safe and secured, the buyer does not access to cancel the transaction under our new Secured Station Service(SSS) and this not a "Scam". You Safe And Protected With PayPal® Service.

Thank you for using PayPal Security !

Help Center
Copyright © 1999-2015 PayPal Canada Pty Limited ABN 93 111 195 389 (AFSL 304962). All rights reserved.

Any general financial product advice provided in this site has not taken into account your objectives, financial situations or needs.

PayPal Email ID PP1525

Had the victim sent the money to the agent, the scammer would either have disappeared with the money or tried to get more with other fees and excuses.

Things to look out for when buying online.

The chapter on fake websites gives a number of things to look out for when trying to decide if a website is legitimate, but here are a few more ways of protecting yourself from being scammed by a fake eCommerce site.

1. Look at the payment methods offered, do they take credit cards, if not then it should be a red flag (but note that the presence of card payments is not a guarantee of legitimacy as some sites will register with card processors.
2. Look for any mention of payment by Western Union, Moneygram or RIA being accepted. None of these methods are designed for business transactions, so if they are offered then it is a major red flag.
3. If the items being sold are unique (such as a particular car or vehicle), then search for the serial number of it is given and the images that are provided. An individual vehicle should not be being sold on various websites in different parts of the world.
4. Research the price the item is being sold for - is it markedly lower than the going rate for the item? There is no legitimate reason for a retailer to vastly undercut the market price for an item, it's reducing their profit.
5. Are you being offered sweeteners on a popular item, such as "Buy 3 get 1 Free"? If an item is new or very popular (particularly brand name electronic items) then there is absolutely no way that a legitimate retailer would be offering such deal as the items will sell without the need for such offers.
6. If you are buying a large item then you should never part with any cash before physically viewing the item. Make the time to travel and view the item and make sure that the person you are in communication with is actually the owner and able to sell the item. If that is not possible, find a trusted person to do it for you.

If you're buying from a classifieds or auction site, then all of the above points apply here as well, particularly viewing the item before parting with any cash. You should also be aware of any specific payment methods that the site uses that offer some form of protection. For example if you buy of eBay and use PayPal through the auction (not just sending the money to an email address that is given to you), then eBay will offer you Buyer Protection. But, step outside of eBay and deal direct with the seller and that protection will be gone.

Things to look out for when selling online.

1. Financial institutions such as banks and PayPal do not hold payments and only release them when an item is shipped or some other specific action has taken place.
2. Any money sent by PayPal will show up in your PayPal account, if someone says they have sent you money and it isn't shown then they haven't sent it to you.
3. Never use a link provided by the seller or in an email claiming to be from PayPal or your bank to check your account. Always log in using your normal link.
4. If someone says they want to have a shipper pick the item up and want you to forward the shipping fee to them, they're a scammer.

The final things to say is to reiterate that whether you're buying or selling online, if there's any mention of you sending money by Western Union, Moneygram, RIA or buying some form of top up card and giving the other person the reference number then it is 100% definitely a scam. If you're dealing with a private individual then selling or buying face to face with cash is the best method.

14. SCAMS TARGETING BUSINESSES

Scammers don't just target individuals, they will try and steal from legitimate businesses as well. Here are a few of the various types of scams that are used to target businesses:

1. Credit card scams – whether you are an online store selling goods of any type, a B&B or hotel or a gym, scammers will come up with a way to use your business to cash in their stolen credit cards.
2. Cheque scams – similar to card scams, scammers with fake cheques will come up with ways to use your business to get funds from their fake cheques.
3. Domain registration scams – popular in China, scammers will approach legitimate businesses telling them that someone is trying to register the Chinese version of their domain name and giving them the chance to register it themselves (at a vastly inflated price).
4. Business directory scams – the scammer approaches victims "inviting" them to register their business in an official looking directory (often implying it is an EU or legal requirement). A few weeks later, the victim will be sent an invoice, often in the 100s of £ or €s for their entry in the "European Business Directory" or similar

Credit Card Scammers

Credit card scammers have a supply of compromised credit cards that they have either bought from a hacker/phisher or have phished themselves. The scammer needs to find a way of converting these cards into cash (or sometimes goods), but obviously can't walk into a local store and buy luxury goods. What they will do instead is to approach small online businesses and fabricate a way where there is a need for the retailer to charge extra and pass the additional payment to a third party. If you are selling something that they are not interested in then they will ask you to use their own (fictional) shipper, if you are a B & B owner or hotelier, the will need a payment made to their travel agent, etc. and will come up with some reason why they cannot pay the third-party directly. Sometimes, if a retailer is selling items that a scammer thinks he can sell (or likes for himself), such as small high value items, they will ask the victim to arrange shipping as well.

Here is an example of a credit card scam targeting a retailer and asking them to use their own shipper. The first email is often vague and spammed to many recipients (both retailers and anyone else who is on the list of emails the scammer was sold), but sometimes may specifically target a retailer and mention specific products.

> Hello, We extend our kind interest to make purchase on some items in your facility. Before we proceed kindly let us know the kinds of credit cards you accept and do you allow private pickup by freight forwarders ? Get back to me at : anthonyadams0012@gmail.com Hope to read from you so soon.
> Anthony Adams

The victim responds with their price list and the scammer will provide his order and the details of his preferred shipper

Hello,

Thank you for the reply and for answering my questions. I have below is my company information for you to setup a new customer account., below is the list of items i want to purchase for:

Product Name : Kidney - £200.00
:............. Order 06 Qty

Product Name : Tongue - £150.00
:............. Order 06 Qty

SHIPPING ADDRESS:
ADAMS VENTURES INCS
Lot 47 Vytauto Str, LT-00101
Palanga, Lithuania
Tel.: (+370 460) 51299

Concerning the shipping , the likes of UPS, DHL and others always don't take care of the charges down here.Charges like handling,customs and duties etc. We have experienced such situation before and i don't want to experience such thing again,you do not need to worry about the stress involve and all documentations because i have a shipping company that have delivered to me in the past,i really like their services so i will like you contact them about the shipping.I will be glad if you contact this shipper (John Trucking Express & Forwarding Services) for the shipping quote. Here is there email address (johntruckingexpress@aol.com) They will take care of everything including handling, customs and duties,Tax, insurance etc,also you will be responsible for payment to John Trucking Express & Forwarding Services then all costs as far as shipping, taxes, duties, and insurance in addition to the costs of the product should be sent to me in a proforma invoice to be paid in advance of shipment.Always send me the copy of email you send to them ,Kindly email them with pick up address,shipping address and the weight of the order.get back to m with the following once you hear back from them..

cost of items..........
shipping cost via John Trucking Express & Forwarding Services........
all additional cost(transfer fee to John Trucking Express & Forwarding Services)....................
total cost (cost of items+shipping cost via John Trucking Express & Forwarding Services agent + transfer fee to John Trucking Express & Forwarding Services agent)..........

so i can send you my credit card details for you to charge the total cost from it and get the shipping fees settled,then my order can be shipped out asap.

Regards,
Anthony Adams.
ADAMS VENTURES INCS
Lot 47 Vytauto Str, LT-00101
Palanga, Lithuania
Tel.: (+370 460) 51299

The victim, will write to the fake shipper, asking for shipping costs and will get a reply with the cost of shipping (which is usually totally unrealistic and often nearly as much as the cost of the ordered goods)

Dear Customer,

  Thank you for contacting John Trucking Express and & Forwarding Services. On checking through our customer database, the address provided below belongs to one of our premium client whom we have made shipments to,however We do deliver to most business outlet worldwide. So getting your shipment to your client won't be a problem. For a shipment moving from your company with the Total weight and dimension you provide, below is the Standard and Express Shipment Air Freight quote.

==========Pick Up===
Pick up Location: NEEDED
==========RECIPIENT-======================================
Address: Lot 47 Vytauto Str, LT-00101
Palanga, Lithuania
==
 Customer ID #TW004223B3
==
Package Containing: 1 Stay Fresh container,
75cm x 75cm x 80cm weight approx 2.5kg
==
(Air freight Cost)
Express Shipment (2 to 3 days)........... GBP 1599.00
Standard Shipment (3 to 5 days)......... GBP 1355.90
==
The freight costs includes:
Collection from your location
Customs clearance fee
Duties & taxes Inland transit to Lithuania
Insured Door To Door Delivery
Including Tax fee
==

Pick up will be made by our agents after payment is confirmed.We will need you to provide us with an estimate pick up date and time so that we can schedule a date and time for you before the item/s are ready for picked up as we normally have numerous shipping request.

As soon as we receive all necessary information from you we will proceed on the pick up at your location,Also we require payment via our Bank account for now prior to pick up and collection of package which is to be paid as soon as the order is ready for pick up.

So you will have to send us the payments via wire transfer so that we can do the pick up and settle the necessary tax and custom duties,this price includes insurance and all there duties,then we will get back to you with the necessary details.We have greatly reduce the price of your shipment. For further information do not hesitate to contact us. We look forward to providing you with the lowest prices and the best customer service possible Customer Service (John Trucking Express and Forwarding Services)

Thank you
JOHN CROGAN

The victim will then provide the scammer with the cost of the shipping and the scammer will reply choosing the more expensive of the options

> Thanks for your email, I also received the copy of the email sent to you from the shipper and i want you to understand that the prices quoted by the shipper is included with the customs and taxes charges. i will prefer to go with the express shipping option and i need you to go ahead to add all cost to my invoice and get back to me with the final proforma invoice for my order showing all cost on it including the total cost for my order plus the shipping cost so i can be happy to forward to you my credit card details to secure the entire payment with you and we can proceed further from there.
>
> (Air freight Cost)
> Note: i prefer for the Express Shipment (2 to 3 days) GBP 1599.00
>
> I await your reply with the proforma invoice for whole payment and i can send you my credit card for the payment asap.
>
> Thanks,
> Anthony Adams

Once the victim provides the total cost, the scammer will start providing his stolen cards in an effort to clear the balance and get the overpayment transferred before the real cardholders notice the fraudulent charges and challenge them with their card company. The scammer won't want card numbers sitting around, so he will often write to ask if the victim is "in the office" or "at their desk", before providing card details.

> Hello Margaret,
>
> Good Morning and how you doing today, I just want to confirm if you are in office right now so i can forward you my credit card payment information.
>
> Thanks,
>
> Anthony.

Once the victim confirms that they are available, the scammer will start sending cards. Sometimes one at a time, but occasionally in batches of 2 or 3 with instructions to split the costs.

> Hello,
>
> Here are the necessary information, Find below is my credit card details below for the total bills and then you advise back with the confirmation of the charges as soon as possible.
>
> CREDIT CARD INFORMATION......
> Name on Card : Anthony Adams
> Card type : Master Card
> Card Number : 5491 2373 1211 ####
> Date Expire : 05/15
> CVV2 :232
>
> Kindly go ahead to make the charges now and I await for the confirmation asap today so we can proceed further.
>
> Thanks ...
> Anthony Adams

Once the victim has been able to charge the full balance, the scammer will ask the victim to contact the shipper for the details to pay the shipping charges. Sometimes these will be requested to be sent by Western Union or Moneygram, but occasionally, the scammer may provide a bank account (usually belonging to a mule)

> Thank you for contacting us, we need to confirm our service charges so we can settle, secure all taxes & duties plus insurance and thereafter we can be happy to come for the collection of the order and delivery to your customer will commence soon. Enlisted below is our accounting information to make the transfer of our charges in amount of GBP 1599.00. via bank wire and once it is done you advise back with the transfer confirmation details so we can schedule the pickup and send our representative to take care of the shipment by Asap.
>
> Below is the bank details for the transfer.
>
> BANK NAME :RICHMOND COUNTY SAVINGS BANK
> BANK ADDRESS : 2424 hyland boulevard Staten Island NY 10306
> NAME ON ACCOUNT : JOSEPH FERRARO
> ACCOUNT NUMBER: 508500116XX
> ROUTING NUMBER: 226071004
>
> Once payment has been wire kindly email us with the transfer details.
>
> We look forward to working hand in hand with you .
>
> John Crogan
> Shipper In Charge

The scammer's hope is that the bank transfer (or Western Union/Moneygram transfer) will, as mentioned earlier, be finalised before any of the card transactions are reversed.

Things to look out for with credit card scams.

1. Never agree to charge extra and forward money on to a third party as a favour to the customer. If you only ever charge for the goods/service that you are providing then you will cover yourself against the vast majority of credit card scams.
2. Beware of any mention of Western Union/Moneygram, perhaps if a customer decides to cancel an order and asks you to refund by a method other than back to the cards originally charged.
3. Watch out for customers who seen to have a large number of cards and will happily provide another card if there is an easily rectifiable problem with a card (incorrect Cvv or expiry for example).
4. If you have a proper eCommerce website, be suspicious of anyone who wants to bypass that and provide cards by emails – they will be hoping to avoid additional security measures such as "Verified by Visa" or "MasterCard SecureCode".
5. If you sell small, high value items (watches, jewellery, small electronics, etc.) then be careful of people claiming to be overseas (particularly in areas know as scam hotspots, such as Eastern Europe, Africa and the Far East). Why would they chose to order from you and not from someone local?

Cheque Scams

Cheque scams can often be similar to credit card scams in that the victim will be asked to take payment for a service provided by a third party and forward money on to them. There are other variations though, such as overpayments made in error with a request to refund the extra back to the "customer" and also delinquent debt collection scams targeting lawyers, where the scammer pretends to be an overseas individual or corporation with a debtor in the lawyers country (perhaps due to a divorce settlement or a cancelled order).

The example below is a delinquent debt collection scam, where the scammer approaches a lawyer and pretends to be a person based overseas, with a debt to be collected.

> Dear Counsel,
> I am seeking for a Divorce Lawyer to assist in a divorce settlement matter. If this is within your line of practice please respond to my email and I will forward you more information. I will also need a referral if this is not your field of practice. I look forward to your response soonest. email: zairahoshiko4477@ymail.com
> Sincerely,
> Zaira Hoshiko

The victim firm responds, confirming that they can assist in the matter and the scammer responds with more details.

> Hello Dwayne,
>
> Thanks for your response, I was married to my ex husband Allen Hoshiko and in March 2010, We mutually agreed under Cool terms to go our separate ways. Allen had agreed to pay me $950,500.00 under terms of the Collaborative Law agreement so that I can settle down and to his credit; he has paid me $251,500.00 with an outstanding balance of $699,000.00. I am hereby seeking your legal assistance in collecting the balance or helping me enforce the agreement, and have him honor the agreement in entirety because the lawyer that helped me in this matter earlier is retired now.
>
> I will be providing further information upon your request. I believe that one of the reasons he has refused to pay is because I am currently living in Japan. I have already advised him that I will be retaining your firm, so he knows I am ready to go any lent to get my money from him.
>
> Let me know if you require consultation fees before you advice or after the case is done, and if so I will require you to send me your retainer terms and agreement so we can start from there, I need to know if I will be able to work with your terms and also I will be sending you our Collaborative agreement and other necessary information will be given to you after I have taken a look at your retainer agreement. I belief a Law firm like yours is needed to help me collect payment from him or litigate this matter if he fails to pay as promised. Thank you and I look forward to your prompt response.
>
> Sincerely,
>
> Zaira Hoshiko

The victim firm sends out a retainer agreement for the scammer to sign and gets this response, with the document on the next 5 pages attached

> Hello Dwayne,
>
> Thanks for your email and the retainer, I will sign and return it back to you shortly. I agree with you because its your profession. However, attached to this email is a scan copy of the Collaborative Agreement for your safe keeping.
>
> I agree to your terms and I know this case will bring out good fruition.
>
> Zaira

Collaborative Law
Participation Agreement
(If Children are included, include III)

ZAIRA HOSHIKO

---and

ALLEN HOSHIKO

--"the Parties"

and their lawyers:

SAKAISUJI KYODO

---and

NAGOYA DAIICHI

--"the Lawyers"

have chosen to enter into this Agreement to use the principles of the Collaborative Law Process to settle the issues arising from the dissolution of their relationship.

I. Purpose
The primary goal of the Collaborative Law Process is to settle the outstanding issues in a non-adversarial manner. The Parties aim to minimize, if not eliminate, the negative economic, social and emotional consequences of protracted litigation to themselves and their family. The Parties have retained Collaborative lawyers to assist them in reaching this goal.

II. Communication
The Parties intend to effectively communicate with each other to efficiently and economically settle the dissolution of their relationship. Written and verbal communications will be respectful and constructive and will not make accusations or claims not based in fact.
It is agreed that communication during settlement meetings will be focused on the economic and parenting issues in the dissolution and the constructive resolution of those issues.
The Parties are encouraged to discuss and explore the interests they have in achieving a mutually agreeable settlement, and each is encouraged to speak freely and express his or her needs, desires, and options without criticism or judgement by the other. Although the Parties should be informed by their lawyers about, and may discuss with each other, the litigation alternatives and the outcomes they might attain, neither Party nor their lawyers will use the threat to withdraw from the process or to go to court as a means of achieving a desired outcome or forcing a settlement.

III. Children's Issues

In resolving issues about sharing the enjoyment of and responsibility for any children, the Parties Agree to make every effort to reach amicable solutions that promote the children's best interests. The Parties agree to act quickly to mediate and resolve differences related to the children to Promote a caring, loving and involved relationship between the children and both parents. The Parties acknowledge that inappropriate communications regarding their dissolution can be Harmful to their children. They agree that settlement issues will not be discussed in the presence Of their children, or that communication with the children regarding these issues will occur only If it is appropriate and done by mutual agreement, or with the advice of a child specialist. The Parties agree not to make any changes to the residence of the children without first obtaining the written agreement of the other Party.

IV. Participation with Integrity

Each participant shall uphold a high standard of integrity, and shall not take advantage of Inconsistencies or miscalculations of the other, but shall disclose them and seek to have them Corrected.

V. Negotiation in Good Faith

The Parties and their lawyers agree to deal with each other in good faith and to promptly provide all necessary and reasonable information requested. No formal discovery procedures will be used unless specifically agreed to in advance by the parties.

The Parties acknowledge that by using informal discovery, they are giving up certain rights, for the duration of the Collaborative Law Process, including the right to formal discovery, formal court hearings, restraining orders and other procedures provided by the adversarial legal system. They give up these measures with the specific understanding that both Parties make full and fair disclosure of all assets, income, debts and other information. The Parties acknowledge that participation in the Collaborative Law Process, and the settlement reached, is based upon the assumption that both Parties have acted in good faith and have provided complete and accurate information to the best of their ability. The Parties agree to provide sworn statements making full and fair disclosure of their income, assets and debts, if requested.

VI. Cautions and Limitations

In electing the Collaborative Law Process, the Parties understand that there is no guarantee that the process will be successful in resolving their case. They understand that the process cannot eliminate concerns about any disharmony, distrust or irreconcilable differences which have led to the current conflict. While intent on striving to reach a cooperative solution, success will ultimately depend on our commitment to making the process work. The Parties understand that they are still expected to assert their respective needs and interests and their respective lawyers will help each of them do so.

The Parties further understand that while the Collaborative lawyers share a commitment to the process described in this document, each of them has a professional duty to represent his or her

VII. Experts and Consultants

When appropriate and needed, the Parties will use neutral experts. The Parties will agree in advance of retaining the Expert as to how the costs of the third party expert will be paid. Unless the parties agree otherwise, the expert report shall be covered by the confidentiality clause.

VIII. Divorce Coaches, Child Specialist, and Financial Planners

When appropriate and as needed, the parties will use the services of one or more of the following professionals: Divorce Coaches, Child Specialist, Financial Planner (Collectively referred to as "the Collaborative Professional"). When a Collaborative Professional is engaged, the parties agree that the Collaborative Professionals and the Lawyers may engage in whatever discussions necessary for resolution of the case. In the event that the Collaborative Law Process comes to an end, the Confidentiality provisions as set out in Paragraph XIV of this Agreement apply to the Collaborative Professionals.

IX. No Court Intervention

Unless otherwise agreed, prior to reaching final agreement on all issues, no writ and statement of claim will be filed or served, nor will any other motion or document be prepared or filed which would initiate court intervention.

X. Disqualification by Court Intervention

The Parties understand that their Collaborative Lawyers' representation is limited to providing services within the Collaborative Law Process. Thus, while each lawyer is the advisor of his or her client and serves as the client's representative and negotiator, the Parties mutually acknowledge that both lawyers, and any one in each lawyers office, will be disqualified from representing them in a contested court proceeding against the other spouse.

XI. Withdrawal of Party from Collaborative Law Process

If a Party decides to withdraw from the Collaborative Law Process, prompt written notice shall be given to the other party through his or her lawyer. Upon termination of the Collaborative Law Process by a Party or a lawyer, there will be a thirty (30) day waiting period (unless there is an emergency) before any court hearing, to permit the parties to retain new lawyers and make an orderly transition. All temporary agreements will remain in full force and effect during this period. The intent of this provision is to avoid surprise and prejudice to the rights of the other Party. It is therefore mutually agreed that either Party may bring this provision to the attention of the Court to request a postponement of a hearing.

If a Party wishes to withdraw from the Collaborative Law Process with their current lawyer, but retain a new lawyer to continue with the Collaborative Law Process, the Party shall give prompt written notice to the other party through his or her lawyer, of their intention to withdraw and obtain a new lawyer. The new lawyer shall execute a new Collaborative Law Participation Agreement within 30 days of the Party giving notice. If a new agreement is not executed within 30 days, then the other party shall be entitled to proceed as if the Collaborative Law Process were terminated as of the date written notice was given.

XII. Withdrawal of Lawyer from Collaborative Law Process

If either lawyer withdraws from the case for any reason excepts those set out in paragraph XIII herein, they agree to do so promptly by a written notice to the other party through his or her lawyer. This may be done without terminating the status of the case as a Collaborative Law case. The party whose lawyer has withdrawn may elect to continue in the Collaborative Law Process and shall give prompt written notice of this intention as well to the other party through his or her lawyer. The new lawyer shall execute a new Collaborative Law Participation Agreement within 30 days of the lawyer first giving notice. If a new agreement is not executed within 30 days, then the other party shall be entitled to proceed as if the Collaborative Law Process were terminated as of the date the first written notice was given.

XIII. Termination of Collaborative Law Process

A Collaborative Lawyer must withdraw from the Collaborative Law Process in the event they learn that their client has withheld or misrepresented information and **continues to withhold and misrepresent such information**, or otherwise acted so as to undermine or take unfair advantage of the Collaborative Law Process. The lawyer withdrawing will advise the other lawyer that he is withdrawing, and that the Collaborative Law Process must end.

XIV. Confidentiality

All communication exchanged within the Collaborative Law Process will be confidential and without prejudice. If subsequent litigation occurs, the Parties mutually agree:

A. that neither Party will introduce as evidence in Court information disclosed during the Collaborative Law Process for the purpose of reaching a settlement, except documents otherwise compellable by law including any sworn statements as to financial status made by the parties;

B. that neither Party will introduce as evidence in Court information disclosed during the Collaborative Law Process with respect to either Parties' behaviour or legal position with respect to settlement;

C. that neither Party will ask or subpoena either lawyer or any of the Collaborative Professionals to Court to testify in any court proceedings, nor bring on an application to discover either lawyer or any of the Collaborative Professionals, with regard to matters disclosed during the Collaborative Law Process;

D. that neither Party will require the production at any Court proceedings of any notes, records, or documents in the lawyer's possession or in the possession of one of the Collaborative Professionals; and the Parties agree that these Guidelines with respect to confidentiality apply to any subsequent litigation, arbitration, or other process for dispute resolution.

The confidentiality clause does not apply in the event that a Party or Collaborative Professional is obliged by law to report to the Superintendent of Family and Child Services information arising out of the collaborative process which gives the party or Collaborative Professional reasonable grounds to believe that a child may be in need of protection.

XV. Rights and Obligations of Settlement

Although the parties have agreed to work outside the court system, the parties agree that:

A. neither Party will dispose of any assets except by an agreement in writing.

B. neither Party may harass the other Party; and

C. all available insurance coverage must be maintained and continued without change in coverage or beneficiary designation.

D. it is further agreed that Allen Hoshiko is to pay Zaira Hoshiko the sum of $950,500.00 USD (Nine Hundred and Fifty Thousand Five Hundred dollars) from the period date February 2, 2010 to July 28, 2010.

XVI. Enforceability of Agreements

In the event that the Parties require a temporary agreement during the Collaborative Law Process, the agreement will be put in writing and signed by the Parties and their lawyers. If either Party withdraws from the Collaborative Law Process, the written agreement is enforceable and may be presented to the court as a basis for an Order, which the Court may make retroactive to the date of the written agreement. Similarly, once a final agreement is signed, if a Party should refuse to honour it, the final agreement may be presented to the Court in any subsequent action.

XVII. Acknowledgment

Both Parties and their lawyers acknowledge that they have read this Agreement, understand its terms and conditions, and agree to abide by them. The parties have chosen the Collaborative Law Process to reduce emotional and financial costs, and to generate a final agreement that addresses their concerns. They agree to work in good faith to achieve these goals.

Dated: March 08, 2010

ALLEN HOSHIKO

NAGOYA DAIICHI ESQ
Lawyer for Allen Hoshiko

Dated: March 08, 2010

ZAIRA HOSHIKO

SAKAISUJI KYODO ESQ
Lawyer for Zaira Hoshiko

The victim confirms that the case should be a simple one and the scammer responds that her ex-husband is now ready to pay the outstanding amount, but wants to send it via the lawyer.

Dear Dwayne,

Thanks for your email and it is good to know that you have received the collaborative agreement I sent to you. This is to inform you that I agree to your terms and have informed my ex-husband that I already hired a Legal Adviser to help me in this case. And because he is now aware that I have already hired you, he is now willing to pay the outstanding . But he confirm that in order to know the legitimacy of my Lawyer, he is going to send the outstanding payment through you to me. Which means once he sends the payment, all you need do is to deduct all your cost, retainer fee and send the balance.

In order to proceed with the payment, you need to re-confirm the information below.

Full name:
Full Contact address:
Direct Tell:

Please respond asap in order for him to proceed with the payment to you. It is good to know that this case is moving successfully.

Zaira

The victim confirms that they are happy with the arrangement and provides the requested details and the scammer responds to say everything has been forwarded to her ex-husband.

Dear Dwayne,

Your email along with the payment information has been received and I have already forwarded it to my ex- husband for immediate payment through you to me .

However, I will keep you posted immediately the Payment is effected to you. Thanks for all your assistance.

Zaira

A week later, the scammer sends another email to say that a cheque for part of the amount is on its way to the lawyer.

Good day DWayne, hope you are doing well. A happy new week to you. This is to kindly inform you that I just received an update from my ex-husband that he has sent a payment of $285,000 issued in you name to your address you sent.

Furthermore, he will be sending the balance outstanding immediately he receives a confirmation from us that we have confirmed this payment. Immediately you receive the payment do inform me at once and also proceed to your bank and cash the payment. Am happy we are progressing as I always told you that this transaction will bring out good fruition.

Await your prompt reply.

Zaira.

In this case, a cheque never turned up, but had it done, the scammer would have asked the victim to deduct their fees and forward the balance to an account that they provide. Eventually, the cheque would have been discovered to be fake and the payment reversed from the victim's account, leaving them with a large amount of missing money. In the case of scams targeting lawyers, a 6 figure fake cheque could have disastrous consequences for a small firm of lawyers.

The best way to avoid being caught in a scam such as this is never to be put in the position where you are receiving a cheque and forwarding part of the money to another party. In the case of a delinquent debt scam, it would be the norm for the person sending the payment to have engaged their own solicitors and it would be them that would be sending the payment. In other cases where a firm is asked to take payment on behalf of a third party, then it is best to refuse, saying that they will only accept payment for the goods or service that they are providing and tell the customer to make arrangements to pay the third party directly. If the scammer is pretending to have sent the wrong amount by mistake and requests a refund of the over payment, then it is best to tell them to cancel the cheque that they have sent and send a new one for the correct amount. If the customer is legitimate then he will understand the reasons for the victims refusal to do as requested. Only scammers will not be happy with the outcome.

Domain Registation Scam

A legitimate business receives an email claiming to be from a domain registration organisation in somewhere such as China or other parts of Asia, claiming that someone is trying to register domains for the business' name. They will then try to sell useless domain names to the business at inflated prices, who may be panicked into buying them to protect the name and reputation of their business from having some unknown foreign company potentially passing themselves off as them.

Here is an example of the initial email that is sent to a victim company

---

Dear "Burke and Hare Ltd",

Having had your name and address from China Council for the Promotion of International Trade,we now avail ourselves of this opportunity to write to you and have something important need to confirm with your company.

We are registration service center authorized by CHINAGOV (THE DEVELOPMENT CENTER OF THE STATE COMMISSION OFFICE FOR PUBLIC SECTOR REFORM) in China.We received a formal application from a company(According to The China Law & Privacy Policy,Hidden The Real Name) is applying to register "burkeandhareltd.cn" as their domain names and internet brand in China and also in Asia on April 20, 2014. Considering domains and internet brand would involve the intellectual property of your company's name,patents,trademarks,and copyright, and in order to avoid confusion between them, so we inform you urgently.

At present, many domain name registries or domain name investment companies in China and even the world register domains and internet brand,and then sell them to the owner of trademark at high prices to make huge profit. Therefore, we remind you particularly that if you considered these domain names and internet brand are very important to you and there is necessary to protect them by registering them first, please let someone who is responsible for trademark or domain name contact me as soon as possible,according to the register principle, the original owner of the trademark has the priority to register.Thank you for you cooperation.

Looking forward to your prompt reply,

Kind Regards,
Dr. Jason Wang
Chief Law Officer,Senior Consulting Director

Internet Brand Justice & Safety Dept.
FireTrust Technology Ltd.
Address: Unit2-602,Building4,Third Qianjiang Community,Hangzhou, China
Tel: +86-571-28927205 ext.805(Mon–Fri,9am to 6:30pm,GMT+8) Fax: +86-571-28926277
Email: Jason.Wang@FireTrust.net.cn Web: http://www.FireTrust.net.cn http://www.FireTrust.org.cn

---

Alan Jones

15. OTHER SCAMS

The preceding chapters have covered some of the more common scams, but there are many other ways that criminals on the Internet will try to steal from you. Here are some details of some other scams that may appear in your inbox or on the web.

Gold seller scams

Scammers will often write claiming to be from small villages in African countries such as Ghana, with supplies of gold from their local mines available to sell. These scammers will try to get their victims to visit them or in some cases visit the victims, so that they can use a small sample of real gold to prove that they are legitimate - they aren't, that small sample is all they've got.

Here is an example of an email exchange from a gold scammer. The initial mail is bulk mailed to as many people as possible, just like most other scam emails

> LOOKING FOR GOLD BUYER,
>
> Dear Buyers,
>
> Our company is looking for real Gold Dust/Gold dore Bar Buyers, Presently We have many Quantity of alluvial gold dust/gold dore bar ready for sale in our mining company office in Accra Ghana Here.
>
> If you are interested, do not hesitate to contact us as soon as possible for us to give you our full co-operate offer (F.C.O). Also even if you are not prepared to buy our Gold now, you can look for a buyer that will buy our Gold through you so that you will benefit a commission from it as well.
>
> Sincerely,
>
>
> Mr Anthony O.
> Accra Ghana.Motor: With God All Things Are Possible.

a reply from a victim will get more details of the gold and how the scammer wants the transaction to take place.

ANTHONY O MINERAL METALS ACCRA GHANA.
Local Mining for Gold & Minerals.
Accra Ghana

Dear Ziege Täter,

Thanks for your mail, Here is the principal/sellers with full legal send And corporate responsibility and under penalty of perjury, with full knowledge of the act, and as seller are ready and able to deliver the herein offered (AU) metal under the following terms and conditions.

PRODUCT: Alluvial Gold Dust
ORIGIN: Ghana
QUANTITY Available: 1200kgs Gold Dust.
Reserved for shipment now: 770kgs
FINENESS/PURITY: 92.05 % Gold Dust for 22 carats.

CURRENT PRICE: USD$32,500/1kg @ 22 carats Gold dust (Local Bush Price)
Not yet-refined and is negotiable.

1. Form: Gold Bar,
2. Purity: 95.67 % like minimum value
3. Price: 32,500 USD for one kg.
4. Quantity Available: 1500kgs.
5. Reserved for shipment now: 850kgs
Origin: Ghana / Liberia /BURKINA FASO.

DISCOUNT: Not applicable
PAYMENT: US$D/ by Wire Transfer
METHOD OF PAYMENT: Total values of the Gold Dust are to be paid
through bank, after 3 days of buyer assay analysis and acceptance of
Gold Dust.

POINT OF DELIVERY: Kotoka International Airport, Accra,Ghana.
to buyer's final Destination.

DELIVERY: Arrangements will be made by seller, with seller's delivery agents to deliver the Gold Dust to buyer's destination by Air Cargo –Europe or USA/Asia etc, before further deliver to buyer's final destination. Delivery took place within 3 days after acceptance/agreed of terms. It is estimated that All Government & Inland Taxes of the Alluvial Gold Dust are to be pay by Seller.

The buyer shall pay only the Transportation charges direct to the transit / shipping company; the shipping cost amount shall be deducted from the Seller's total value Gold dust money after assay, and must be paid to the delivery Shipping Company at optional method of payment agreed with the shipping company.

The buyer will provide a refinery where the shipping company will deliver the Gold Dust. We transact on this procedure because we have lost so much products to people who claimed to be buyer while they are not but only use the claim to run away with our quality product
without any trace.

Moreover we deliver to buyers to be pay after refinery test/assay, while buyers pay only for the shipment of the gold dust to their refinery. If you are prepared to work with us accordingly we therefore advise you to look for reputable buyers and then update us with their following information to enable us send them our FCO:

---

1. The quantity you need to purchase for first shipment
2. Your Company/Refinery Address for delivery
3. Your direct Tel/Fax No.
4. Name of contact person for document processing
5. Country / Air port for delivery.

I want you to know that as soon as we receive your information, it will enable us send your buyer our FCO, Invoice for the quantity they need to purchase from us and then sign NCNDA / IMFPA with you. Meanwhile we do ship our products with a reliable shipping/transit Company that cargo our merchandise through Airline.

THE SELLER CONFIRMS THAT EACH CONSIGNMENT WILL BE ACCOMPANIED BY THE FOLLOWING DOCUMENT'S to Europe or buyer's final destination point:

1. Commercial Invoice made out to BUYER
2. Certificate of Origin
3. Packing List
4. Assay Report
5. Certificate of Ownership
6 Master Air waybills etc at buyer's request

please forward your Letter of Interest to our company. As soon as terms agreed on by all parties, we will begin delivery procedures via Europe or USA. We look forward to establishing a long-term relationship with you by supplying Alluvial Gold Dust to you on a long-term basis. If you have any questions please call or email us anytime. We look forward to your prompt reply and are ready, willing and able to deliver upon your request.

Best regards,
Seller: Mr Anthony O.
Accra Ghana. Motor: With God All Things Are Possible
We will give you a phone number upon your response.

In many countries, the sale of gold is regulated and takes place through specific markets, so anyone approaching you by email offering gold for sale is almost certainly a scammer or in possession of stolen gold.

Death Threat or Hitman Scam

The premise of the death threat scam is that the scammer claims to have been paid to kill the victim, but will offer them a chance to live, if they pay the "assassin" some money.

Here is an example of a set of mails from a death threat scam.

ATTN.

LISTEN VERY CAREFULLY ,THIS IS THE ONLY WAY I CAN CONTACT
YOU, my TEAM HAS BEEN PAID TO ASSASINATE YOU, I HAVE EVERY REASON TO
CARRY OUT THE CONTRACT,BUT I DECIDED TO GIVE YOU A CHANCE AND SAVE YOUR FAMILY
THIS PAIN,THIS YOUR ALTERNATIVE,I WISH TO HELP YOU UNLESS YOU
DONT WANT TO HELP YOUR SELF,I WILL SEND YOU ENOUGH EVIDENCE YOU NEED ON A VIDEO TAPE RECORD
TO NAIL MY EMPLOYER DOWN WITH THE LAW.

BEFORE THAT YOUR REQUIRED TO MAKE AVAILABLE THE SUM OF $100,000. USD
AFTER WHICH I WILL DIRECT YOU ON WHAT TO DO NEXT TO SAVE YOUR SELF AND
YOUR FAMILY FROM THIS PAIN THAT WOULD HAVE BEFALLED YOU FROM MY

> EMPLOYER,THE MONEY WILL BE USED TO SETTLE THE TEAM MEN INVOLVED TO GO BACK TO THERE DESTINATIONS AND YOU BETTER KEEP THIS INFORMATION TO YOUR SELF BECAUSE YOU DONT KNOW WHO IS WHO WHERE YOU ARE NOW,IF HE FINDS OUT I HAVE BETRAYED HIM TRYING TO HELP YOU,YOU WILL HAVE YOUR SELF TO BLAME, I HAVE ORDERED MY MEN TO SATY AWAY FROM YOU.
>
> DO WE HAVE A DEAL OR NOT ?
>
> NOTE: YOU HAVE TWO OPTIONS HERE, (1)YOU HAVE TO GET HIM ARRESTED WITH THE INFORMATION I WILL GIVE YOU AFTER THE PAYMENT OR (2)YOU HAVE HIM KILLED TO SAVE YOUR SELF.
>
> I WILL VISIT YOUR HOUSE AGAIN BUT NOT NOW,MY BOYS EYES ARE ON YOU SO GET BACK TO ME AS SOON AS POSSIBLE

The scammer has no real script, he will just send empty threats that he is watching and preparing to kill the victim, in the hope that he can persuade them to pay him the money he demands.

Here is another example of a mail from him

> This is the only way I could contact you for now,I want you to be very careful about this and keep this secret with you until I make out space for us to see. You have no need of knowing who I am or where I am from.I know this may sound very surprising to you but it's the situation. the problem is, if i do'nt KILL YOU somebody else will. i have been paid some ransom in advance to terminate you with some reasons listed to me by my employer.It's someone I believe you call a friend, Do not contact the police or try to send a copy of this to them,because if you do, I will know,and might be pushed to do what I have been paid to do, this is the 1st time I turn out to be a betrayer in my job. I took pity on you,that is why I have made up my mind to help you if you are willing to help yourself.

The whole premise behind this scam is totally ridiculous, why would the "killer" be in possession of the victims' email address, but receiving such a mail can be a cause of great concern for victims, especially if they are elderly.

Black Money AKA "Wash Wash" Scams

In black money scams, the scammer will claim he has a huge sum of money, but that it has been dyed black to disguise it so it can be snuck through customs or otherwise evade detection. The scammer will offer to share it with the victim if the victim will pay for the chemicals needed to "clean" the money, or, may offer to sell it to the victim for a fraction of its claimed value, if the victim is willing to deal with the job of "cleaning" it. Either way, there is no real cash and all the victim will end up with is a load of worthless black paper. Black money scams will often take the form of advance fee scams, where the victim will have paid various fees before he receives his money.

Where this scam is particularly nasty is that the scammers will actually meet the victim to show them the money and perhaps demonstrate how it can be cleaned (using a real bill and some slight of hand or chemical "magic"). This is often enough to convince the victim that there really is millions of dollars of currency sitting in front of them. Once the victim has paid for the currency or the chemicals to clean it then he is an easy target for other scammers who claim to be offering cleaning solutions to allow them to clean their "black money" and can end up in an endless cycle of looking for a solution to getting all of those dollars that are in their possession cleaned.

Here are a few of the key phrases to look out for that indicate that you are dealing with a black money scammer

- The defaced money
  - Anti-breeze bank notes
  - Black Money
  - Defaced Currency
- The chemical
  - S.S.D. Solution
  - Vectrol Paste
  - Tebi-Manetic
  - Humine Powder
    - solid solution
    - Shiba / Fay
    - Motion
    - Decharge
    - Sahualla

Black Magic scammers

Black magic scammers will claim to be able to produce spells and potions to help solve all manner of problems from love to money and even health problems. The scammer will send out a format offering the list of spells that are available, but will require payment up front to prepare the required potion.

Here is an example of a few black magic scammer's opening mails, where they pretend to be happy clients.

> OMG!!! I am so proud and happy to be out here sharing this remarkable, awesome and extraordinary review of your work Dr Royal. I just can't believe this now my ex Husband is really back to me today feb 14th "VALENTINES DAY" on his knees presenting a ruby rose begging me to take him back and he was feeling regretful and sorry for leaving me and for causing me pains after the divorce which occured last year. And this whole miracle happened after i ordered an urgent 48hours of Dr Royal powerful spell which he cast on me and my husband. Sir I am the happpiest woman today in this whole wide world. Dr Royal you really did it..Yes.. Its a miracle and everlasting pleasure and cheerfulness for me and my family today.. I am so happy now and i dont know how much to convey my thankfulness and appreciation to you sir. And to the whole world, contact him if you need urgent help(Royallovespell@gmail.com)(Royallovespell@yahoo.com) or his website (http://Royallovespell.webs.com) or call him on +2349037171626, now because its guaranteed that he will help you.

> Am here to testify what this great spell caster done for me. My Name is JEFF ANITA, i never believe in spell casting, until when i was was tempted to try it.. i and my husband have been having a lot of problem living together, he will always not make me happy because he have fallen in love with another lady outside our relationship, i tried my best to make sure that my husband leave this woman but the more i talk to him the more he makes me feel sad, so my marriage was falling leading to divorce because he no longer gives me attention. so with all this pain and agony, i decided to contact this spell caster DR JAME to see if things can work out between me and my husband again. this spell caster DR JAME told me that my husband is really under a great spell that he have been charm by some magic, so he told me that he was going to make all things normal again. he went ahead and cast the spell for me, after 2 days of casting the spell my husband changed completely he came apologizing saying the way he treated me that he was not himself, i really thank you DR JAME for bringing back my husband to me i want you all to contact him for those who are having any problem related to marriage issue and relationship problem he will solve it for you.You can email him on drjamespelltemple@gmail.com for instant SOLUTION
>
> He cast spells for different purposes like
> (1) If you want your ex back.

(2) if you always have bad dream
(3) You want to be promoted in your office.
(4) If you want a child.
(5) You want to be rich.
(6) You want to tie your husband/wife to be yours forever.

HELLO EVERYBODY AM LIZZY FROM IRELAND I AM FULL OF JOY FOR WHAT DR AGBALAGBA DID FOR ME, I NEVER TAUGHT SPELL CASTING WAS REAL BECAUSE I HAVE CONTACTED ALOT OF SPELL CASTERS AND THEY ALL COLLECTED MY MONEY WITHOUT GIVING ME RESULT, SOMEBODY TOLD ME OF AGBALAGBA SO I GAVE IT A TRY, BEHOLD! I WAS SUPRISED OF EVERYTHING MY HUSBAND LEFT ME FOR 11YRS BUT AGBALAGBA TOLD ME NOT TO WORRY THAT HE WILL RETURN HIM BACK TO ME . TODAY AM THE MOST HAPPIEST WOMAN IN THE WORLD BECAUSE AGBALAGBA RESTORE JOY BACK TO ME BY BRINGING HIM BACK, AM GREATFUL FOR EVERYTHING BECAUSE I NEVER TAUGHT I WILL EVER FEEL THE WARM TOUCH OF MY HUSBAND AGAIN, I PROMISED HIM THAT I WILL ALWAYS SINGS HIS PRAISES EVERYWHERE I GO AND TELL THE WHOLE WORLD OF HOW POWERFUL HE IS.... CONTACT HIM THROUGH THIS EMAIL FOR ALL THOSE OF YOU WHO WANTS TO BE HAPPY LIKE ME AGAIN.. AGBALAGBATEMPLE@YAHOO.COM

While black magic is a real belief of many people the world over, the scammers writing these mails have no magical knowledge or powers, they are just after the money that they can steal by charging for their spells.

16. FAKE WEBSITES

Scammers will often set up fake websites to make their scam look more convincing. These can range from fake sites selling non-existent plant machinery, to fake sites to back up an employment scam (such as a money mule or reshipping mule scam) or fake banks and courier companies for Advance Fee, Romance or Pet Scams. Often, the sites will be a copy of a legitimate site, but sometimes they will be for a non-existent business or organisation. Just because you are given a website, don't be fooled into thinking that what you are involved in is legitimate. Domains and hosting can be easily and quickly purchased and a fully functioning site quickly installed on it (particularly if it is a replacement for a recently suspended website).

In this chapter, we will look at a few of the signs that you can use to check whether the sites you are visiting are legitimate. Taken individually, some of these signs may just be a minor red flag, but when you encounter a few of them together, the likelihood that a site is fake grows.

The domain name

While businesses will often register misspelled domains to prevent cybersquatting, they will not use these as their main domains and give them to customers. So, for example, if you are given a domain (or written to from one) that claims to belong to Wells Fargo that is welllsfargo.com, then you guarantee it is a scam. The same goes for abbreviations, such as wfargo.com or including "bnk" or "bk" in the name, such as wellsfargobnk.com - legitimate businesses have no need to do this as they will own a proper domain name. The suffix of the domain name will also give a sign that it is a scam - businesses will use .com (or .co.xx for countries such as the UK) domains, so if you are directed to barclays.org or even barclays.me then that is a scammer trying to look like he is the legitimate domain. Some scammers won't even bother registering a proper domain, they will use hosting from one of the free website providers and end up with a free sub-domain such as bankofamerica.webs.com.

If you are dealing with a major bank or well-known business then Googling their name will usually bring up their legitimate domain as the first result. Also, Google the domain that you have been given, does it appear in posts on anti-scam websites or is it listed in the Artists Against 419 (aa419.org) database as fraudulent? If so then it is definitely fake – note though that the fact it does not appear is not a guarantee that it is legitimate, it may just not have come to the anti-scam community's attention yet.

The WhoIs

Every domain that is registered has a WhoIs record that displays details of when it was registered and by who. You can check WhoIs records at a number of sites, such as www.whois.com. Here is an example of a domain for a fake bank.

```
Domain Name: BARCS-PRIVATE.COM
Registrar: PDR LTD. D/B/A PUBLICDOMAINREGISTRY.COM
Sponsoring Registrar IANA ID: 303
Whois Server: whois.PublicDomainRegistry.com
Referral URL: http://www.PublicDomainRegistry.com
Name Server: OURL147694.EARTH.ORDERBOX-DNS.COM
Name Server: OURL147694.MARS.ORDERBOX-DNS.COM
Name Server: OURL147694.MERCURY.ORDERBOX-DNS.COM
Name Server: OURL147694.VENUS.ORDERBOX-DNS.COM
Status: clientTransferProhibited http://www.icann.org/epp#clientTransferProhibited
Updated Date: 14-feb-2015
Creation Date: 14-feb-2015
Expiration Date: 14-feb-2016

Domain Name: BARCS-PRIVATE.COM
Registry Domain ID:
Registrar WHOIS Server: whois.publicdomainregistry.com
Registrar URL: www.publicdomainregistry.com
Updated Date: 2015-02-14T08:20:17Z
Creation Date: 2015-02-14T08:20:16Z
Registrar Registration Expiration Date: 2016-02-14T08:20:16Z
Registrar: PDR Ltd. d/b/a PublicDomainRegistry.com
Registrar IANA ID: 303
Registrar Abuse Contact Email: abuse@publicdomainregistry.com
Registrar Abuse Contact Phone: +1-2013775952
   Domain Status: clientTransferProhibited
   (http://icann.org/epp#clientTransferProhibited)
Registry Registrant ID:
Registrant Name: David
Registrant Organization: fedres
Registrant Street: newyork
Registrant City: newyork
Registrant State/Province: New York
Registrant Postal Code: 1
Registrant Country: US
Registrant Phone: +1.21257585
Registrant Phone Ext:
Registrant Fax:
Registrant Fax Ext:
Registrant Email: mohamamed119@yahoo.com
```

This domain was claiming to be the UK bank Barclays. There are a few things of note in the WhoIs that show the domain to be likely to be fake.

First, the recent registration. At the time the details above were copied, this domain was only a week old. Banks and existing businesses do not tend to regularly register and use new domains, they stick with the one that they have had registered already.

Then there is the details of the registrant. There are a number of things wrong here.

1. This is a domain of a UK bank, they would not register it using details of an individual in the USA.
2. The address is clearly incomplete - there is no street and the post code is fake
3. The phone number is invalid as it is the wrong length for a US phone number.
4. A business would not register their domain using a Free email address such as the Yahoo one here, or one that has a name that bears no relationship to the business.

Here is a section of the WhoIs of another domain claiming to be a bank in the Caribbean.

```
Domain Name: CABROYALOFFSTT.COM
Registry Domain ID:
Registrar WHOIS Server: whois.publicdomainregistry.com
Registrar URL: www.publicdomainregistry.com
Updated Date: 2014-10-28T02:22:16Z
Creation Date: 2014-08-28T17:11:52Z
Registrar Registration Expiration Date: 2015-08-28T17:11:52Z
Registrar: PDR Ltd. d/b/a PublicDomainRegistry.com
Registrar IANA ID: 303
Registrar Abuse Contact Email: email@publicdomainregistry.com
Registrar Abuse Contact Phone: +1-2013775952
Domain Status: clientTransferProhibited
(http://icann.org/epp#clientTransferProhibited)
Registry Registrant ID:
Registrant Name: Domain Admin
Registrant Organization: Privacy Protection Service INC d/b/a PrivacyProtect.org
Registrant Street: C/O ID#10760, PO Box 16 Note - Visit PrivacyProtect.org to contact
the domain owner/operator Note - Visit PrivacyProtect.org to contact the domain
owner/operator
Registrant City: Nobby Beach
Registrant State/Province: Queensland
Registrant Postal Code: QLD 4218
Registrant Country: AU
Registrant Phone: +45.36946676
Registrant Phone Ext:
Registrant Fax:
Registrant Fax Ext:
Registrant Email: email@privacyprotect.org
```

You can see here that the registrant is hiding their real details by using a Privacy Protection Service. A real business would have no need to do this - they would be happy to display their real address and contact details. The scammer doesn't want to display the fake details he used to register the site. Here is the WhoIs of the same site, a few days later when it was suspended for fraud and the Privacy Protection was removed.

```
Registrant Name: Nicole Charles
Registrant Organization: N/A
Registrant Street: 523 12th Ave E
Registrant City: Vancouver
Registrant State/Province: British Columbia
Registrant Postal Code: V5T 2H6
Registrant Country: CA
Registrant Phone: +1.6048739875
Registrant Phone Ext:
Registrant Fax:
Registrant Fax Ext:
Registrant Email: nicole.charles2@aol.com
```

As you can see, once again, it is a totally unrelated registrant to the claimed business.

Security

Banks and businesses will use a secure web page for any pages that are used to collect or display personal information such as account or credit card details, including login pages. That means that they will have an https:// prefix in the address bar and display a padlock sign in the browser. Most scammers do not bother to do this, so you will see this information being collected or displayed on pages using normal http:// transfer.

Some sites will also display logos from sites such as Mcafee to indicate that the site is secure or virus free. On legitimate sites, these logos will link to the actual checker's site and display details to confirm the information on the logo. On the scammer's sites, these logos will often just be an image, with no link to the actual site that claims to do the checking.

Site Content

The content of the site can also often tell you a lot about the legitimacy of a site, both from what is on the site and what is missing.

- Claimed longevity of the site - Footers will often have © dates showing the site existing far longer than it has actually been registered, or there will be a claim that a business has been established for a number of years. It would be unusual for an established business to have only registered its domain and set up a website in the last few months or year.

- Inconsistencies of the claimed business. Many countries allow the online searching of registered companies, so if a website claims to be run by a Ltd, Plc, LLC, etc. then always check that countries company registration site to see if the company actually exists and, if it does, whether it is still trading, is registered for the type of business its website shows and whether the details match.

- Confusion over the name of the business. Many scammers will use the same basic fake website template over and over again (or copy from a legitimate site), as their fake sites are suspended for fraud, often changing the name. Sometimes in their rush to get a new site live, they will miss changing some of the names, leaving them inconsistent or will even end up creating nonsense, such as the extract below that was taken from a site of a fake investment company calling itself Alison Capital.

> In rock climbing, an Alison is a steel spike hammered into a crack to act as an anchor, protecting against the consequences of a fall and assisting upward progress. This iconography describes our firm well: we all are or have been keen mountaineers or climbers; the journey to the summit is interesting and exciting; it requires teamwork; and a Alison is something that helps you manage risk.

The site that the fake was copied from belonged to a company called Piton and if you replace the word "Alison" with "piton", you will see that it now makes sense.

- Missing images. In the example given in the point above, next to the text on the real site was a picture of some pitons with the word piton in the filename. This image was missing on the fake site because, in their rush to replace all mentions of "Piton" with "Alison", they changed the filename as well, meaning that the file the page was looking for no longer existed.

- Contact details:
    - Legitimate businesses have nothing to hide, so they will provide a full set of contact details, including addresses, telephone numbers and email addresses. Any business that just provides a form for contact and no physical address should be viewed as suspicious.

    - Google Maps searches and normal searches of the claimed addresses can also give a lot of evidence that the site is not legitimate, fake or partial addresses (missing building numbers or floor/suite numbers in a large multi-occupancy building) and addresses that do not fit with the type of business (large companies do not operate from small residential properties) are a good indication that the site is fake. A non-multi-occupancy address being used by another business (particularly a UPS or mailbox type business or a firm of solicitors that may have been used to register a company) is a good indication that the business does not really exist, as is the property being listed for sale or rent on various property websites.

    - Major businesses also use proper landline phone numbers, they will not have a mobile, VoIP or personal redirect numbers (such as the +4470 UK numbers) for their main point of contact or give an invalid number. Phone numbers can be checked on my www.scamnumbers.info website to see the type of number, where it is located and also if it has been previously used in a scam. In some countries (such as the USA and Canada), it is also possible to use directory sites such as WhitePages to tell the type of number, or even a site such as Wikipedia to look at the format of phone numbers,

    - Businesses also do not tend to use an email address on a different domain to their websites or use free Gmail, Yahoo or Outlook email addresses. Scammers do this so that if their main domain is lost, there is still a possibility that existing victims will still be able to contact them.

- The information that is not on the site can also give a good indication that something is not right. In many countries, there is information that sites legally have to display, particularly if they are in a regulated industry. So sites that are missing privacy policies, cookie policies or regulatory details should be viewed with suspicion.

- If the site is an eCommerce site, then see what payment options are available. Sites that only offer payment by non-reversible or anonymous methods such as Western Union, Moneygram, Bitcoins or even Bank Transfer should be deemed suspicious. A legitimate eCommerce site will offer payments by Credit Card or PayPal. Scammers like to avoid this as firstly, it would be difficult for them to get card processing facilities and secondly, there is a chance for victims to be able to reverse the fraudulent payments.

- If a site is selling/renting items such as vehicles or properties, where you would only expect to find one site selling them or they are specific to a particular area, then Google's reverse image search will often prove useful to show the exact same picture being used on another site (sometimes in a totally different country) to sell/rent the item at a much higher price or a similar price if the sites are both fake.

- Items tend to have a price at which the market sells them at (be they brand name electronics or a second-hand car of particular age and mileage). Anyone selling the item at a price that is way below the norm or is offering deals such as "Buy 2 get 1 free" on popular brand name electronics, is almost certainly a scammer. At best, you will end up getting a cheap poor quality and possibly dangerous fake that is worth far less than you paid and at worst, you will just be outright scammed and get nothing at all.

As mentioned at the start of the chapter, many of the points raised above, on their own are red flags that something might be wrong, but when you start seeing many of them together then the likelihood that the domain is fake grows.

If the domain is fake then the person that gave it to you and any deal that they are involving you in is also fake and part of a bigger scam.

17. MULES

Scammers need a way to collect the money that they are stealing, but obviously do not want it to be traceable back to them. Many scammers will use the fact that services such as Western Union and Moneygram use independent agents, such as small stores, to their advantage. They will either find one with poor ID checking or one where they can bribe the agent to turn a blind eye to the fact that they are collecting money without providing a legitimate ID.

Many people though are now becoming more suspicious of being asked to use services like Western Union and Moneygram send money to countries in scam hotspots such as Africa and the Far East. Also, the services themselves are becoming more pro-active in highlighting the possibility of fraud.

The scammers therefore need to find a way to collect the money, but still avoid being directly connected to it. To achieve this, they will recruit overseas "money mules", who will receive the Western Union/Moneygram transfers for them or allow their bank accounts to be used to receive the funds and then forward it on to the scammer using a service such as Western Union.

Mules were mentioned in the chapter on Employment Scams, in connection with the sophisticated websites set up to recruit mules using titles such as "payment agents". Those type of operations are often run by major crime gangs, looking for large numbers of mules to launder the proceeds of their various crimes. However, even small time scammers will try to recruit mules, either through less sophisticated employment scams, or possibly by using an existing victim (often of a Romance Scam), who is no longer able to pay them money and persuading them to receive funds for them.

Usually, the mules will be in countries such as the UK or USA, to make the sending of the funds less suspicious, but sometimes the scammer will use a bank account in their own country, perhaps even belonging to a friend or family member as they know that the risks of being caught are low.

Many mules are, as mentioned above, innocent scam victims themselves, but some do know what they are involved in and do not care. Either way, the implications are the same. When a victim realizes that they've been scammed and reports it to the authorities, the only **real person** he has details of is the mule and it is them that will be investigated for and possibly charged with fraud or money laundering. The real scammer will be sitting in his Internet café using the anonymity of his fake email addresses and names, with no worry about being caught and no concern for the fate of the mule, except that he will have to find and groom a new one.

18. STAYING SAFE ON THE INTERNET

Here are a few hints and tips for general Internet safety.

1. Banks, email providers, retailers and other online businesses do not send unrequested emails asking you to click a link to reactivate your account. If you receive an email alerting you to a problem with your account and you actually hold an account with that business then open a new browser and manually type in the URL of the business concerned – if there really is a problem with your account then you will be alerted to it on the proper website. The link will either be to a phishing page to steal your personal details or to the download of a virus or other malware.

2. Similarly to 1., companies do not send unrequested attachments with statements, orders, invoices etc. Care should be taken with any attachment that is sent, even if it appears to be from a trusted source. This is particularly true if the attachment is a .zip, .exe, .htm or .html file. Again, these will be virus, malware or phishing attacks.

3. Companies will **never** email you asking you to reveal personal information such as passwords, PINs, or memorable information such as mother's maiden name.

4. Webpages to log in to a secure area such as Internet banking or email will **always** be a secure page and not a standard web page. Secure pages are denoted by the prefix in the address bar being https:// and will also display an icon such as a padlock.

5. Search everything – the email address, the names used, telephone numbers, chunks of the email that appear to be strangely worded. You will often find the email addresses and telephone numbers already listed on anti-scam websites, or the exact same email sent by a different email address.

Key phrases and themes to watch out for in Internet Scams

Internet scammers often do not have the intelligence or language skills to be able to write in the styles that the people they often pretend to be would use, so their emails will often contain signs that show them to be fakes. Here are just a few things to look out for.

- Overly religious emails.
- Overly personal emails.
- Use of slang and text speak in business mails.
- Poor language skills, misspelling, and typos in what are meant to be official emails and documents.
- Vagueness of how your details were obtained.
- Vagueness of what they are writing about.
- The phrase "your outstanding fund"
- The writing out of monetary amounts in words as well as numerically and the use of "USD", "EURO" or "GBP" etc. in addition to the standard symbols..
- Placing amounts, names or places in parenthesis, such as "my son (Brian)".
- Any mention of "Western Union" or "Moneygram" – these money transfer services are intended for use by individuals to transfer money to people that they know personally overseas. They are never used by businesses, governments or the military.
- The phrase "Transfer payment slip" or similar. If you send money by bank transfer in the course of a legitimate transaction, the recipient will not ask for a copy of any receipt given to you by your bank. They will have no need for it as they will see the money in their account. Scammers ask for these so that they can prove to the person whose bank account they have given that the money has been sent for them.
- The use of mobile, VoIP and personal redirect phone number (in particular United Kingdom **+4470** phone numbers).
- Emails sent from one address, but with the "reply-to" address being totally different, or a request in the body of the mail to reply to the sender's "private email box".

ABOUT THE AUTHOR

"Alan Jones"/"B8er" has been scambaiting since 2009 and is an established member of the scambaiting community. In addition to scambaiting he is also a member of the Anti-Scam & Internet Anti-Fraud Information Centre www.scamwarners.com, where he is one of the Support Team who advise victims and potential victims on scams.

"Alan" is also the owner of two anti-scam websites:

- www.scamnumbers.info, a database of phone numbers used by Internet scammers in emails and on fake websites, which allows you to search numbers and see if numbers have previously been previously reported for use in scams, as well as giving information on the type of number it is.
- www.itsascam.email, a small site, providing anti-scam soundbites and descriptions for common types of scams.

"Alan's" online scambaiting personas are many and varied, such as Burke & Hare Ltd (Edinburgh's leading purveyor of fine and exotic meats), the North Korean Tourist Board, Swiss aristocrat Conte Capra Ábusante, తిపి యొాన the Indian au pair, and many more

In real life, "Alan" is in his forties and has a varied career background in Financial Services and Corporate IT. He is married with a son, a cat and possibly a rabid pet squirrel called Slightly.